I0493506

PREVAILING WESTERLIES

PREVAILING WESTERLIES

Fine Art Photographs

Ed Lavino

Sastrugi Press
San Diego • Jackson Hole

Copyright © 2015 by Ed Lavino

All rights reserved. No part of this book may be reproduced or transmitted in any form or by any means, electronic or mechanical, including photocopying, recording, or by any information storage and retrieval system without the written permission of the author, except where permitted by law.

Sastrugi Press / Published by arrangement with the author

Sastrugi Press: PO Box 1297, Jackson, WY, United States
www.sastrugipress.com

Prevailing Westerlies: Fine Art Photographs

The author has made every effort to accurately recreate conversations, events, and locales from his memories of them. To maintain anonymity, some names and details such as places of residence, physical characteristics, and occupations have been changed. All photos and text contained herein are copyrighted by the author and registered with the United States Copyright office. As such, they may not be reproduced, copied, distributed, reprinted, published, displayed or broadcast without the written permission from the author and/or publisher. The publisher does not have any control over and does not assume any responsibility for author or third-party websites or their content.

Poetry by Gerard Manley Hopkins (1844–1889)
Poetry by Rainer Maria Rilke (1875–1926)

Library of Congress Catalog-in-Publication Data
Library of Congress Control Number: 2015939578
Lavino, Edwin
Prevailing Westerlies: Fine Art Photography / Edwin Lavino - 1st United States edition
p. cm.
1. Photography—Black-and-White photography 2. Photography—Artistic 3. Photography—Still-life photography
Summary: This collection of fine art, black and white photographs by Edwin Lavino features landscapes, portraits and still lifes from the Rocky Mountain West of North America.
ISBN-13: 978-0-9960206-8-8

770'

10 9 8 7 6 5 4 3 2

Dedication

For Jane, my wife and my terra firma

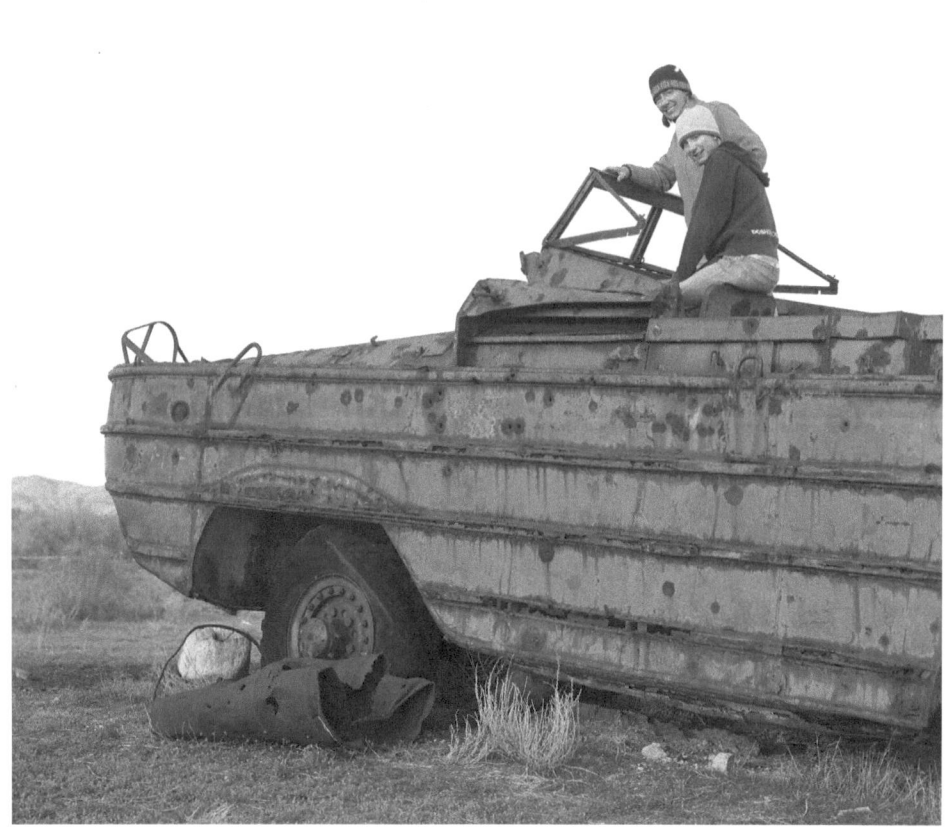

Jane and Hillary in an abandoned amphibious vehicle.
North shore of the Great Salt Lake, Utah, 2005

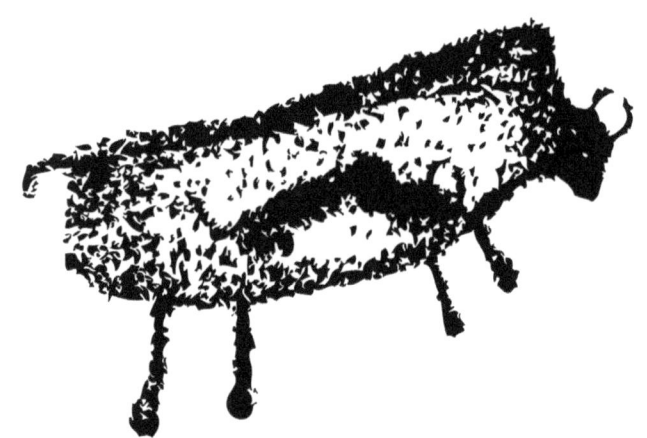

Foreword

As you leaf through this manuscript, notice how Ed Lavino organizes his photographs and documents his world. Ed creates a remarkable collection of nature, human figure portraits, landscapes and still life photographs. The quantity of high caliber images is inspiring. The most effective words to say are: you must see the photos yourself. Compare this artist's works with the technical depth of Ruth Bernhard, Edward Weston, Paul Strand and Ansel Adams. The vocabulary speaks about man and his environment. Texture becomes the focal element on some images, conveying a tranquility of interactions between humankind and nature. Apply a critical eye and see how humanity is illuminated. Ed was raised in the Catskill Mountains, which obviously helped formulate his sensitivity to the bucolic world of Mother Nature.

As a photographer myself, it is very natural for me to take pictures and tell my story. In this I can identify with Edwin Lavino. Can you do the same? Select a photo and study it.

What do Ed's photographs say to you? How do these photographs tilt your perceptions? Explore his creations. He captures shapes and shadows, suspends time and light, unveiling skin tones and nature's textures throughout the black to white spectrum.

Lavino blends textures of the environment, humans, metal, farms, forests, plains, plant life, the western big sky and found objects.

The world today affords us the ability to document with smart phones. Our day, our friends, and our selfies now dominate the screens we view. Look at Ed's photographs and his method of large format negatives in the technique of mid–20th century black and white photography. Appreciate how he captures humanity and the environment.

Photography was once pushed away like a prodigal son of fine art. "Unacceptable," they said. Today photography is ordinary and celebrates birth, documents life experiences, travel, objects of value and wars.

An enormous amount of space would be required to list all the artistic photographers who have contributed to the growth of making photographs. If Edward Weston were around today, Ed Lavino would have been recruited into Weston's "Group f/64."

Consider this book a text—a mobile gallery for the devotee, collector or scholar. It is the work of an artist. Now go ahead—flip forward to the pages of beautiful pictures.

What do Ed's photographs say to you?

Philip J. Milio
Professor/Counselor, Fashion Institute of Technology (retired)
State University of New York

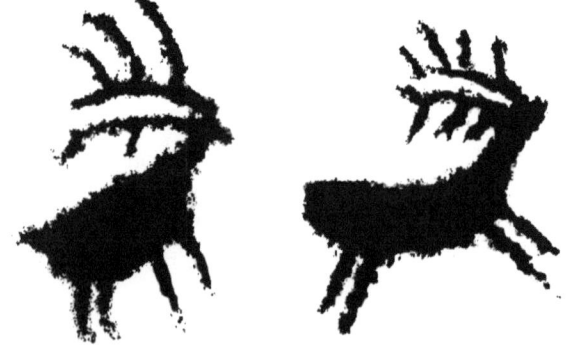

Preface

When I initially began working on sequencing the photographs for this book, I presumed my landscapes, portraits and still lifes needed to be separated into distinct sections. An exhibit of my work at the Lander Art Center, in 2011, presented my photographs in three categories: People, Places and Things (also the title of that exhibition). This book is the first instance in which I have intentionally mixed the categories. The act of integrating my photos felt like shuffling a deck of playing cards; I gradually became more confident with the process. Ultimately, I acquired a whole new language in which to speak. I am amazed at how the pairing of images creates a synergy that strengthens my overall message.

Landscape photography is my oldest love. I gain inspiration from the influence of photographers Robert Adams and Mario Giacomelli. I am awed by the landscape paintings of Leonardo da Vinci and Pieter Bruegel the Elder. I spend significant amounts of time outdoors land surveying, fly fishing, and backcountry skiing. Through these connections, I have acquired an intimacy with the land that is difficult to explain. I read the terrain and sky the way some read human expressions—capturing subtle moods and nuances. I never tire of it.

Photographic portraiture is an art I have experimented with on and off for decades. Significant influences include Edward Weston, Andrew Wyeth and Michelangelo. I live for those moments behind the lens when my model and her environment merge to become one poetic statement. This goal requires patience. I spend time with people to build rapport, slowing down enough to honor both the place and the person.

I discovered my love of photographing still life arrangements more circuitously, during times when neither landscape nor portraiture adequately conveyed an idea or feeling I wanted to express. I have long admired still life art by Giorgio Morandi, Paul Outerbridge, and Frederick Sommers. I collect intriguing artifacts. Whether bushwhacking in the wilderness, or walking through a cityscape, I keep a keen eye out for flotsam that describes the people and animals inhabiting the space. Still life arrangements of objects and materials have the power to spark associations, trigger memories, and provide insight into abstract ideas.

The most challenging aspect of assembling this book has been writing the text—particularly the descriptive captions for the photographs. I am a visual person and have always believed my photographs should speak for themselves. Ultimately, I believe my words add value because they articulate my ideas and choices. The accompanying prose and poetry will pique your interest, provoke you to look more closely, and answer a few of the questions that will arise as you turn the pages ahead.

Ed Lavino
Jackson, Wyoming

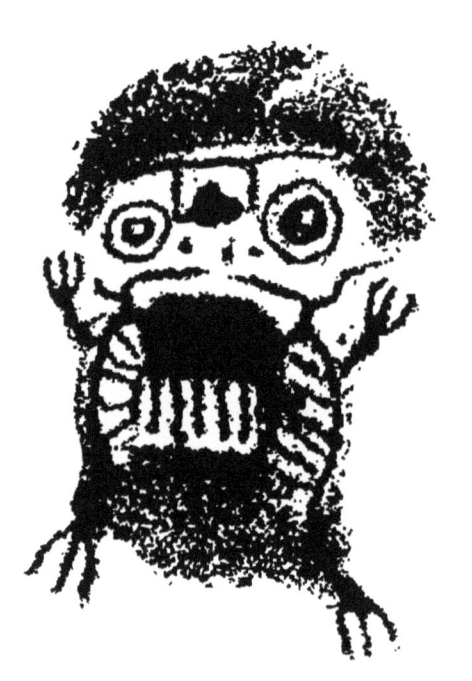

Acknowledgments

I am indebted to a great group of people for their roles in the realization of this book. This group includes: My publisher, Sastrugi Press, for proposing the creation of this book and expertly leading me through each step of the process; My wife, Jane Lavino, for her essential help with writing and editing; My daughter, Hillary Torrey Lavino, for her perceptive critiques; My sister-in-law, Cathy Petrick, for her patience and expertise in piecing together and crafting my biography; My sister-in-law, Ellen Petrick, for her insightful and intelligent text edits; David Sabio for his helpful advice regarding my first attempt at poetry; Bob Mullins and Shane Shibayama for their photographic printing prowess; Chris England for his friendship and the petroglyph graphics; Corrie Ellis and Hunter Grosse for consistent support and generosity; and Nancy D. Wall for her efficient copy editing skills.

I'd also like to thank the following people for their important influence and support: Meg Daly, Maria and Ed Hajic, Andy Kincaid, George and Beverly Leys, Thomas Macker, Dan McCormack, Bronwyn Minton, Camille Obering Musser, David Swift, Jennifer Tennican, and Gregory Zeigler.

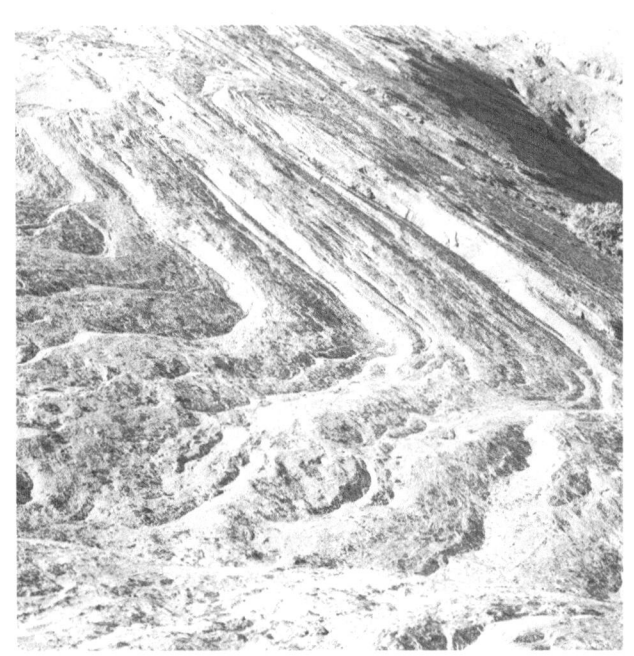

God's Grandeur

The world is charged with the grandeur of God.
    It will flame-out, like shining from shook foil;
    It gathers to a greatness, like the ooze of oil
Crushed. Why do men then now not reck his rod?
Generations have trod, have trod, have trod;
    And all is seared with trade; bleared, smeared with toil;
    And wears man's smudge and shares man's smell: the soil
Is bare now, nor can foot feel, being shod.

And for all this, nature is never spent;
    There lives the dearest freshness deep down things;
And though the last lights off the black West went
    Oh, morning, at the brown brink eastward, springs-
Because the Holy Ghost over the bent
    World broods with warm breast and with ah! bright wings.

— Gerard Manley Hopkins

Darwin
Rustic Pine Tavern, Dubois, Wyoming

Indoor and outdoor environments merge at the Rustic Pine Tavern in Dubois, Wyoming. Darwin, a wrangler, sits beneath a trophy mule deer mount. The light streaming through the window vanished as a fierce squall moved in, bringing the first snow of the season.

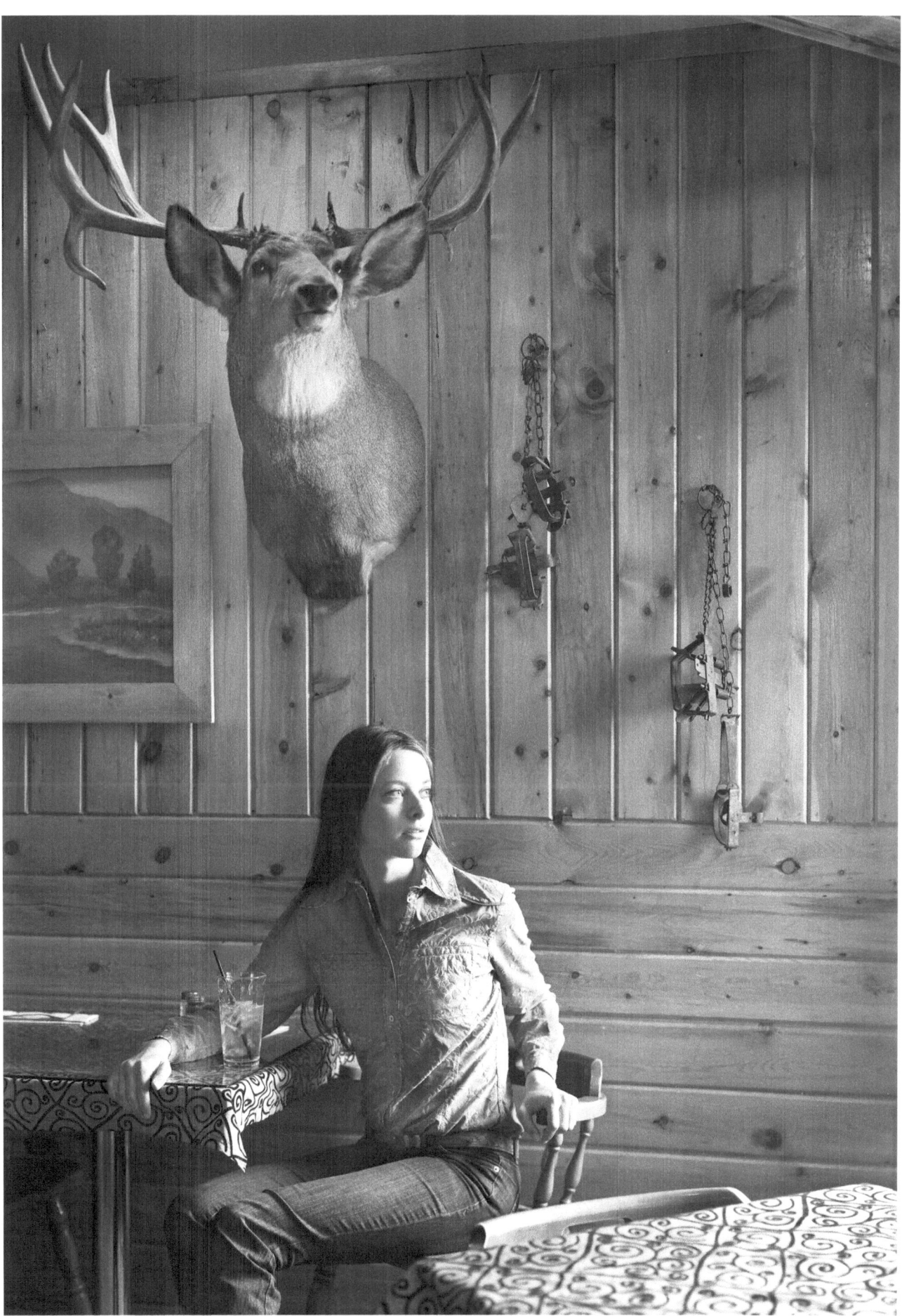

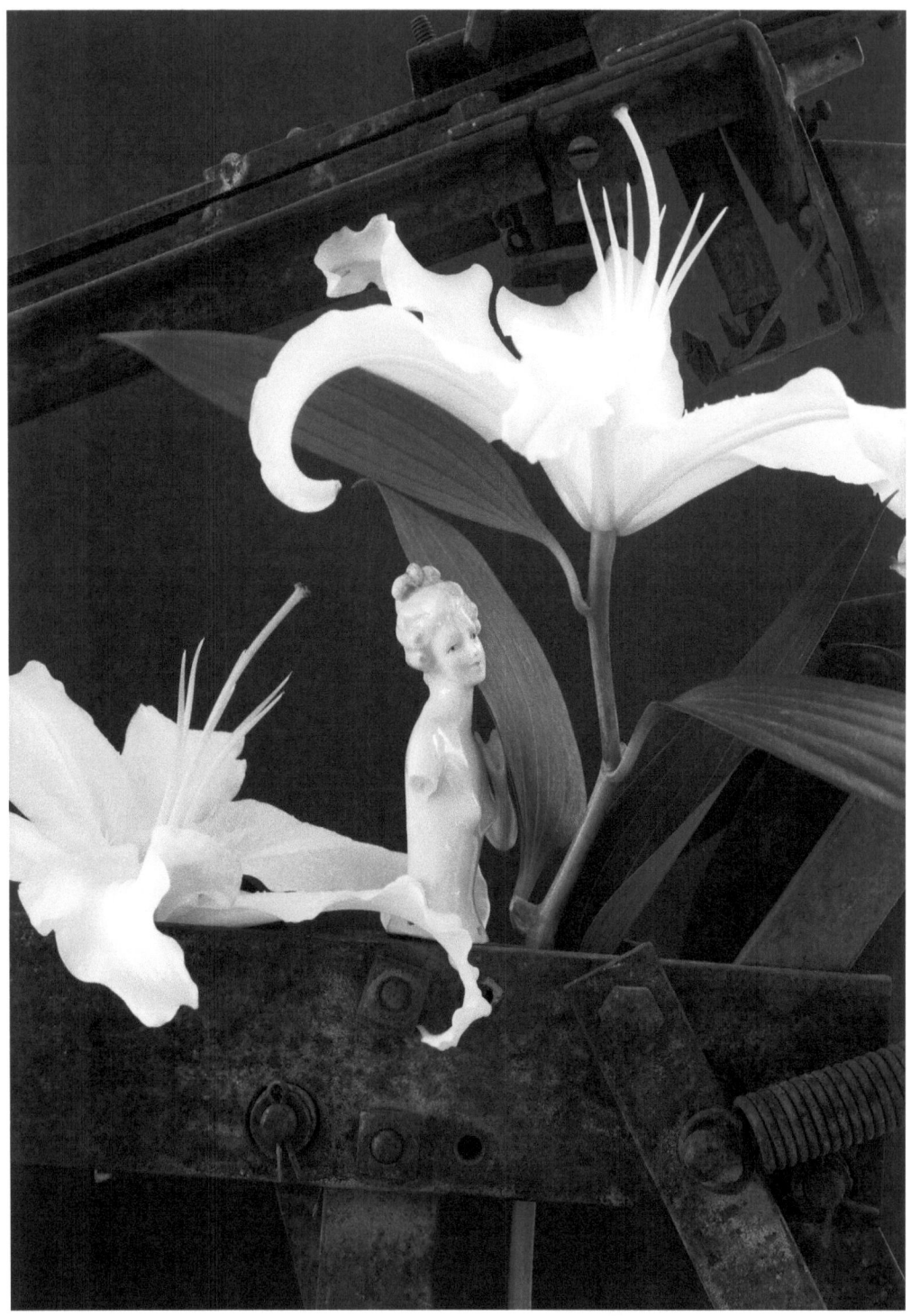

Lily and Dresden Doll

The lily accentuates the fragile, ephemeral qualities of female beauty. The rusted machinery provides a counterpoint, symbolizing the destruction of war and its effect on humanity, particularly women.

Torso and Stag

The female torso is a chance form, suggested in the twisted trunk of a tree. My neighbor, George, found this anomaly while out gathering firewood and wisely set it aside. The pairing of this feminine oddity with the atypical, asymmetrical antlers of a mule deer seems fitting.

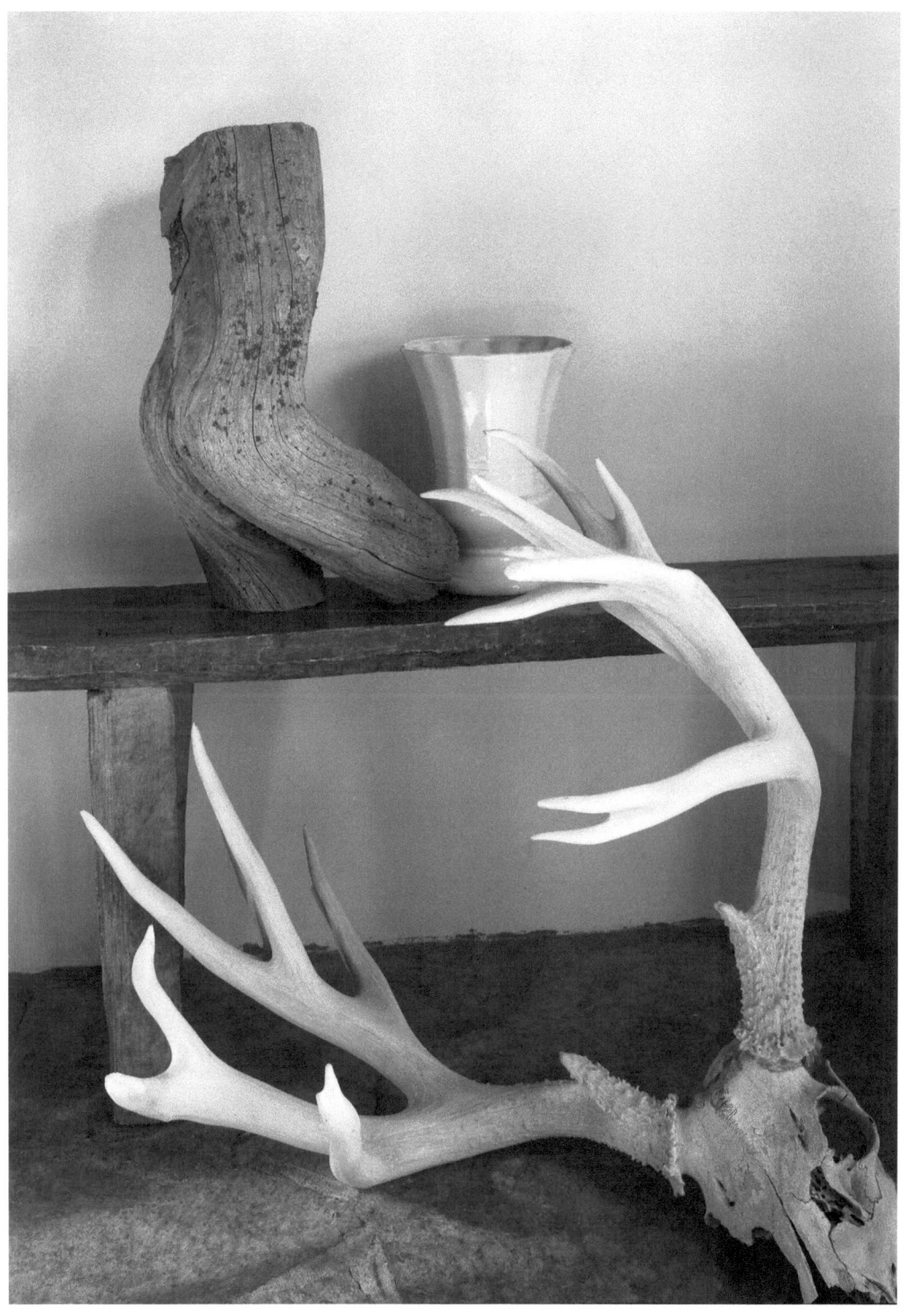

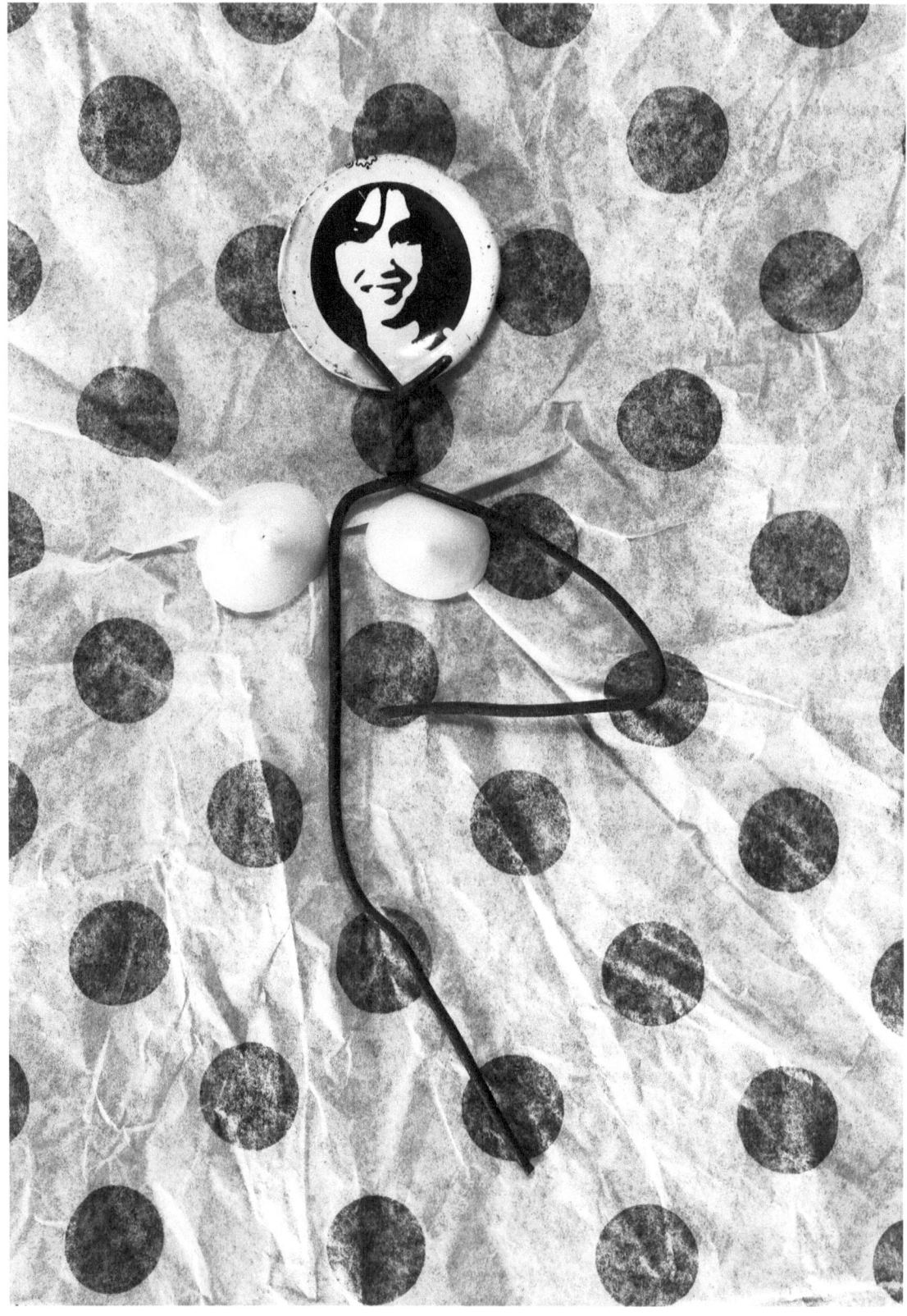

Soda Cap Girl

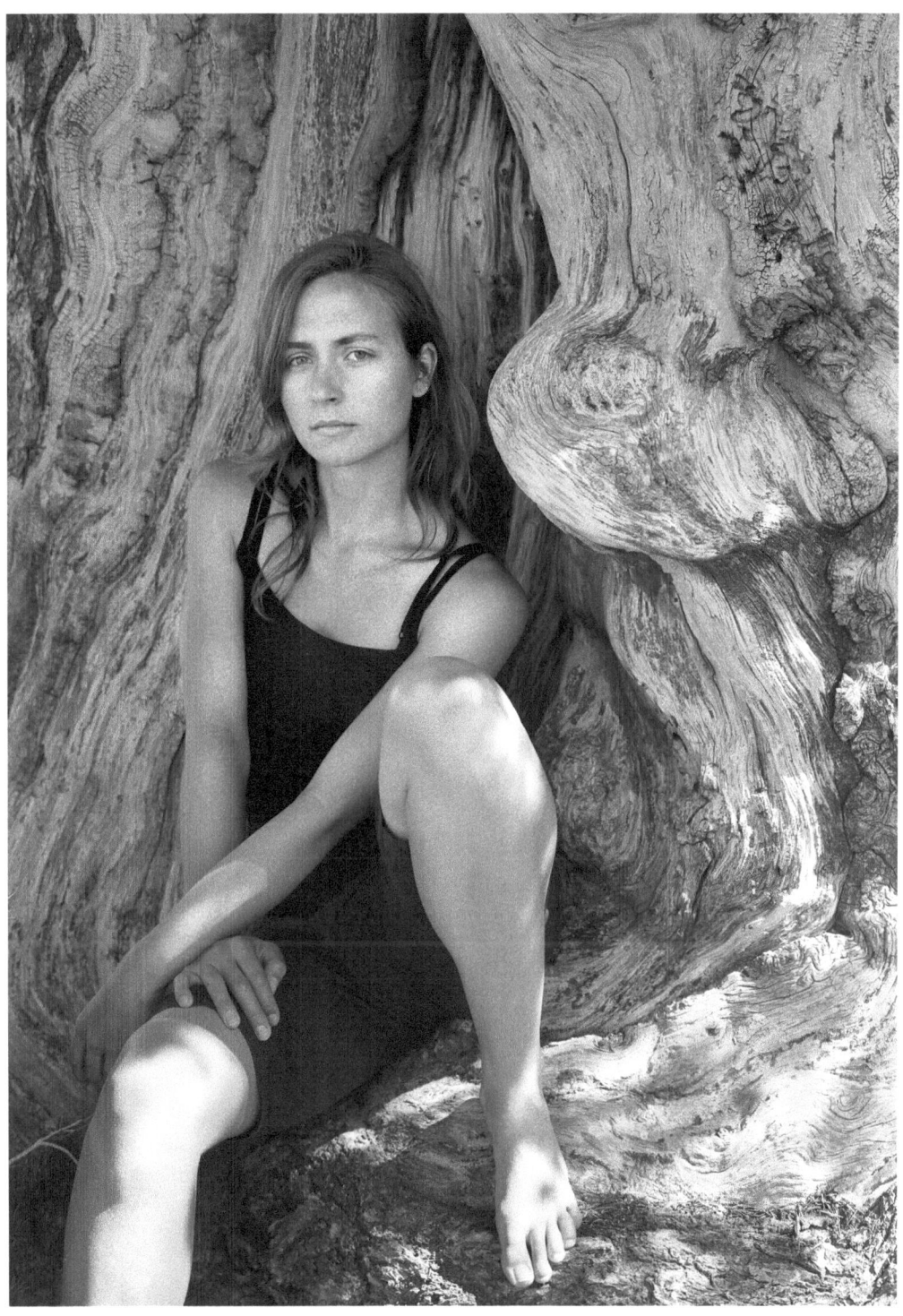

Corrie and Twisted Pine

Corrie was the perfect model: at ease in the outdoors, invested in the process, and self-possessed with a thoughtful intelligence. The massive pine tree encircles her with its sinuous, knotted lines. She appears confident and comfortable, enveloped in nature.

Ed Lavino

Five Eggs and One Tulip

The central stalk is rhubarb, pulled from a wild garden behind our house. I borrowed the tulip from the kitchen table bouquet. I am pleased when seemingly unrelated objects forge new meaning in context with each other. A fanciful organic form bears new fruit.

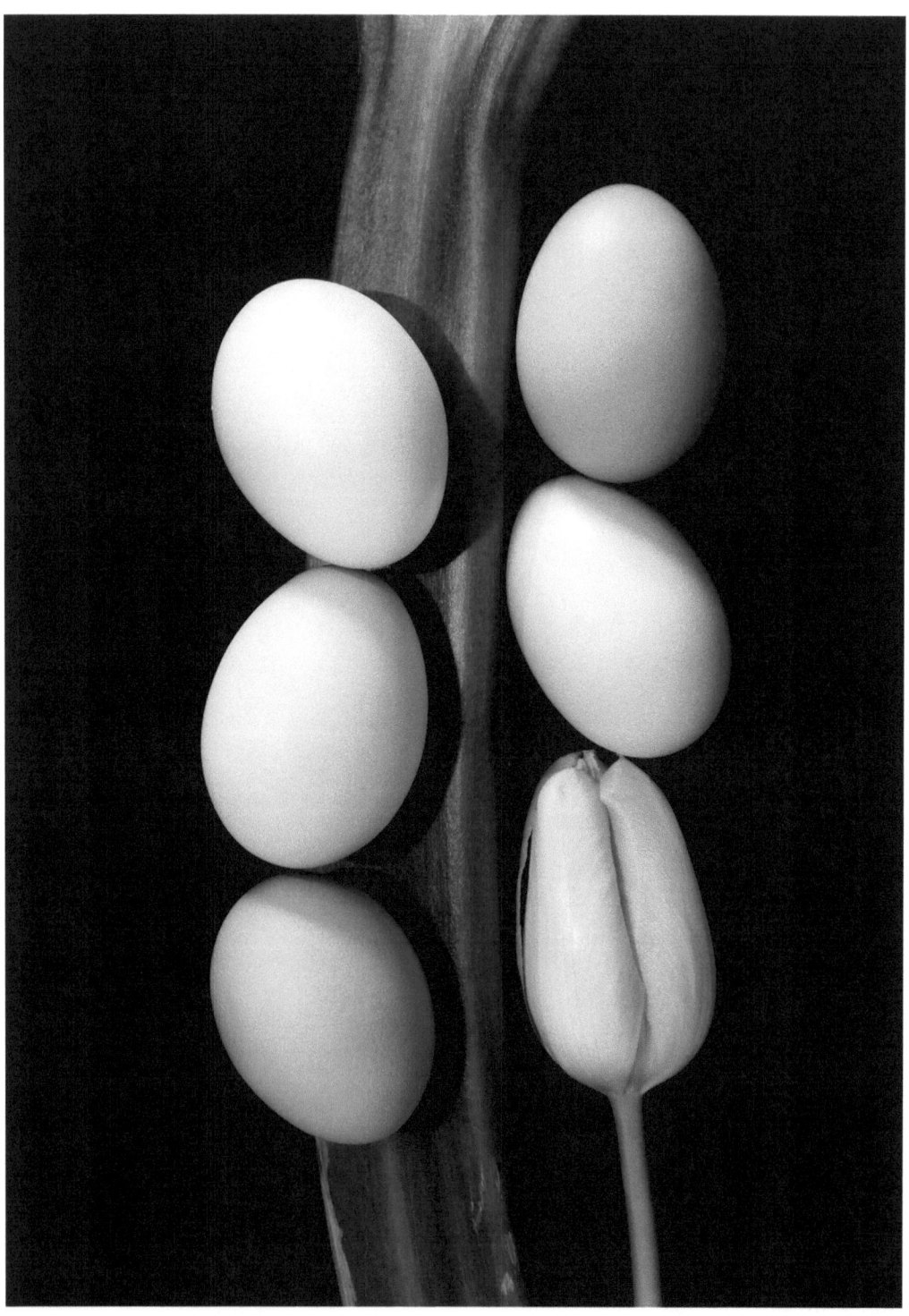

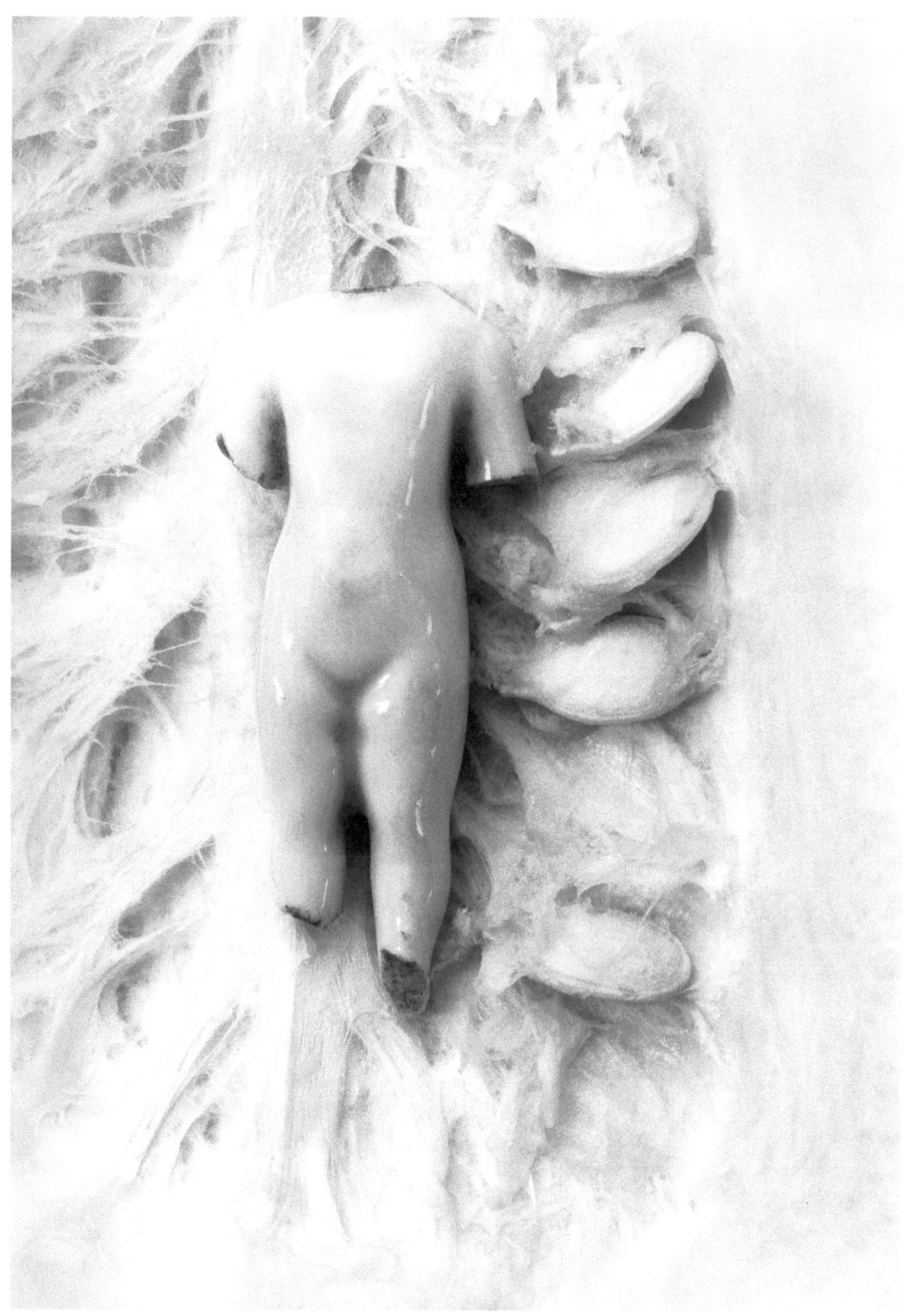

China Doll on Pulp

A white pumpkin, split lengthwise to harvest the seeds, revealed soft, pulpy flesh. It seemed an appropriate matrix on which to place the smooth porcelain doll.

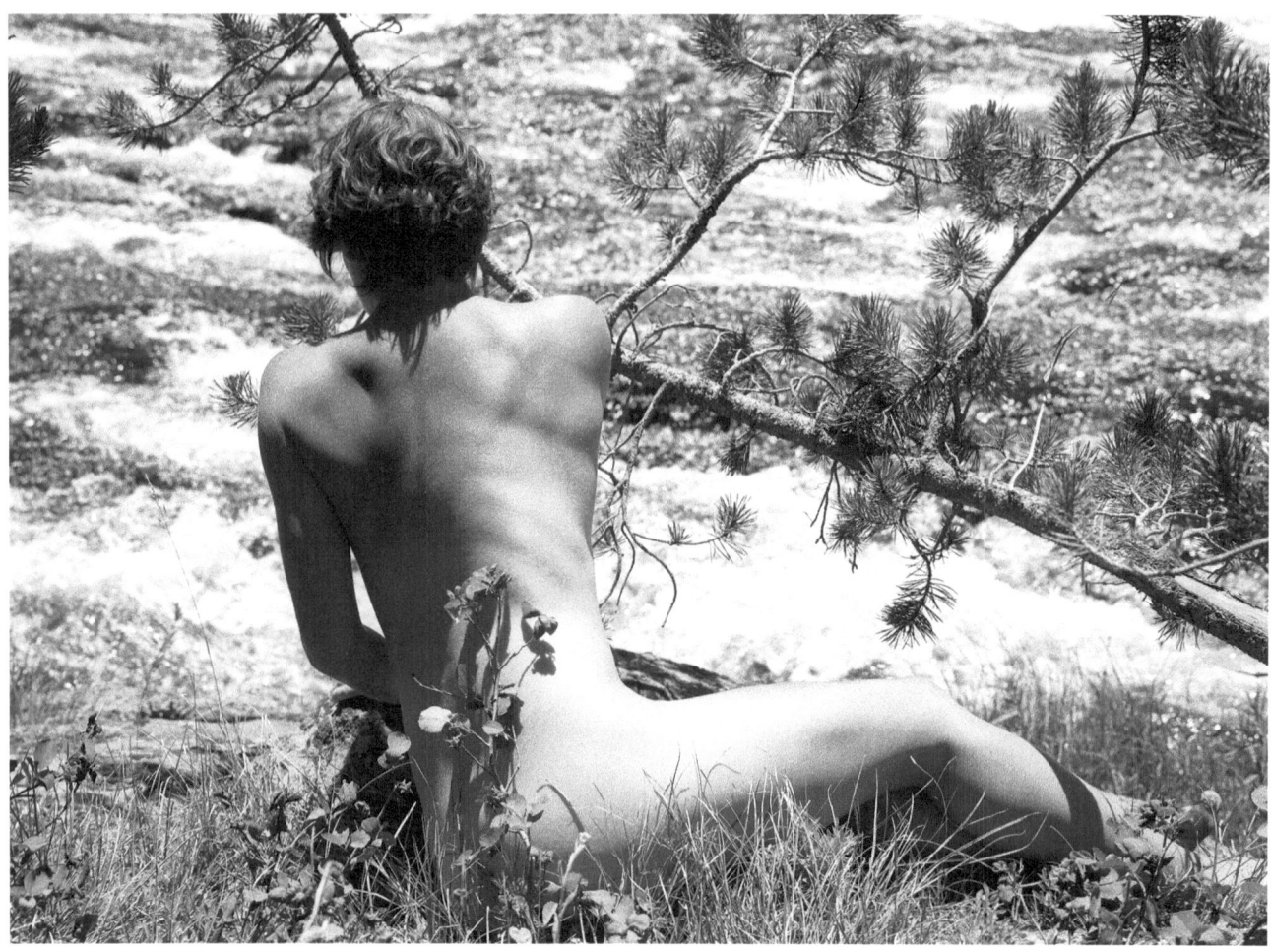

Emma Against the River

The format of paired images enables me to play with repetition for emphasis. The subjects of these two photographs are decidedly different, yet each has similar torqued lines that catch the eye and dominate the composition. Both reference strength under pressure. Emma was unperturbed by modeling outdoors, even when it entailed bushwhacking across muddy flats full of mosquitoes.

Prevailing Westerlies

This photo was taken on a backpacking trip in a remote area of the northern Wind River Mountain Range. A Shoshone tribal member told me about a shortcut to Roberts Mountain used by reservation hunters in the fall. As I tried to follow it, I found myself in a thickly wooded area, with stone cairns spaced at considerable distances.

Gradually, the trail became nonexistent. A huge bank of fog moved in as I arrived at this dry, primordial pond, ringed with boulders. I watched the fog ebb and flow, as if the mountain were breathing. I took this photograph as the fog receded.

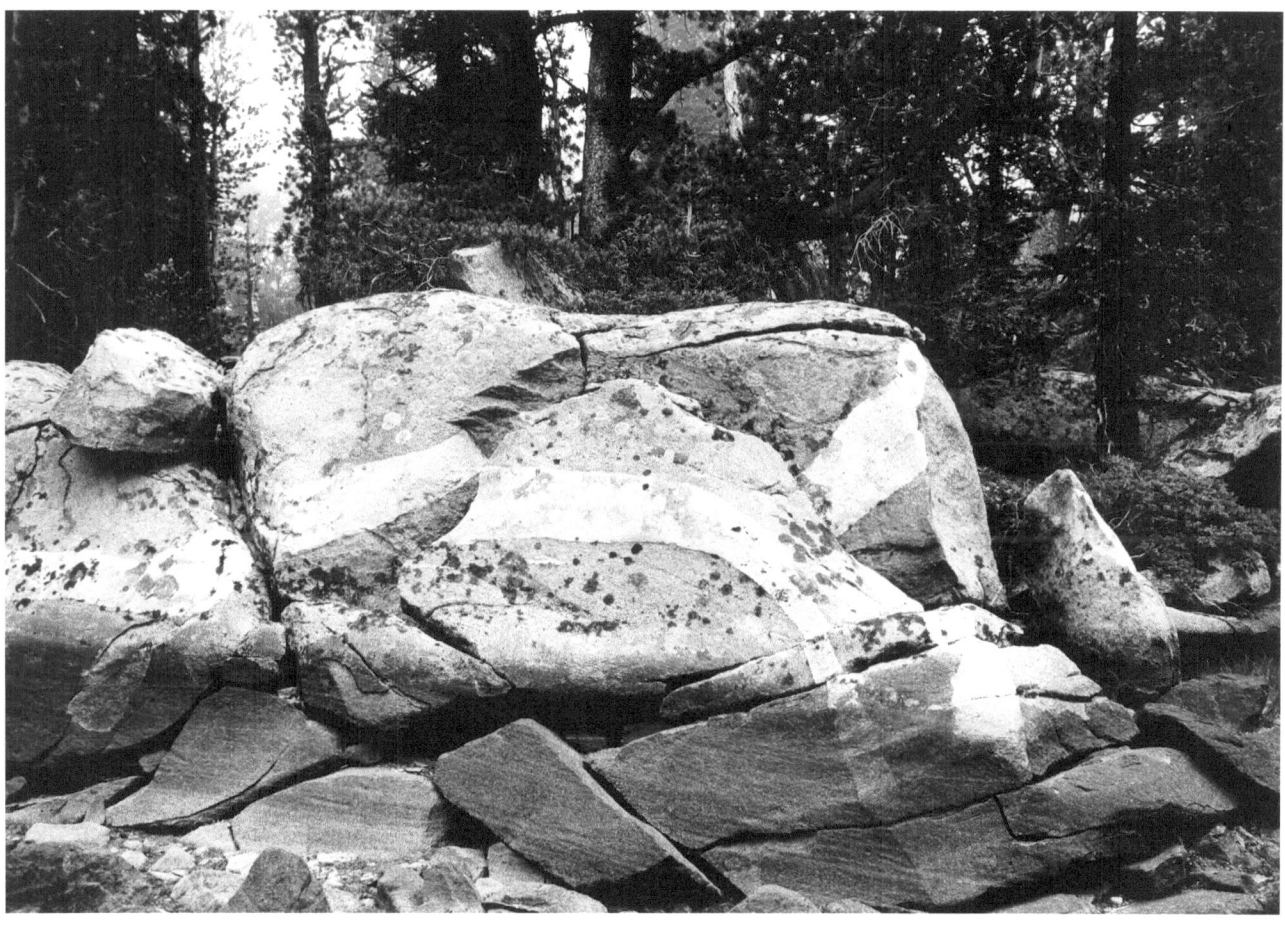

"It's possible, I'm moving through the hard veins of heavy mountains, like an arc, alone; I'm so deep inside, I see no end in sight, and no distance: everything is getting near and everything near is turning to stone."
— Rainer Maria Rilke

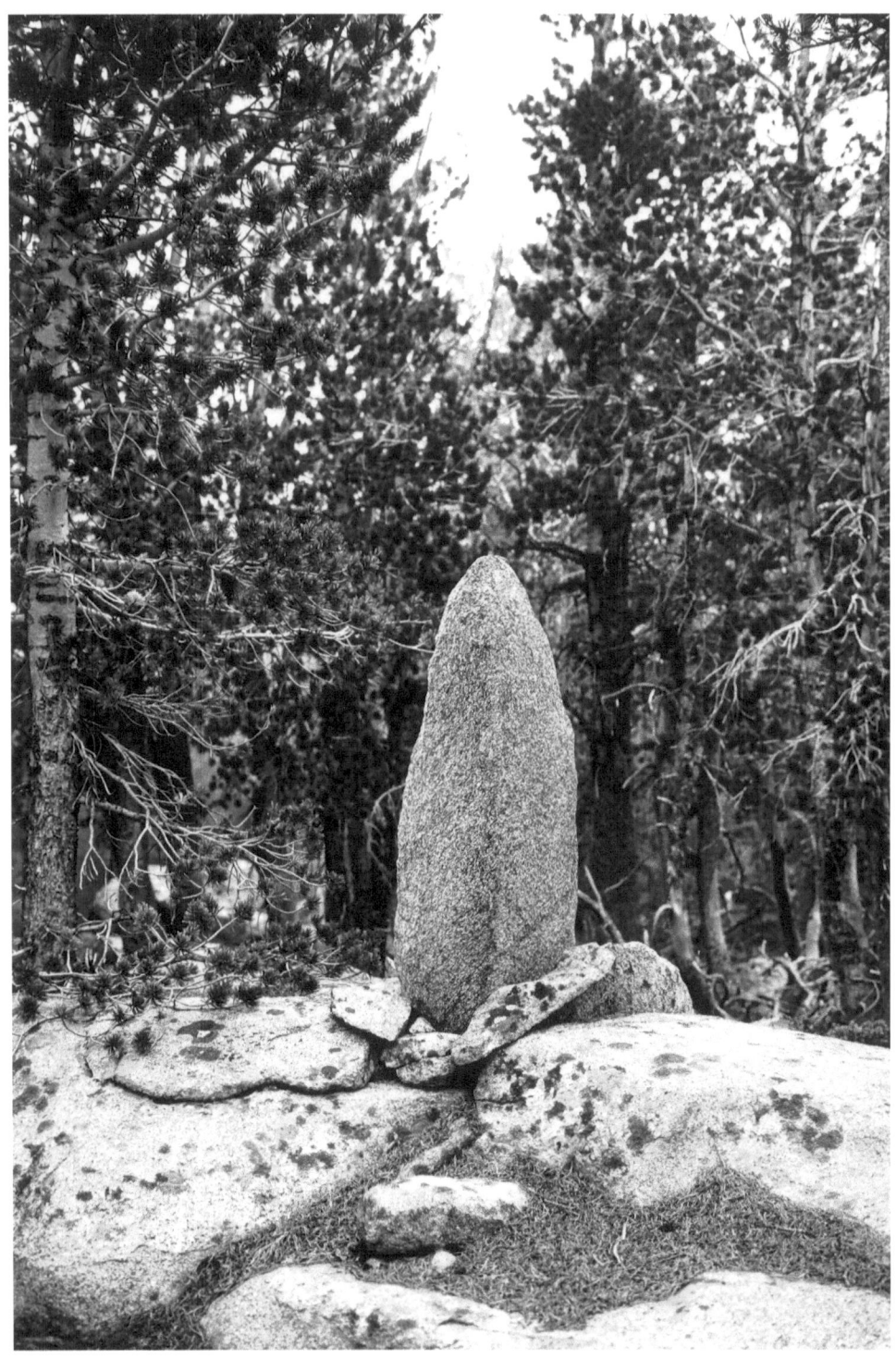

Stone Cairn
Wind River Indian Reservation, Wyoming

This stone cairn, in the shape of an arrowhead, was found within the Wind River Indian Reservation, marking an ancient hunting trail.

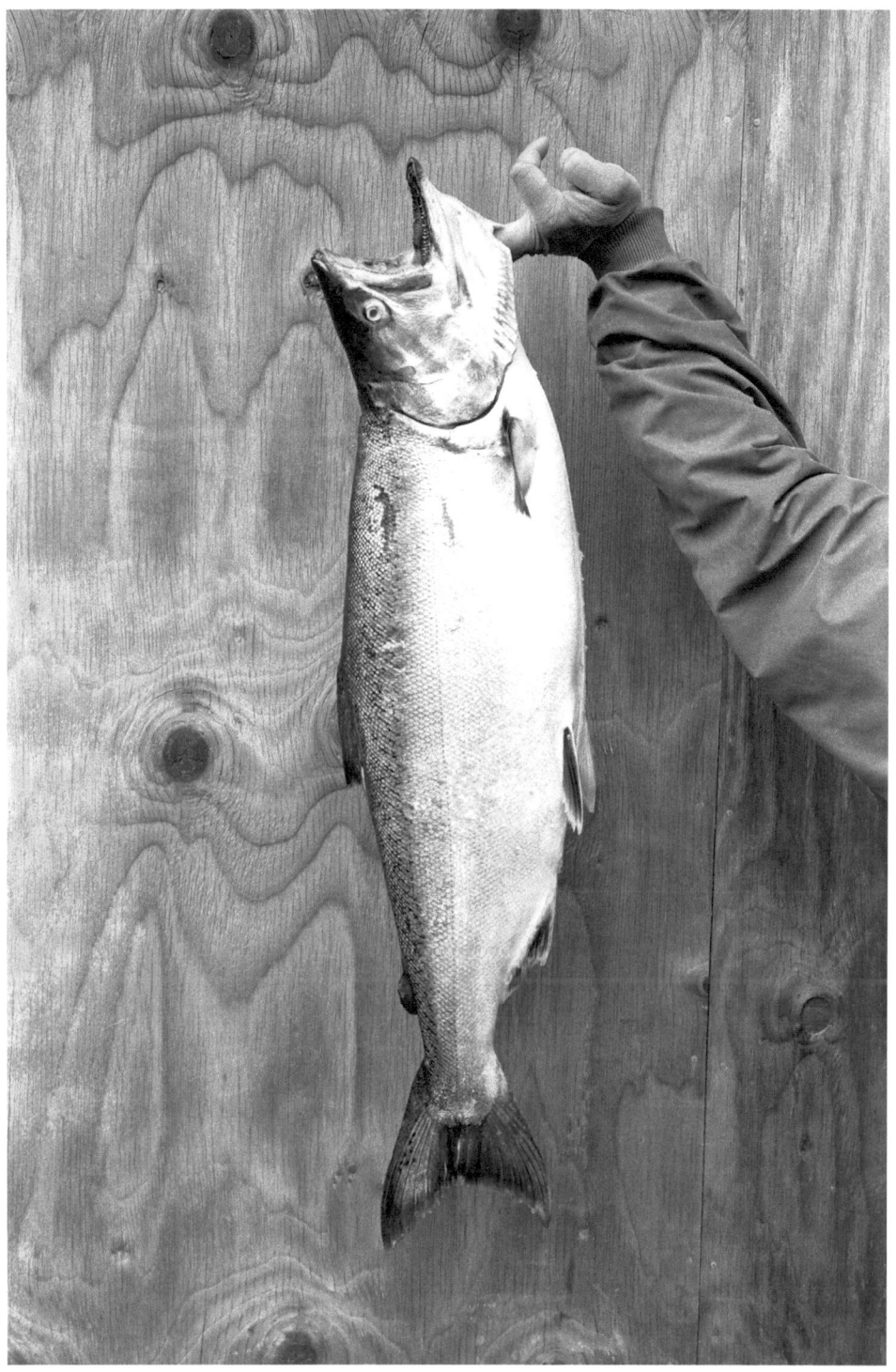

Pacific Salmon

This 14-pound salmon was caught during its long spawning journey off the coast of California. Each year fish make the trip from kelp forests in the Pacific Ocean, up streams braiding through coastal rainforests, to channels carving the high arid plateau. Their journey ends in the shadow of the Rocky Mountains.

Ed Lavino

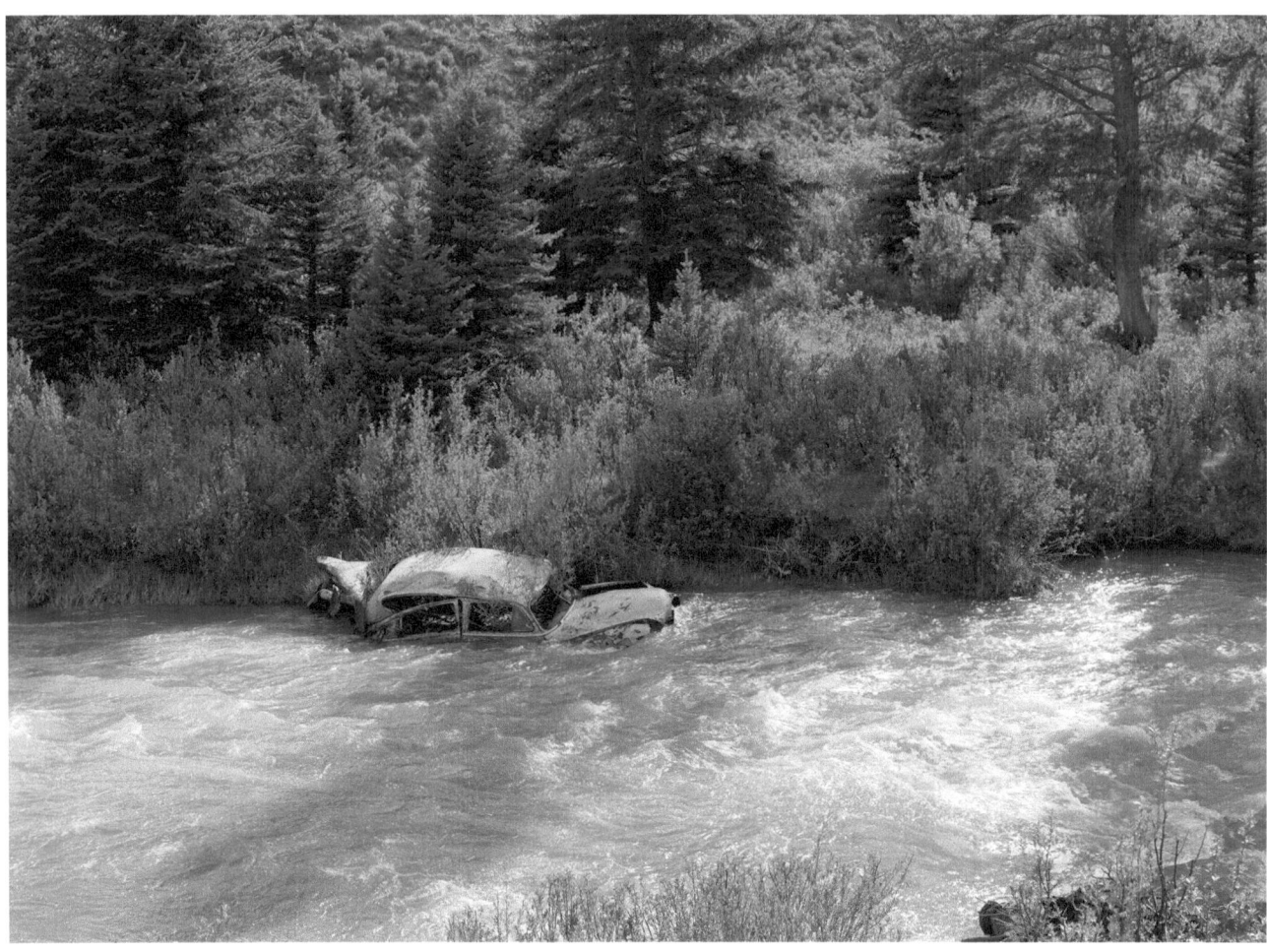

Rusted Car
Little Wind River, Wyoming

On repeat visits to this spot over a span of twenty years, I observed this abandoned car gradually shifting down the river. It struck me that this automobile was moving downstream on the same highway the juvenile salmon were using on their annual migration to the ocean.

Chinese Tea Tin and Pliers

The rock backdrop is Idaho Bitch Creek "Jade," heavily polished by thousands of years of submersion, imbuing it with a reflective surface glimmer. The brass tea box was found in the desert outside Elko, Nevada. It is likely a relic abandoned by Chinese laborers who laid track for the transcontinental railroad.

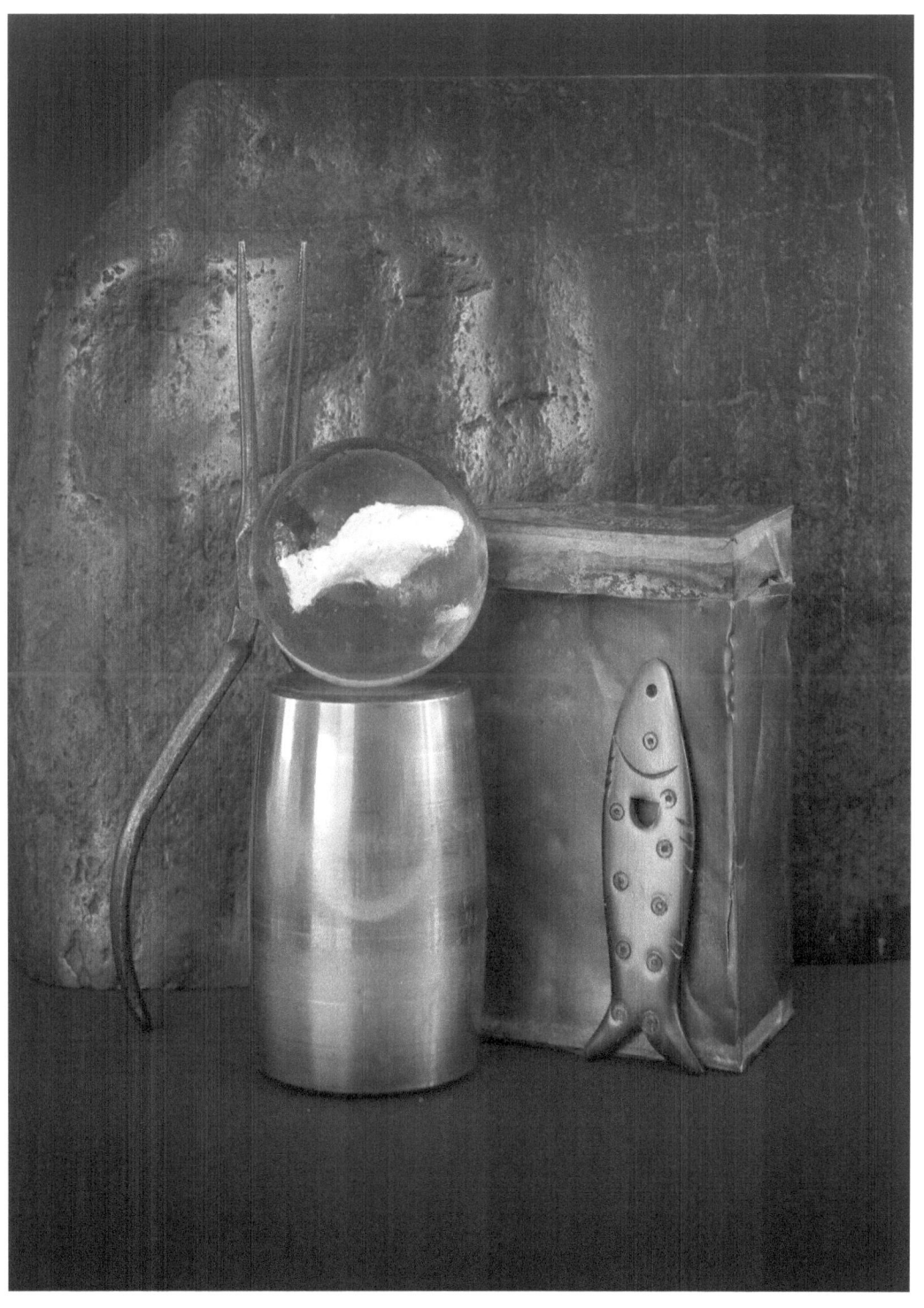

Ed Lavino

Turtle Skull and Cable

This human-sized sea turtle skull caused me to reflect on the myriad, potentially lethal obstacles sea turtles face on their migrations. It's incredible this one survived to reach such size. I constructed a sandy shoreline and inserted references to hazards. The curved piece of steel cable complements the shape of the skull, while exposing sharp, dangerous edges. The large metal object, a discarded dump truck hitch, is placed in close proximity to the skull, suggesting the brutal impact which too often occurs when sea turtles and ships collide.

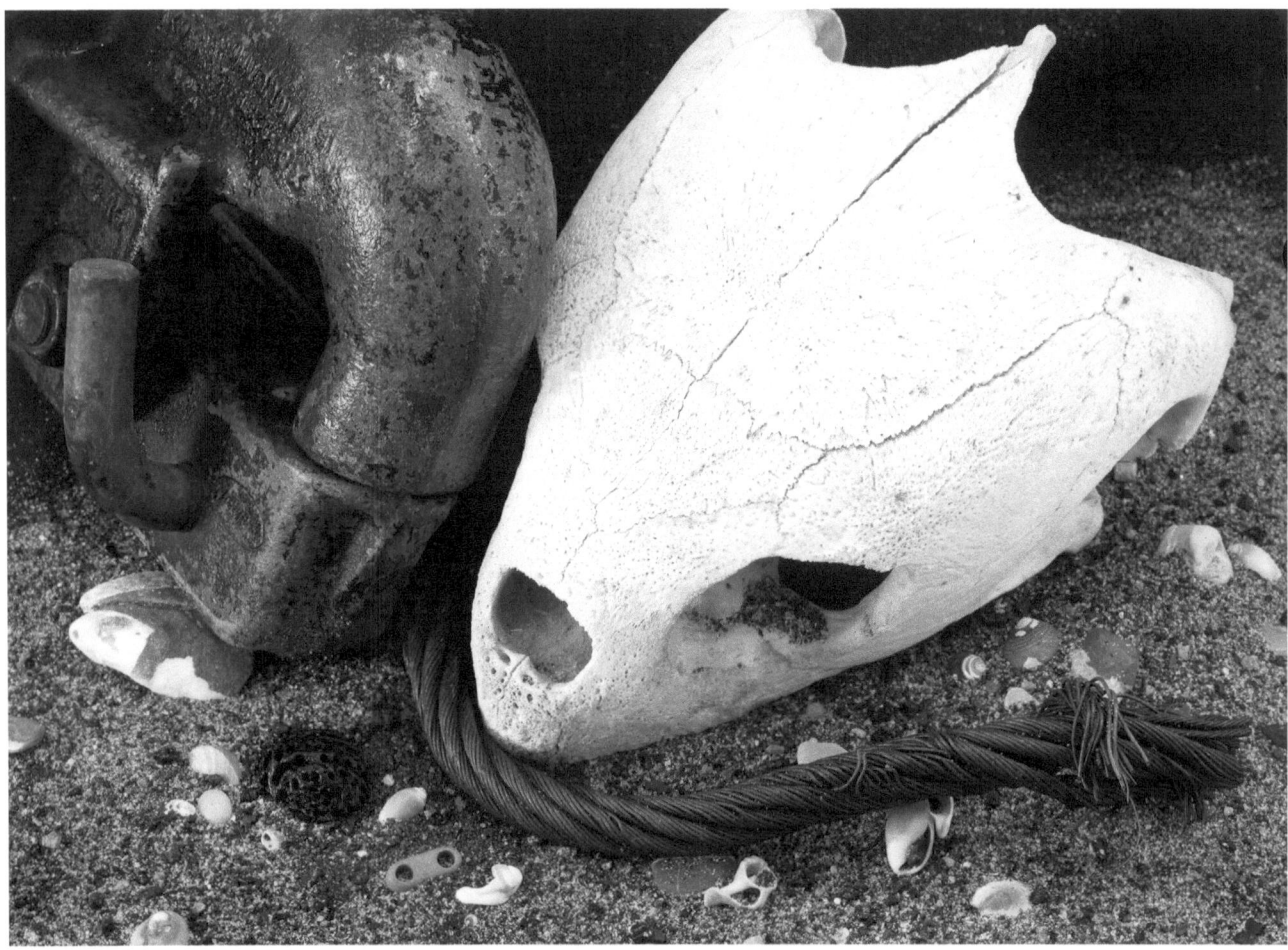

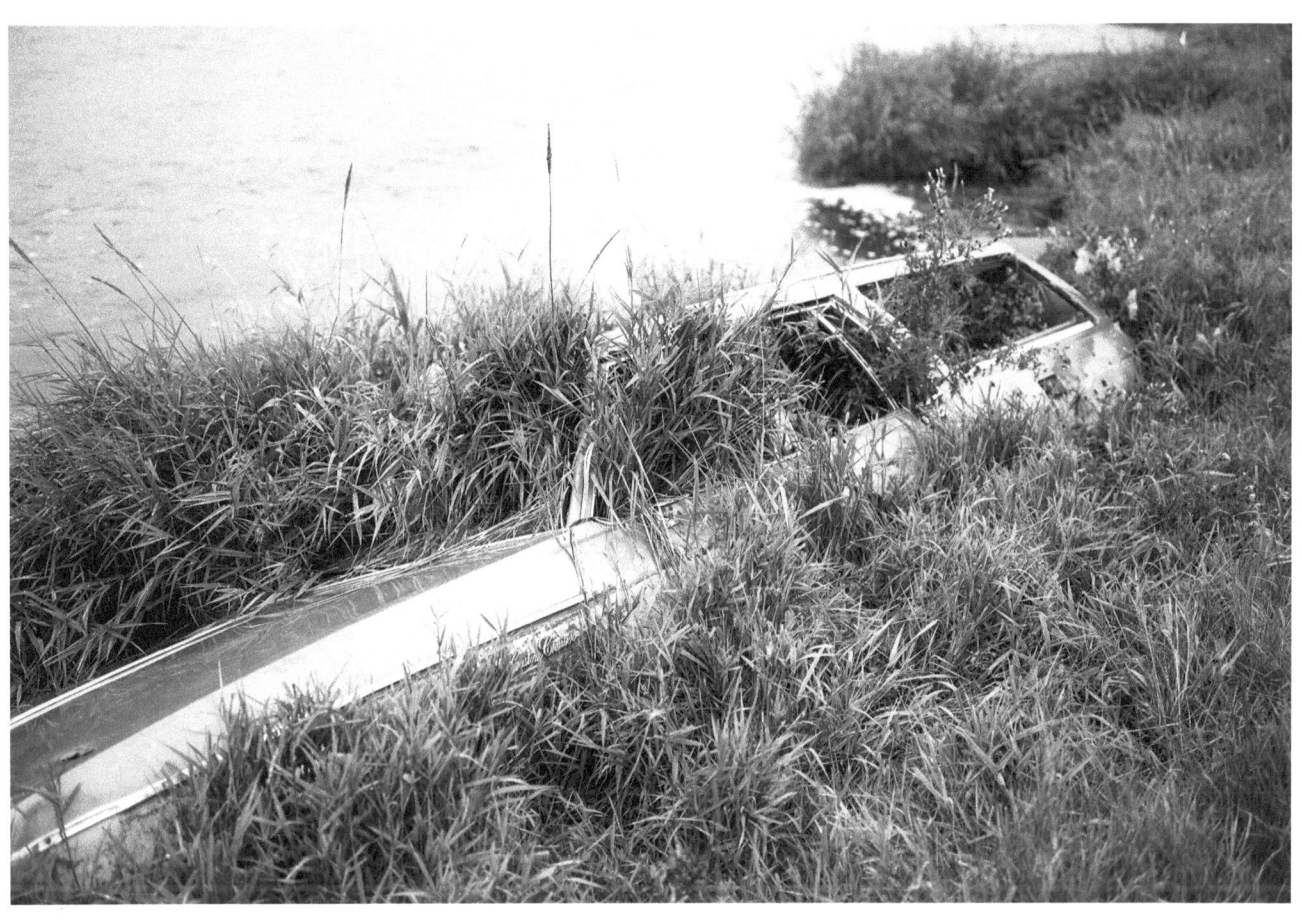

'67 Plymouth
Salt River, Wyoming

I discovered this sunken, overgrown car while land surveying along the banks of the Salt River. The farmer whose land I was on planted the Plymouth station wagon to stabilize an eroding riverbank. The native wetland grasses embrace the car, slowly pulling it into the earth.

Ed Lavino

Three Canadian Dimes

The broken glass fragments here represent ice sheets, under which centennial dimes with fish emblems are placed. I reference the once plentiful cod fishery off the shores of Canada. Individual fishermen, in wooden rowboats, using single hand lines, were replaced by large scale, floating factories. The ensuing decimation was fast and furious.

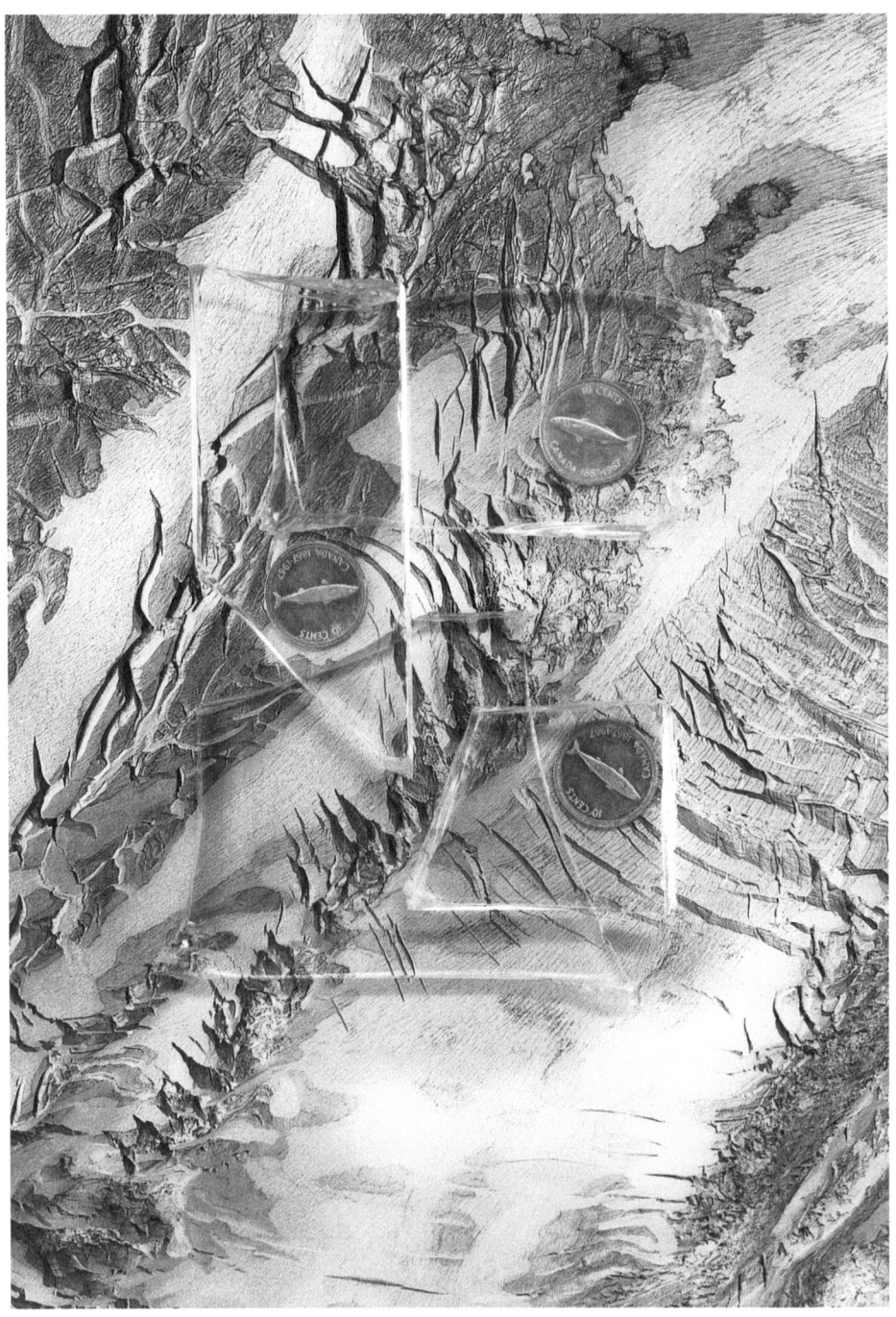

Three Chocolate Fish

I was attracted to these foil-covered chocolate fish while traveling in France. The broken paintbrush handle closely mimics the fish in form. The lead tire weight at the top balances the composition, but is also symbolically significant. Lead is harmful to aquatic ecosystems. Waterfowl, having no teeth, ingest gravel to grind up their food. Lead sinkers and jigs, easily mistaken for pebbles, are swallowed. The dose of lead in one sinker can prove deadly for a swan or loon, as it attempts to digest a meal of fish.

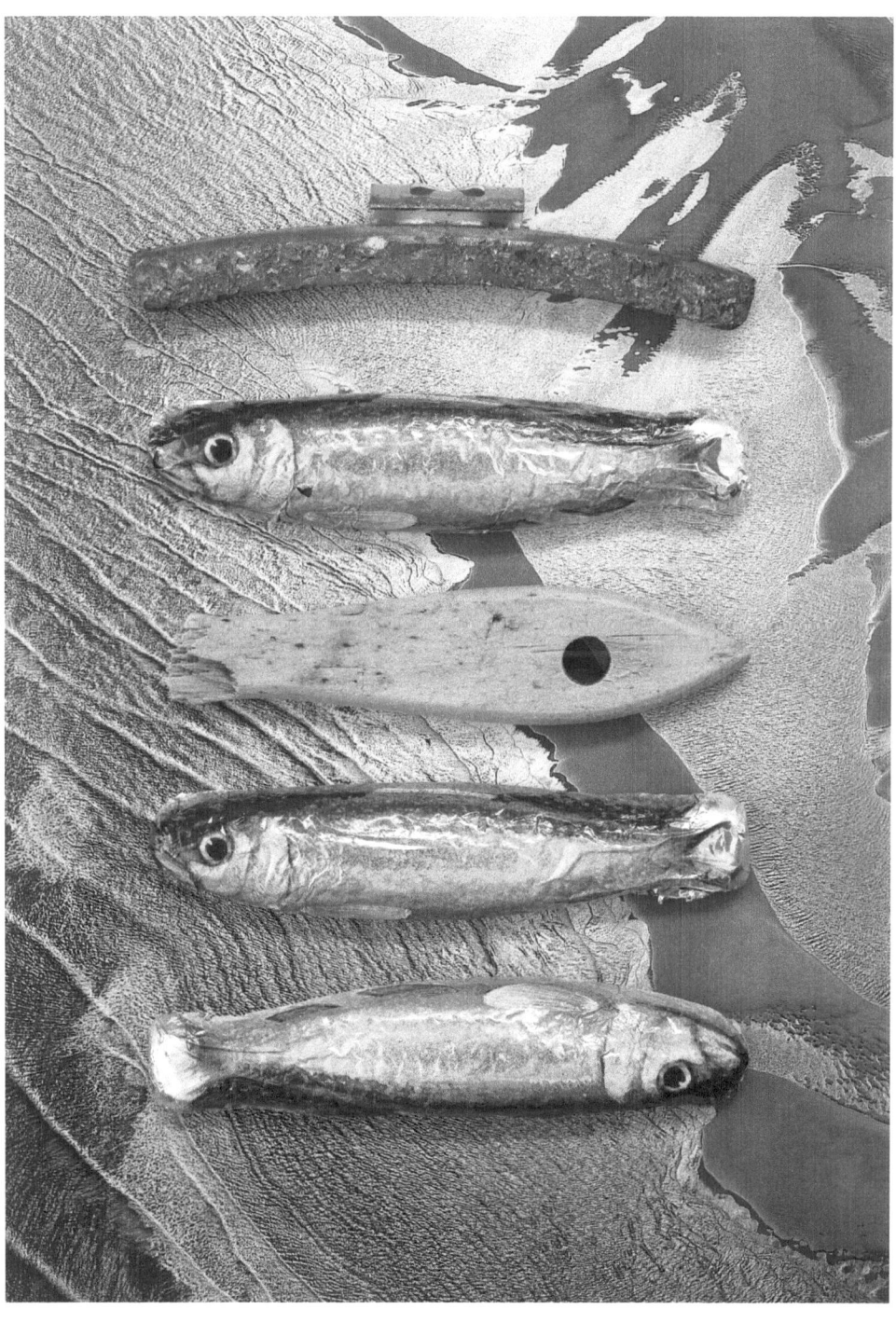

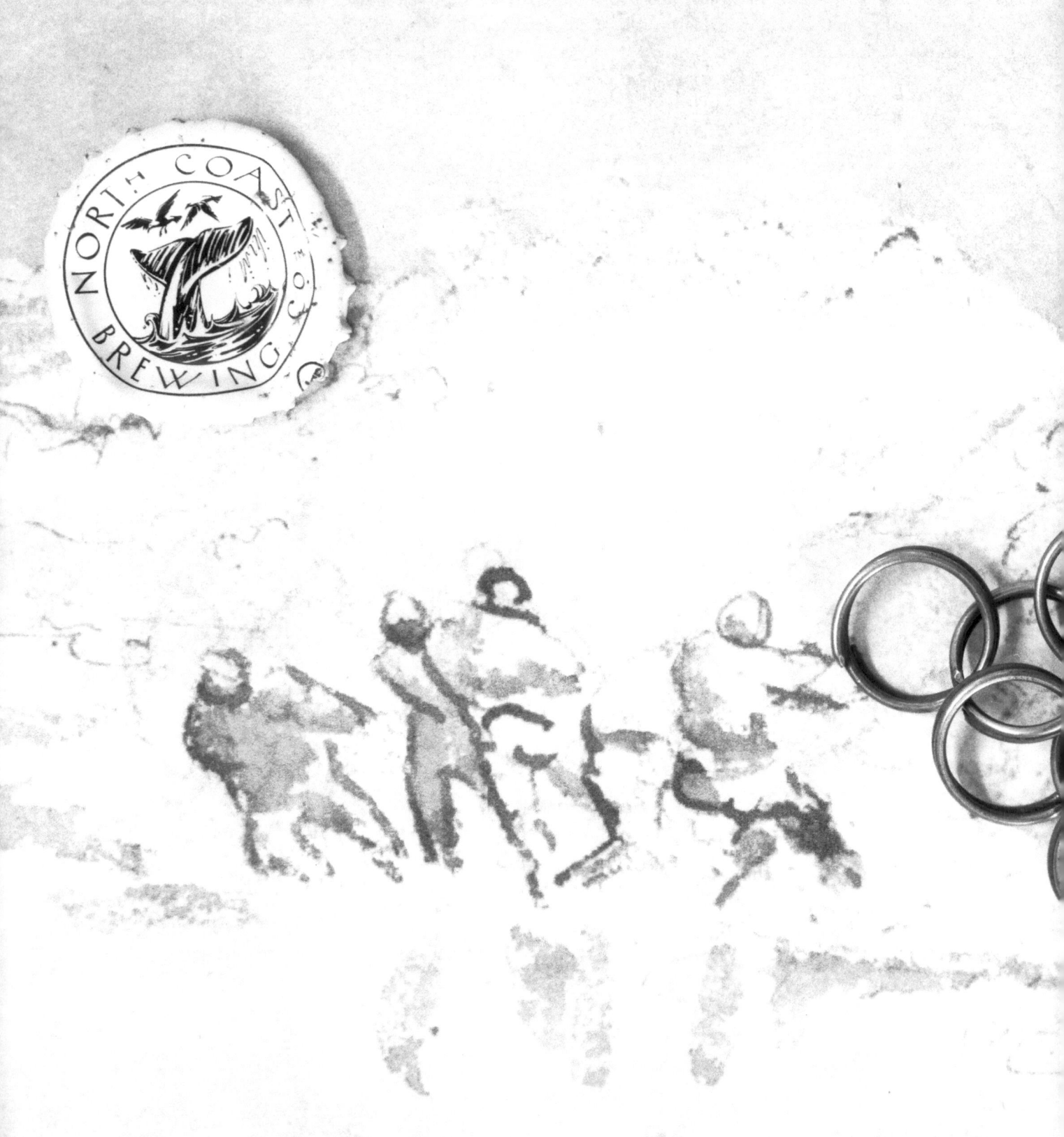

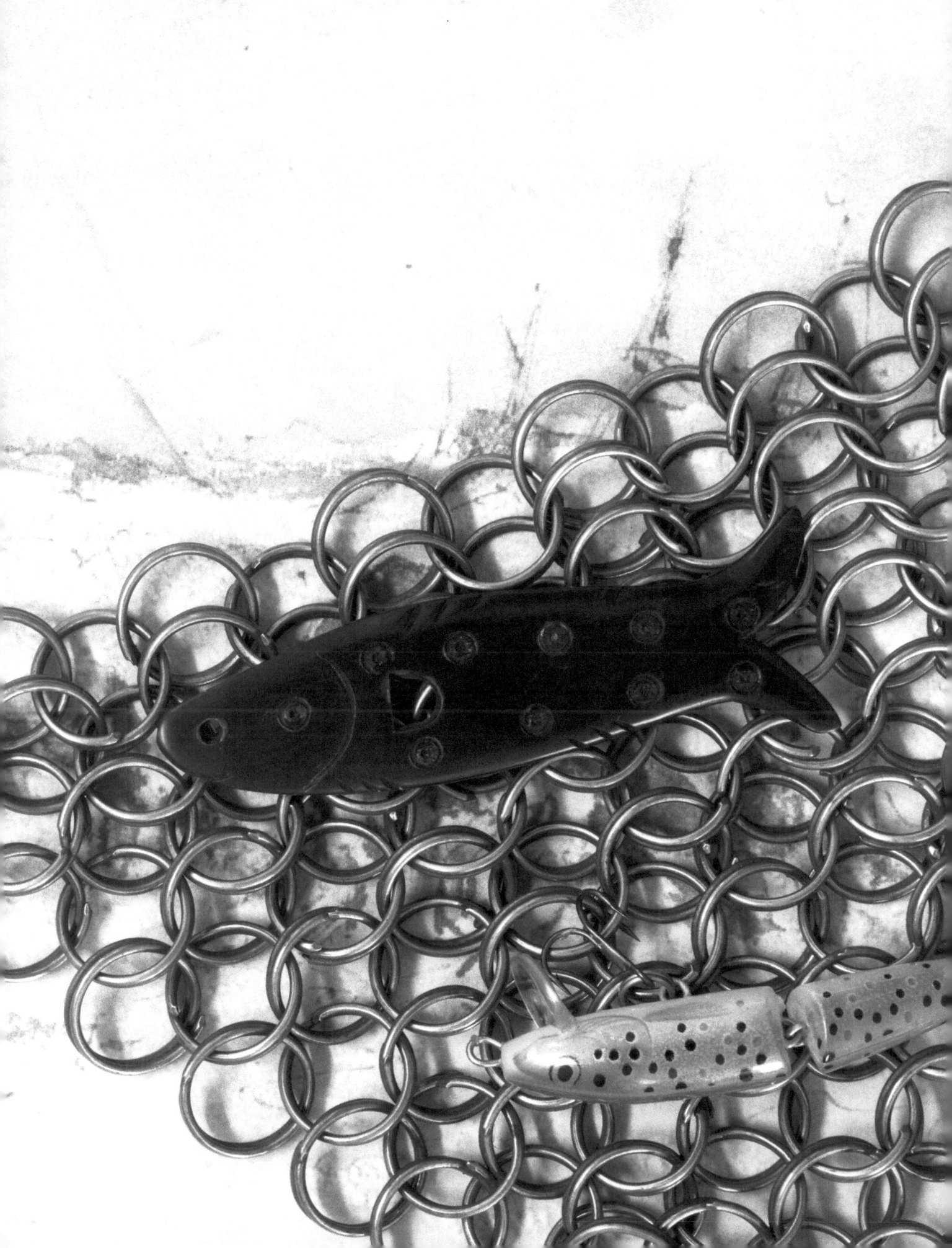

Ed Lavino

(Previous page) Whale's Tail and Fishermen

This object-enhanced image reflects a time when men caught fish by hand, in contrast to today's mechanized ships that dredge life indiscriminately off the ocean bottom.

Owl Petroglyph
Ring Lake Ranch, Wyoming

This petroglyph is located on a rocky hillside near Torrey Creek, in northwest Wyoming. The thousand-year-old owl design is pecked into the stone patina. Archaeologists speculate that the dotted line surrounding the bird may reference a spirit sighting during a vision quest. Once perhaps a bold emblem, now a mere trace of people long gone.

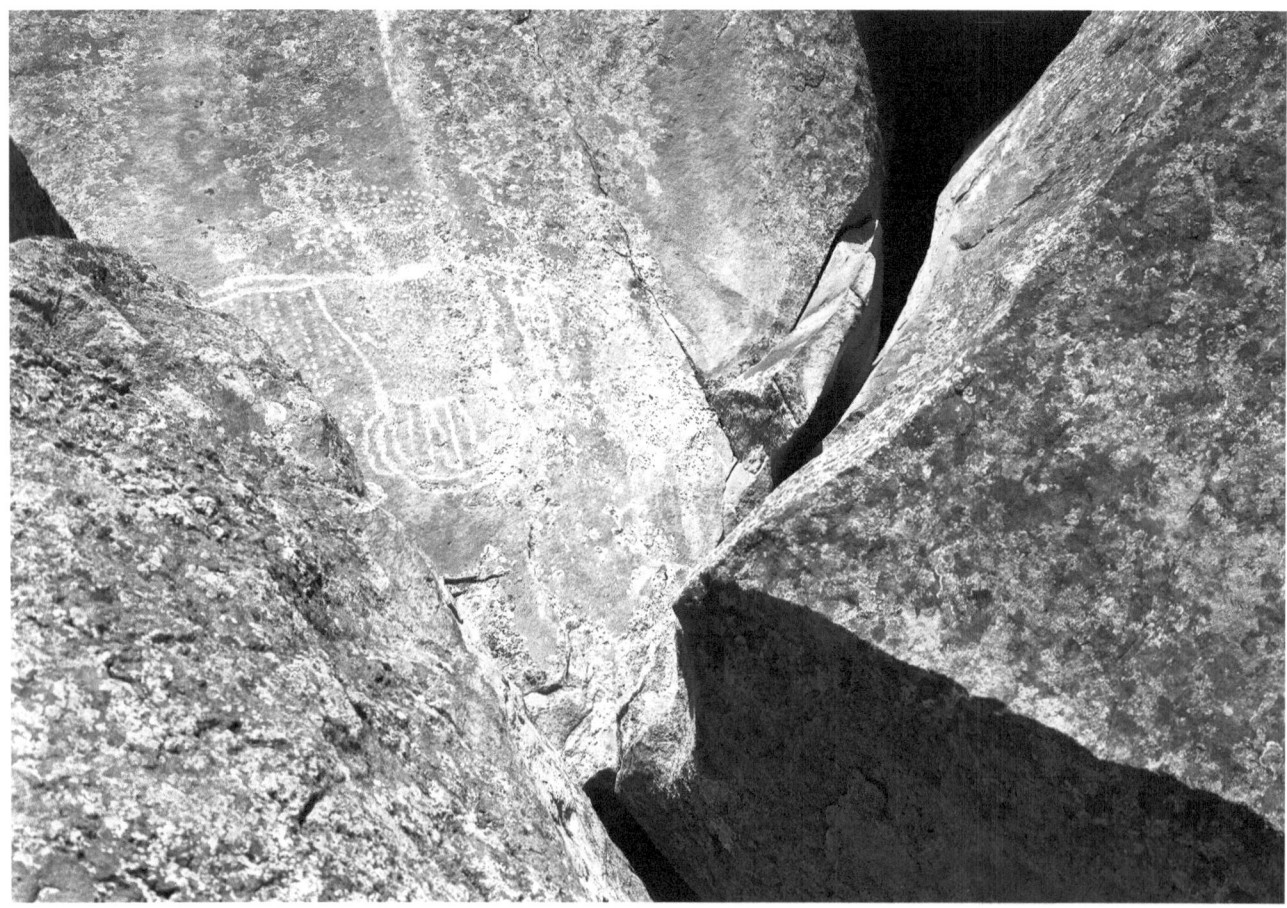

Prevailing Westerlies

This curtain hangs in a deserted log cabin on the grounds of an abandoned Christian mission, south of Fort Washakie. The butterfly pattern repeated in the lacework caught my eye. Sunlight transforms the curtain into a veil or filter, softening the world outside.

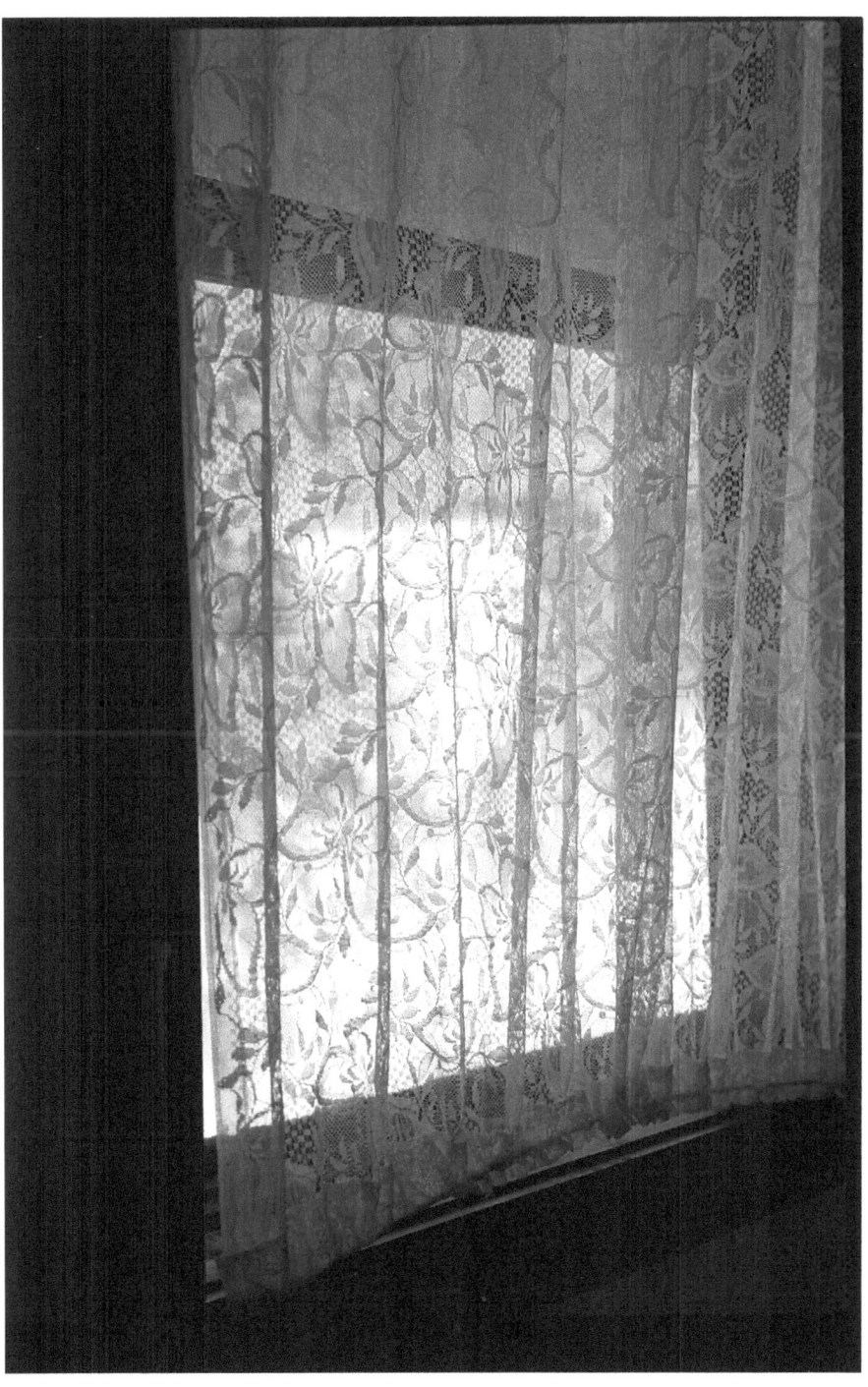

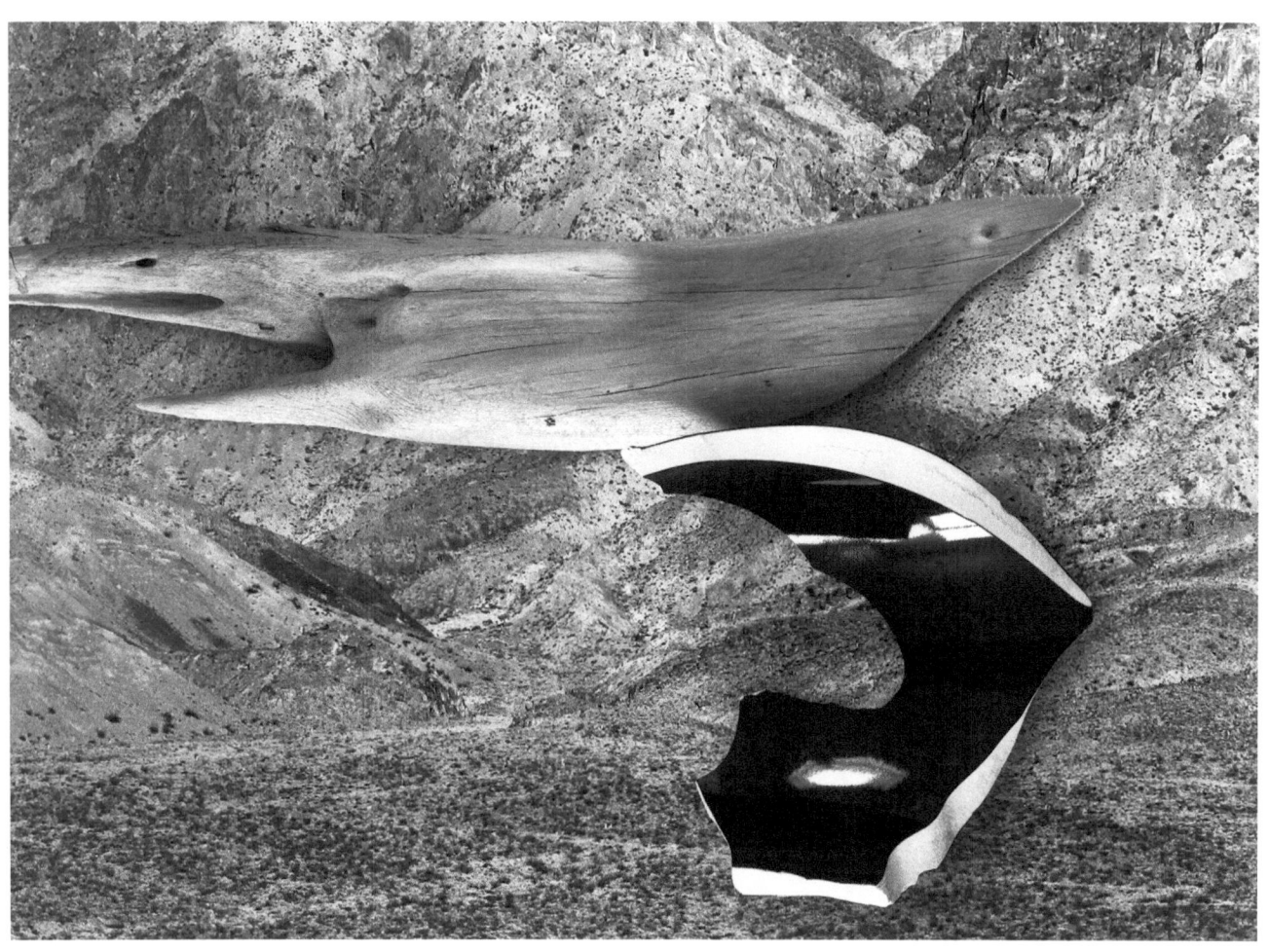

In Flight

This piece of driftwood reminded me of a bird in flight. Together, the two forms create a synergy that enhances the sensation of soaring. A concocted universe, with disparate objects, creates a new visual logic.

Prevailing Westerlies

The title of this piece references the lyrics of a song by the same name describing a hobo's paradise. As with the song, this composition is whimsical. A vintage illustration on a box of French chocolates sets the stage. The pine cone is a delicate, glitter-encrusted glass ornament. I think the songwriter and I would agree that playfulness and serendipity make life's struggles more palatable.

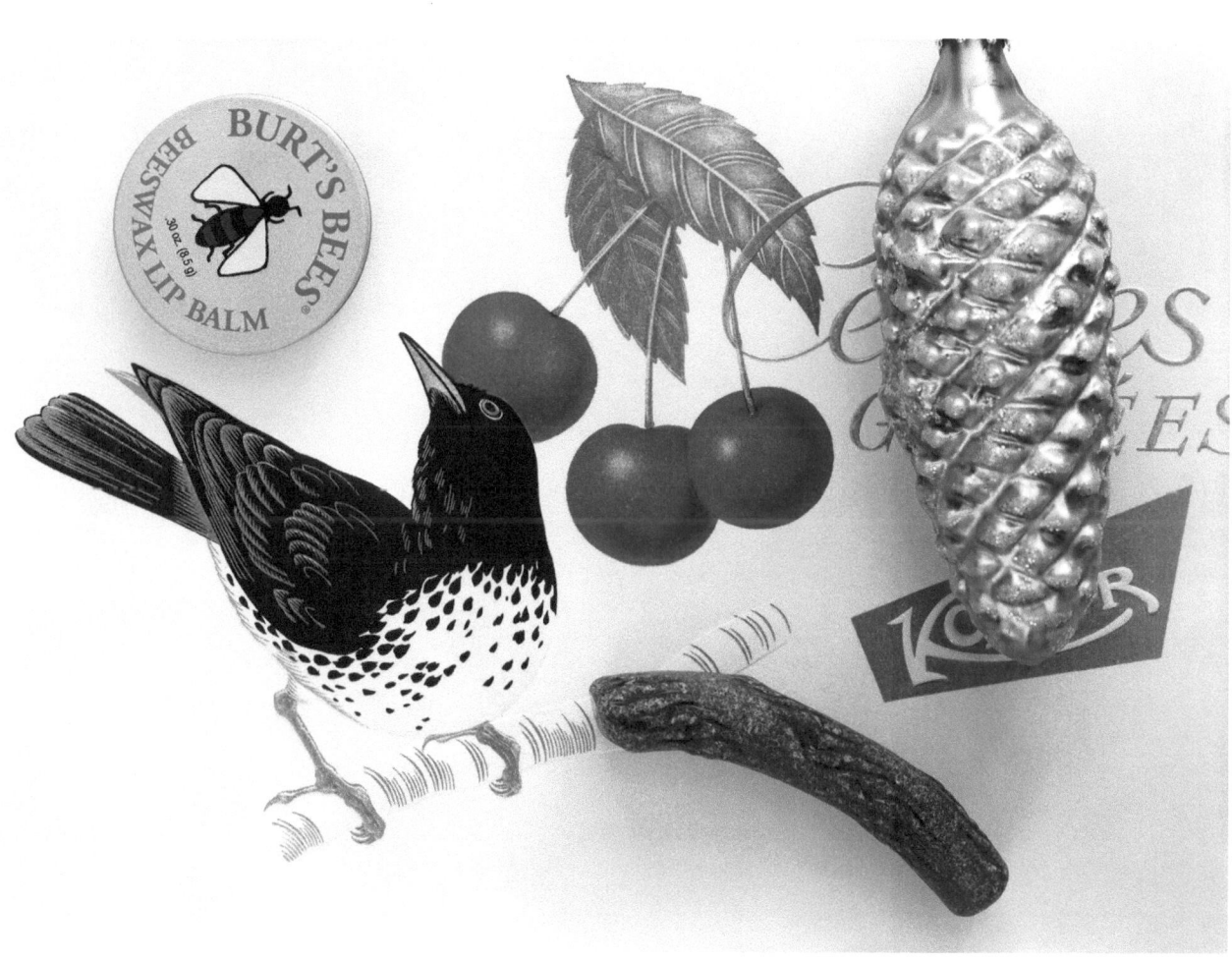

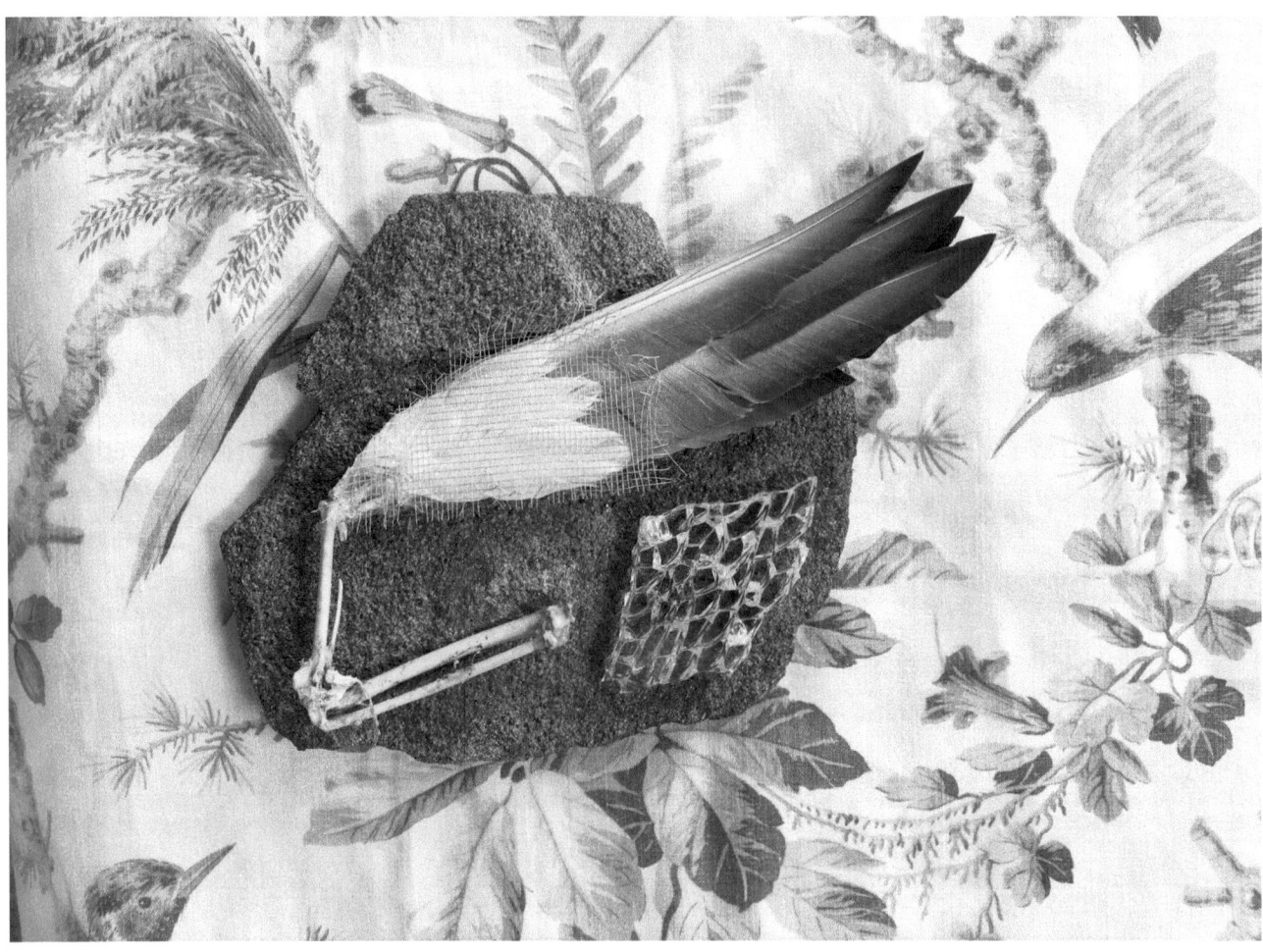

Duck Wing on French Fabric

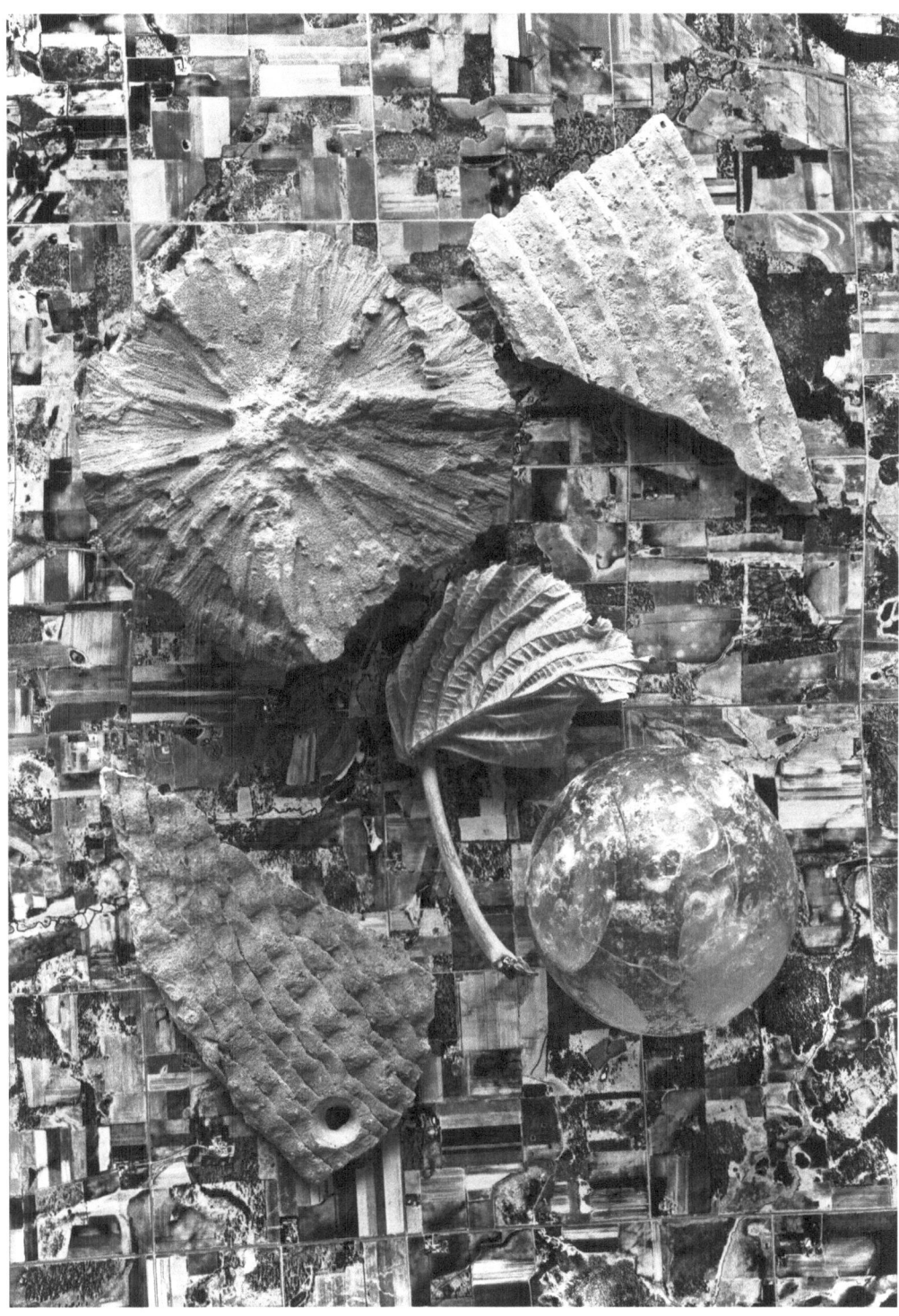

Revolving Tenants

Some ideas are better articulated visually than verbally. Much of my art addresses layers of meaning. In this image, the cyclical nature of life on earth is reflected in an assortment of objects. Some natural, and others man-made, they appear to float above the earth, hinting at their origins.

Ed Lavino

Elegy for a Mallard

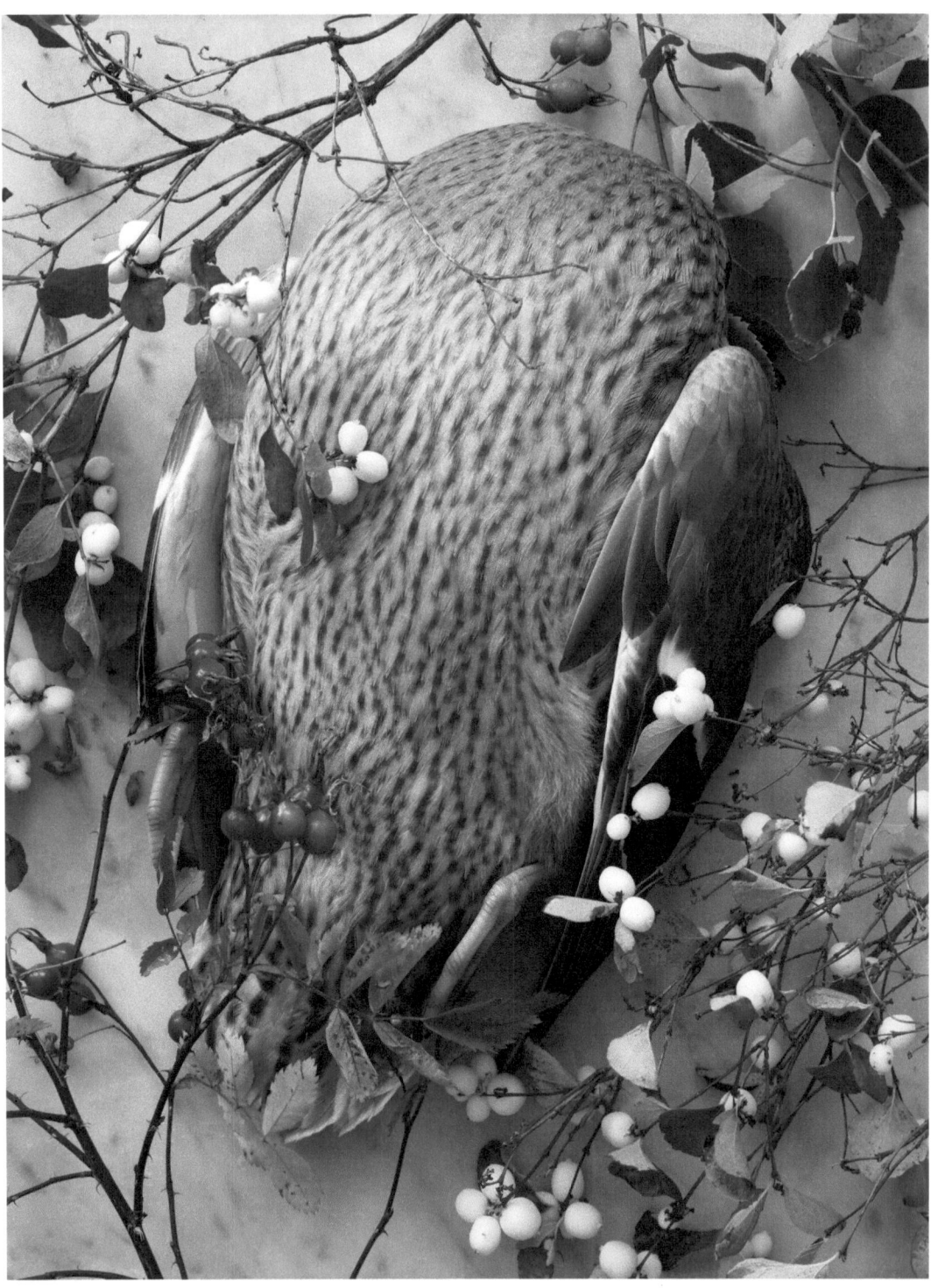

Out walking, I found this duck lying at the edge of the road. It likely hit an overhead utility line, broke its neck, and fell to earth. In homage to this bird's life, I shrouded its exquisite form in a funerary arrangement of snowberries and rosehips.

Prevailing Westerlies

Milkweed Pods and Brown Packing

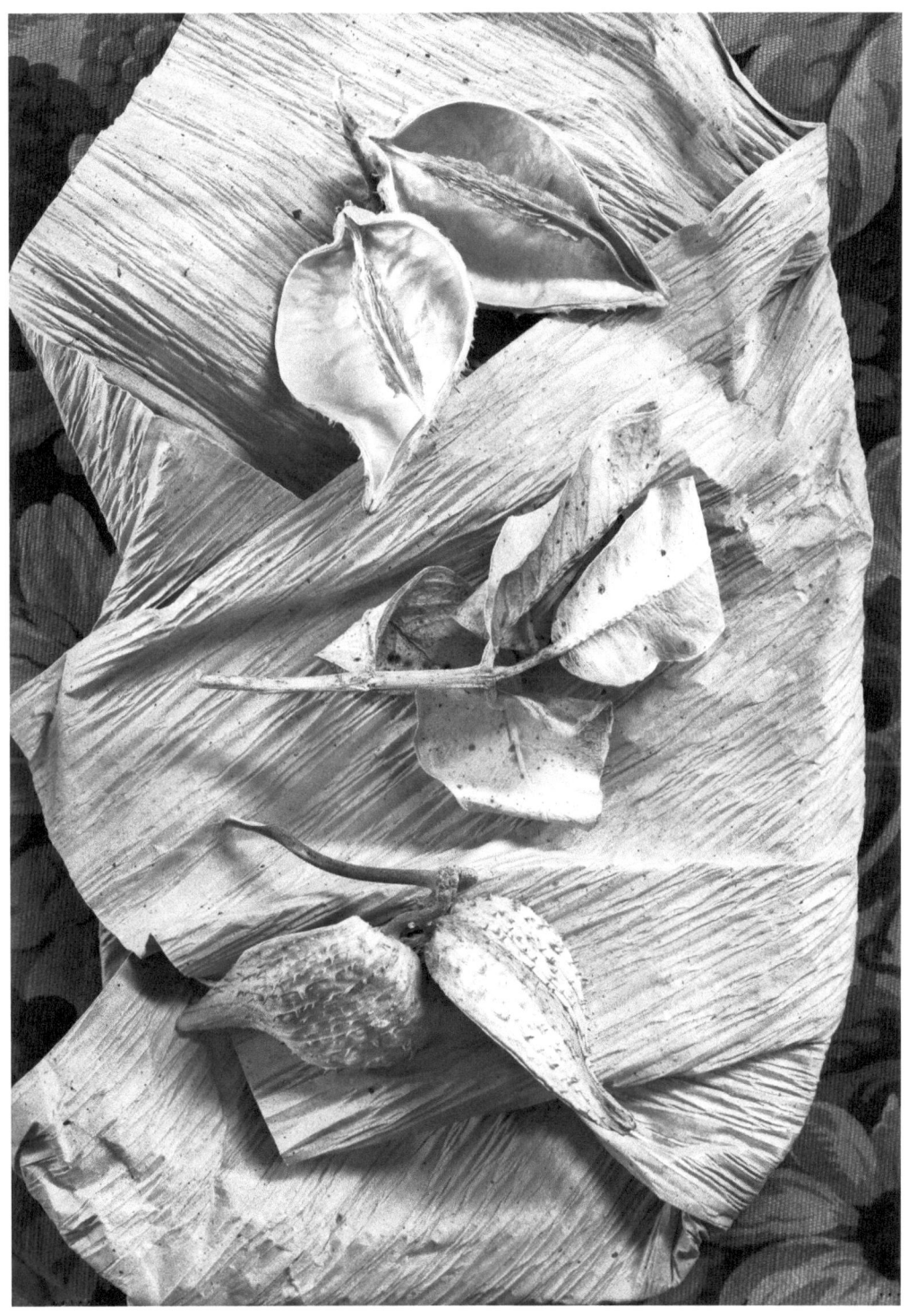

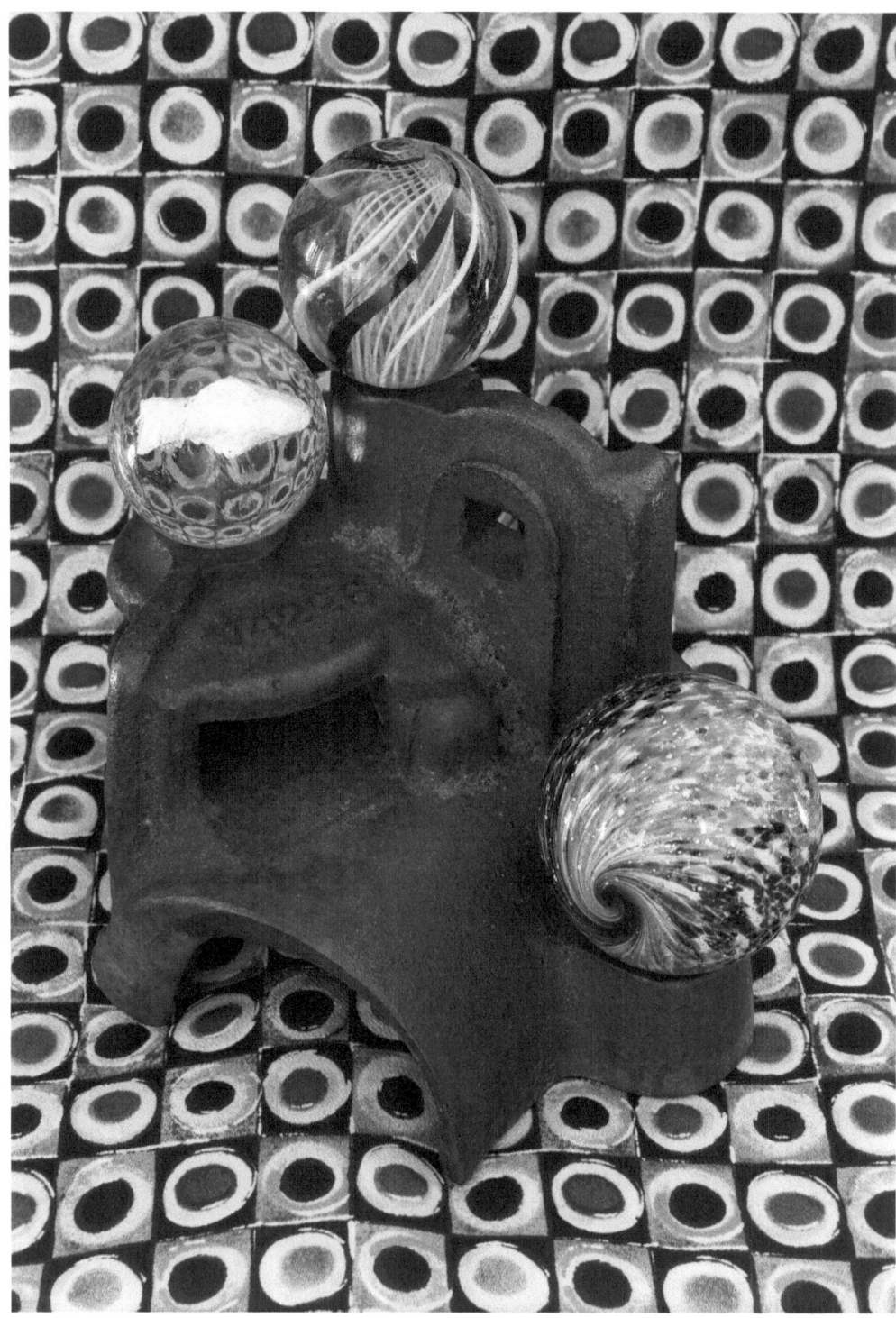

Black Holes in Two Dimensions

The purpose of art is not to copy life, but to create a different truth. The new opus is even more potent in its power to transfix, and to reveal alternate realities.

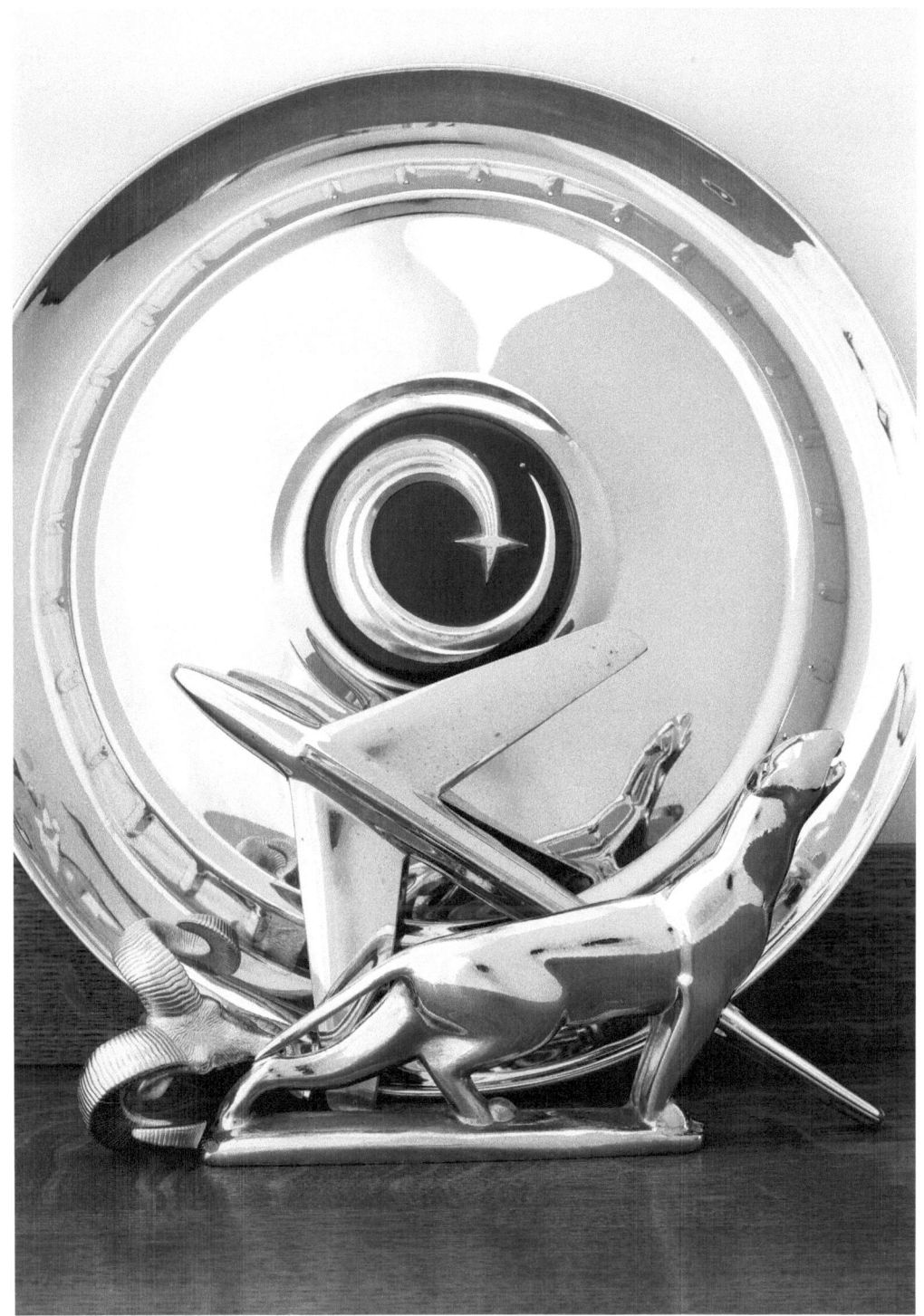

Chromed Nature

The chromed hood ornaments and hubcap of this still life create a shiny universe: celestial heavens with idealized creatures living beneath.

Ed Lavino

Eternal Wake

This taxidermy mount was created in the early 1900s, from one of the last free-roaming bison to graze the upper DuNoir valley of Wyoming. The lifelike preservation and display create the impression of an eternal wake for this long-gone bison.

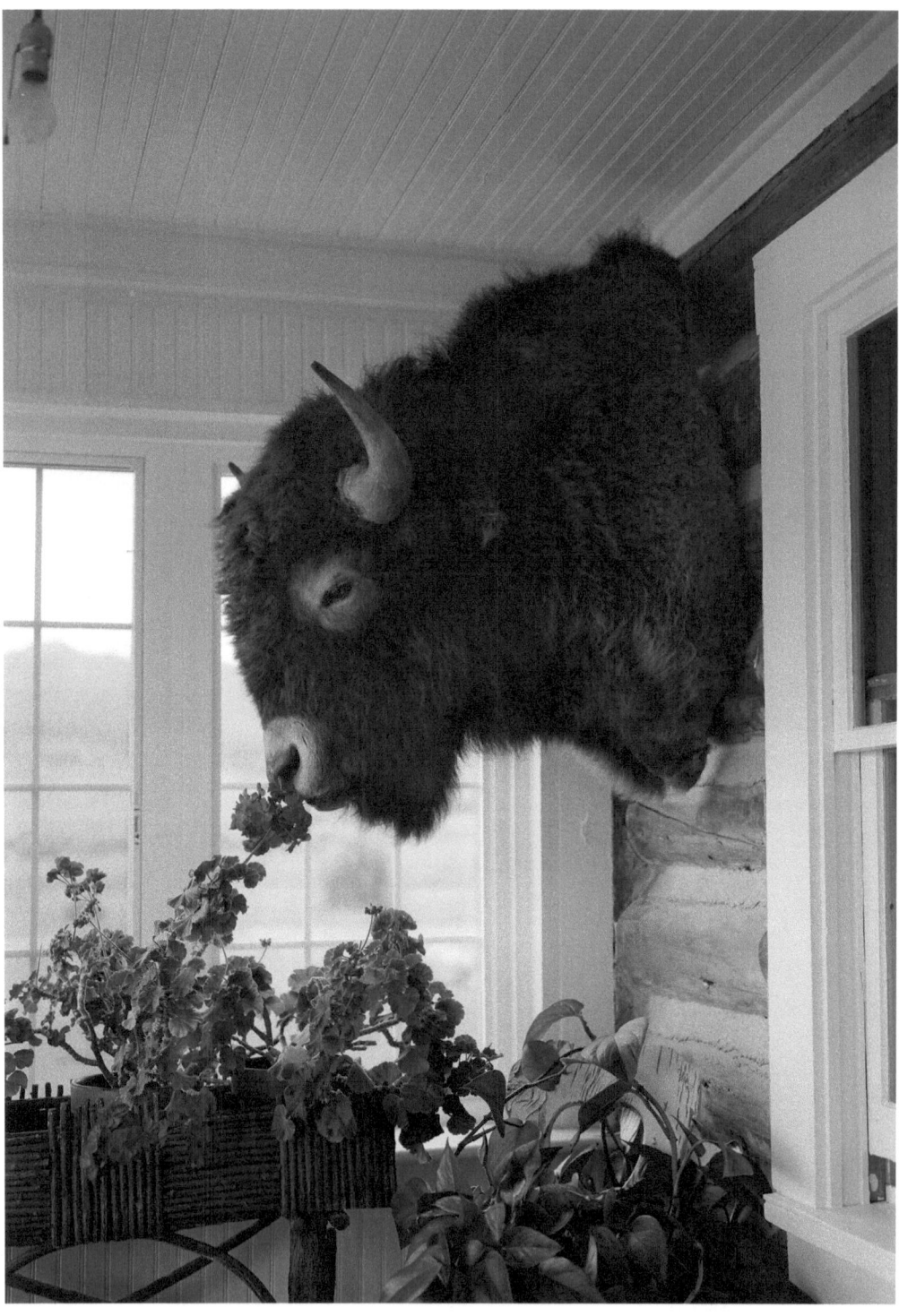

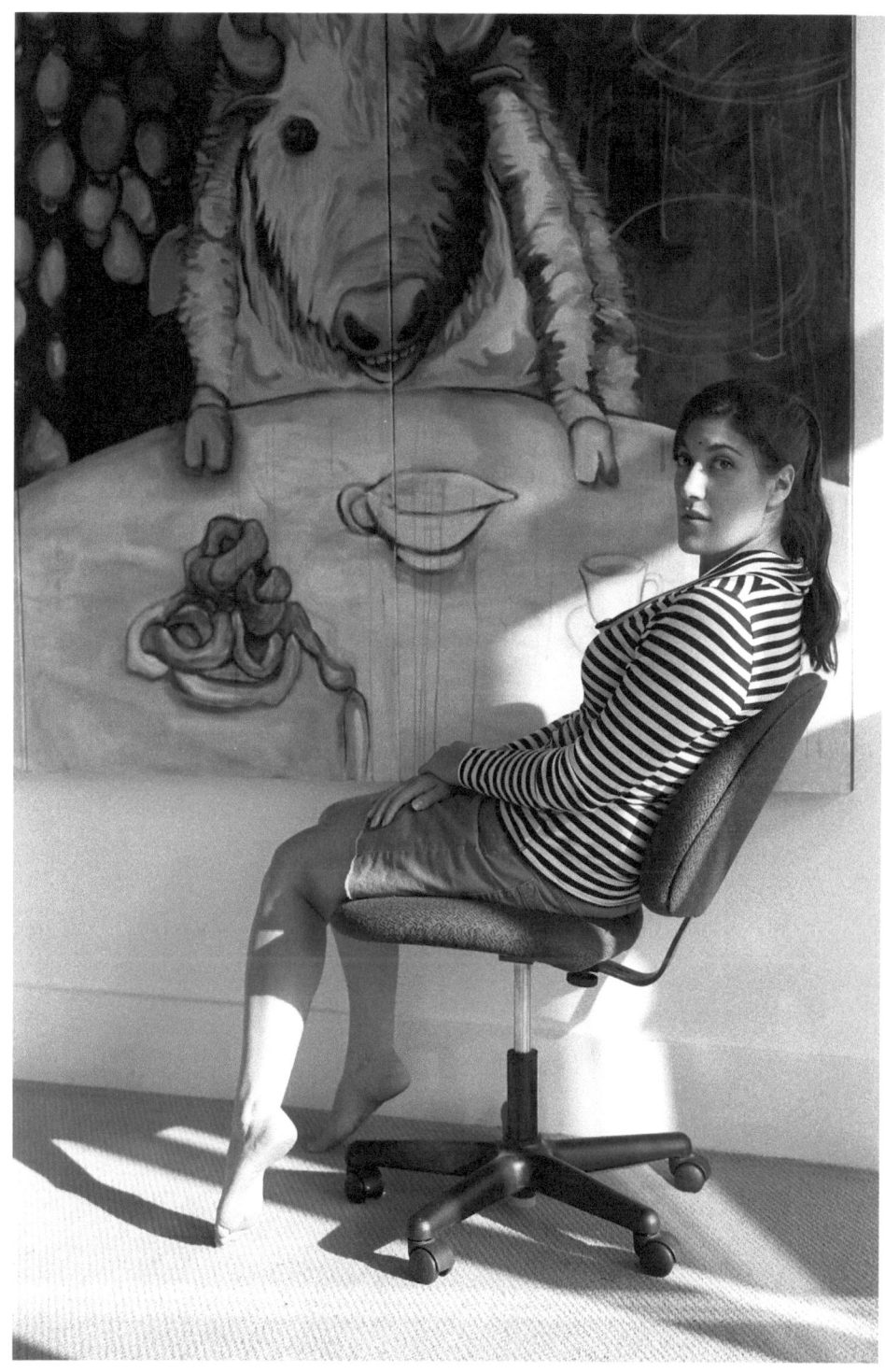

Danforth Gallery,
Livingston, Montana

Soussan, the art gallery receptionist, humored me by posing as if she were seated at the table with the bison in this life-sized painting.

Ed Lavino

Drop Tine Taxidermy
Sheridan, Wyoming

Unpretentious, folksy displays of objects fascinate me. When photographed exactly as they are found, they sometimes prove to be the most prophetic and surreal things I have seen.

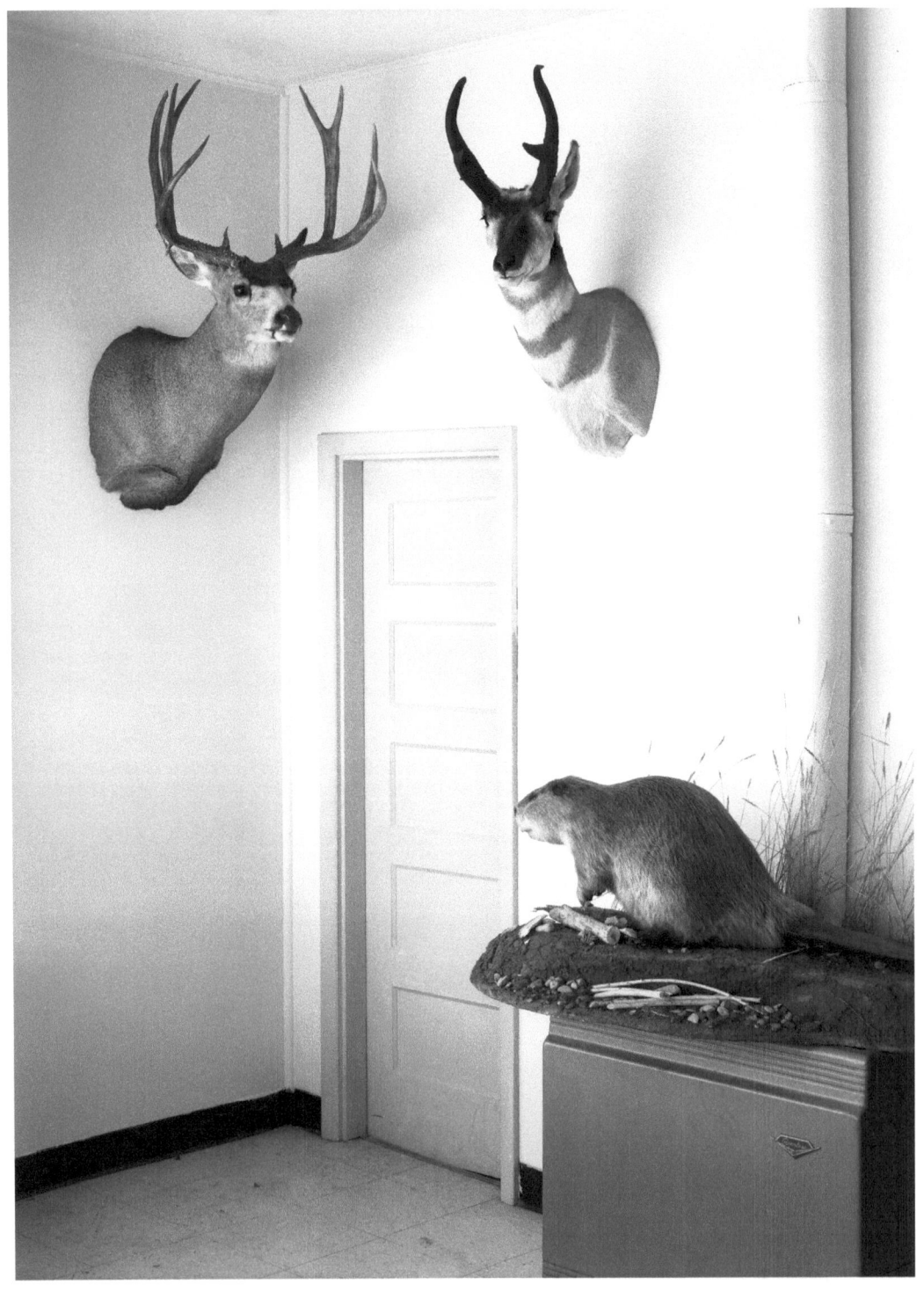

Prevailing Westerlies

This dusty mountain goat mount stands above the main entrance of the Murray Hotel in Livingston, Montana. My 5"x7" view camera was set up in the lobby, looking out on the sun-filled main street. It was off-season, so few people came and went during the twenty-minute exposure necessary to capture detail in this shadowy niche.

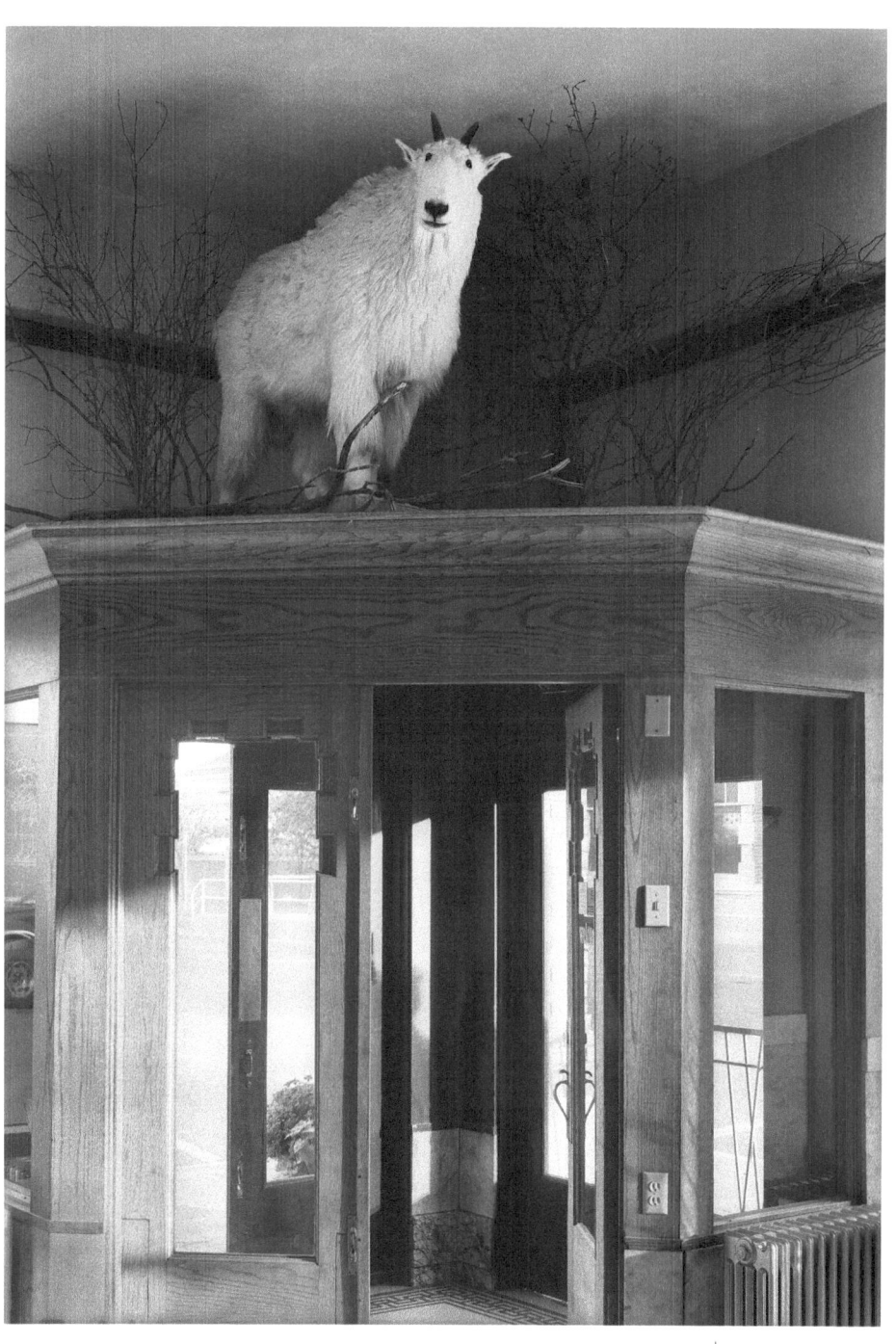

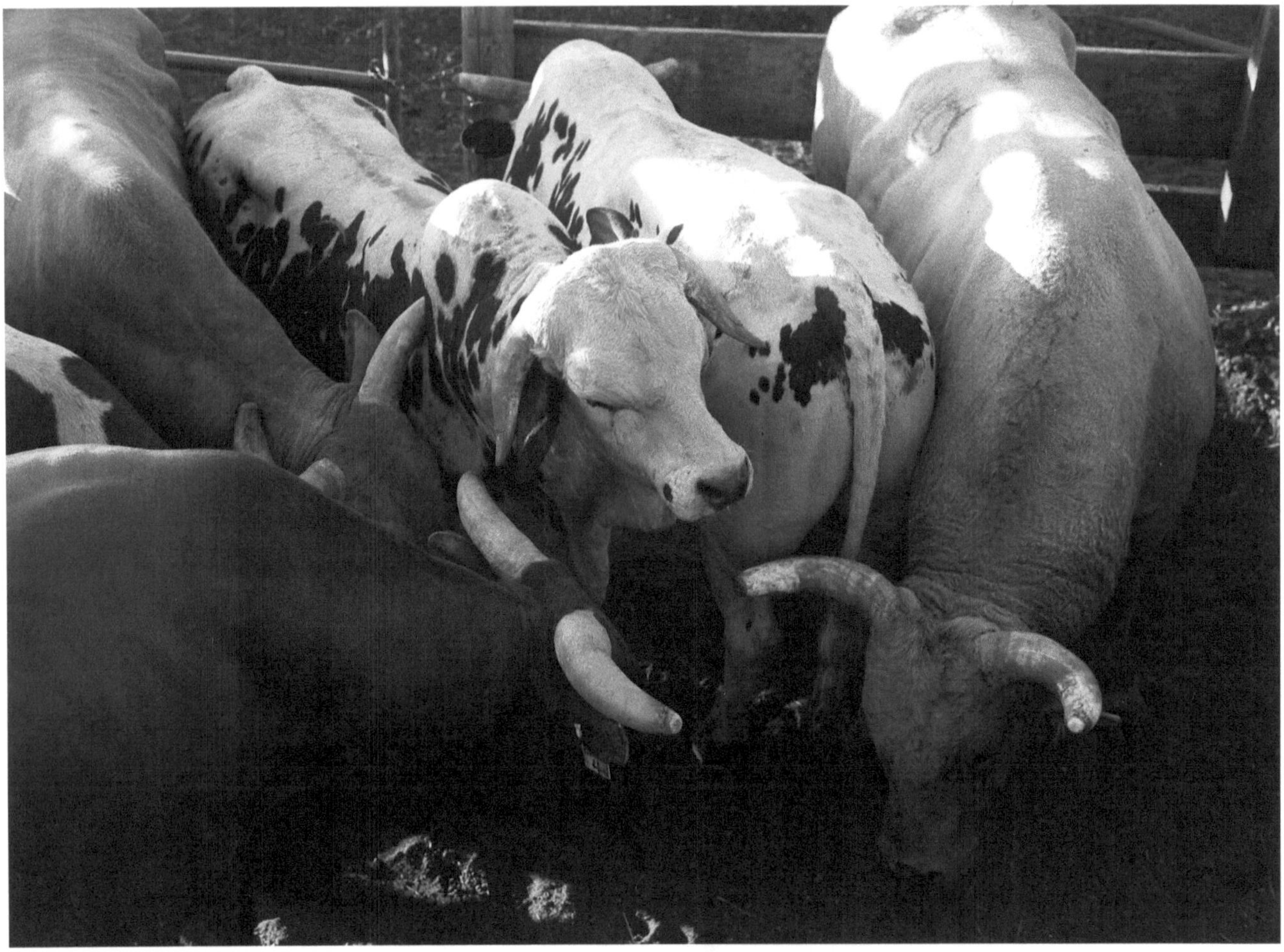

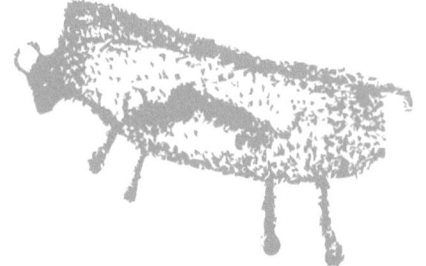

Rodeo Stock
Big Timber, Montana

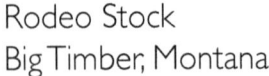

The tightness of this shot allowed me to capture the rising tension between the bulls, as they worked out their dominance hierarchy within the pen. The pent-up aggression right before the animals were pushed into their individual holding chutes was palpable. I empathized with the anxious, young cowboys who would soon be on their backs.

Prevailing Westerlies

The framed photograph of Old Faithful is by Frank J. Haynes, a famous turn-of-the-century Yellowstone photographer. The taxidermy buffalo head is unusually well executed in its realistic nature, and especially its expression. My photograph comically juxtaposes these two Yellowstone icons.

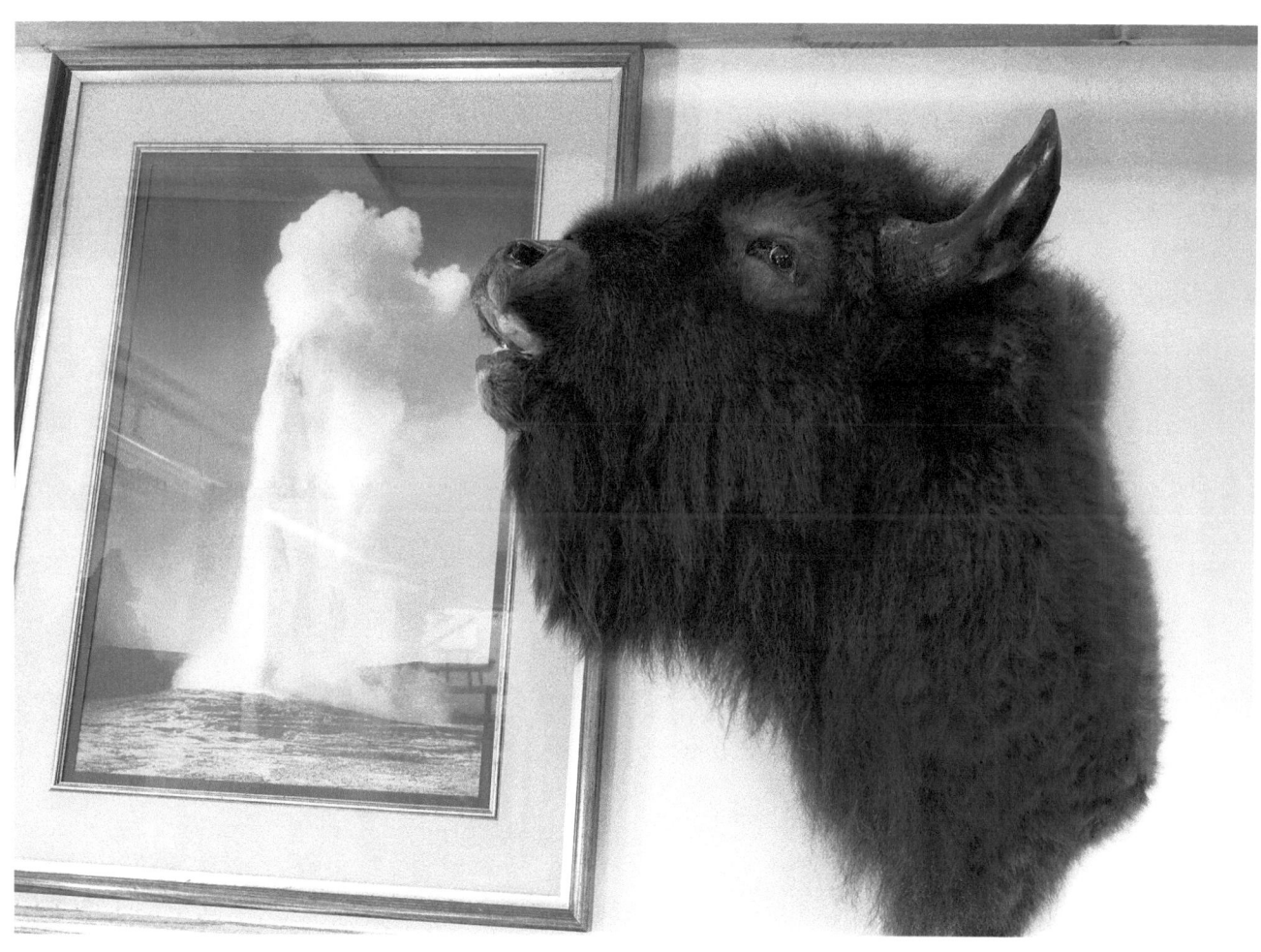

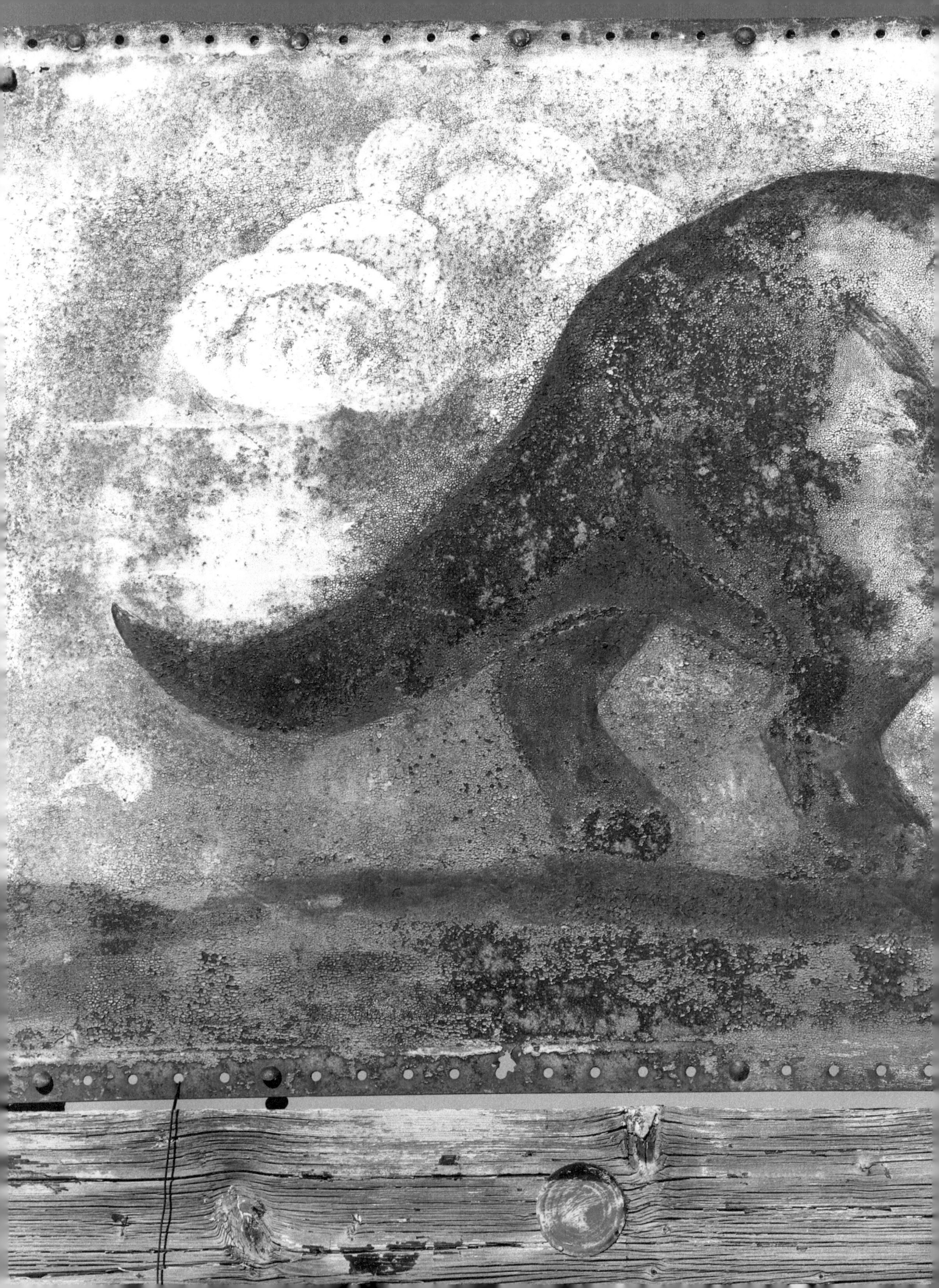

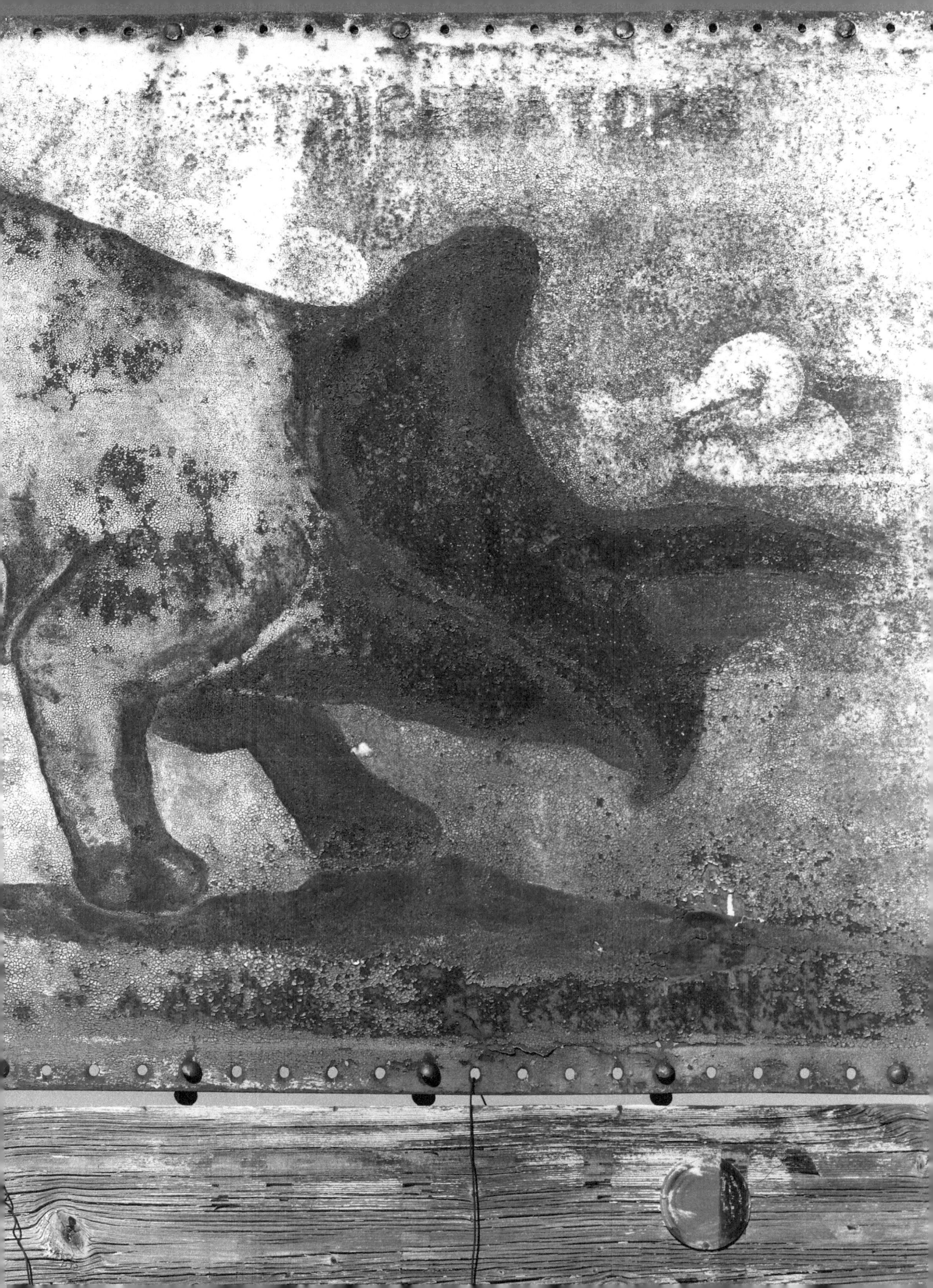

Ed Lavino

(Previous page) Triceratops Sign
Medicine Bow, Wyoming

This hand-painted tin sign advertises a former roadside attraction: a one-room museum or "fossil cabin" constructed entirely of dinosaur bones in the early 1930's. The private museum closed over 20 years ago, but the cabin still stands near the Como Bluff dinosaur bone beds. The rusted sign has long since been removed.

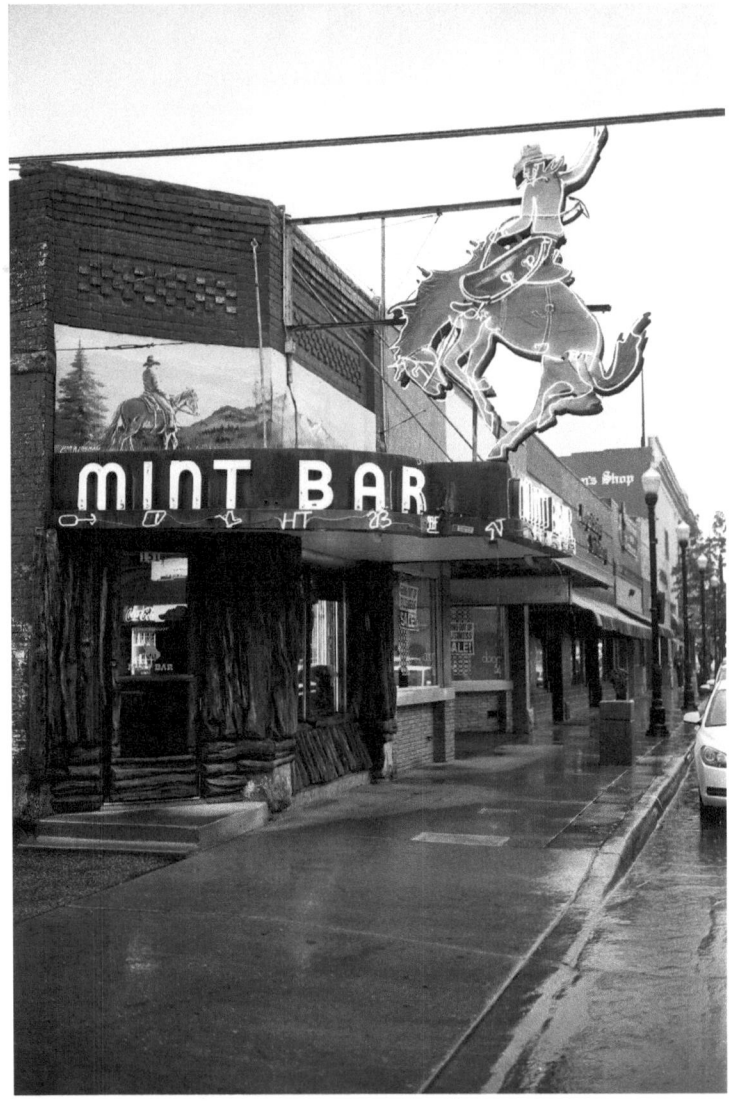

Mint Bar
Sheridan, Wyoming

This photograph was taken on a rainy evening just before dusk. The string of local cattle brands, reproduced in neon at the base of the sign, reflects a long history of local ranching. The image of a cowboy on a bucking bronco is a cliché of the old west, yet working cowboys remain a vital and relevant part of our western heritage. Not much has changed in this line of work since the days of the open range.

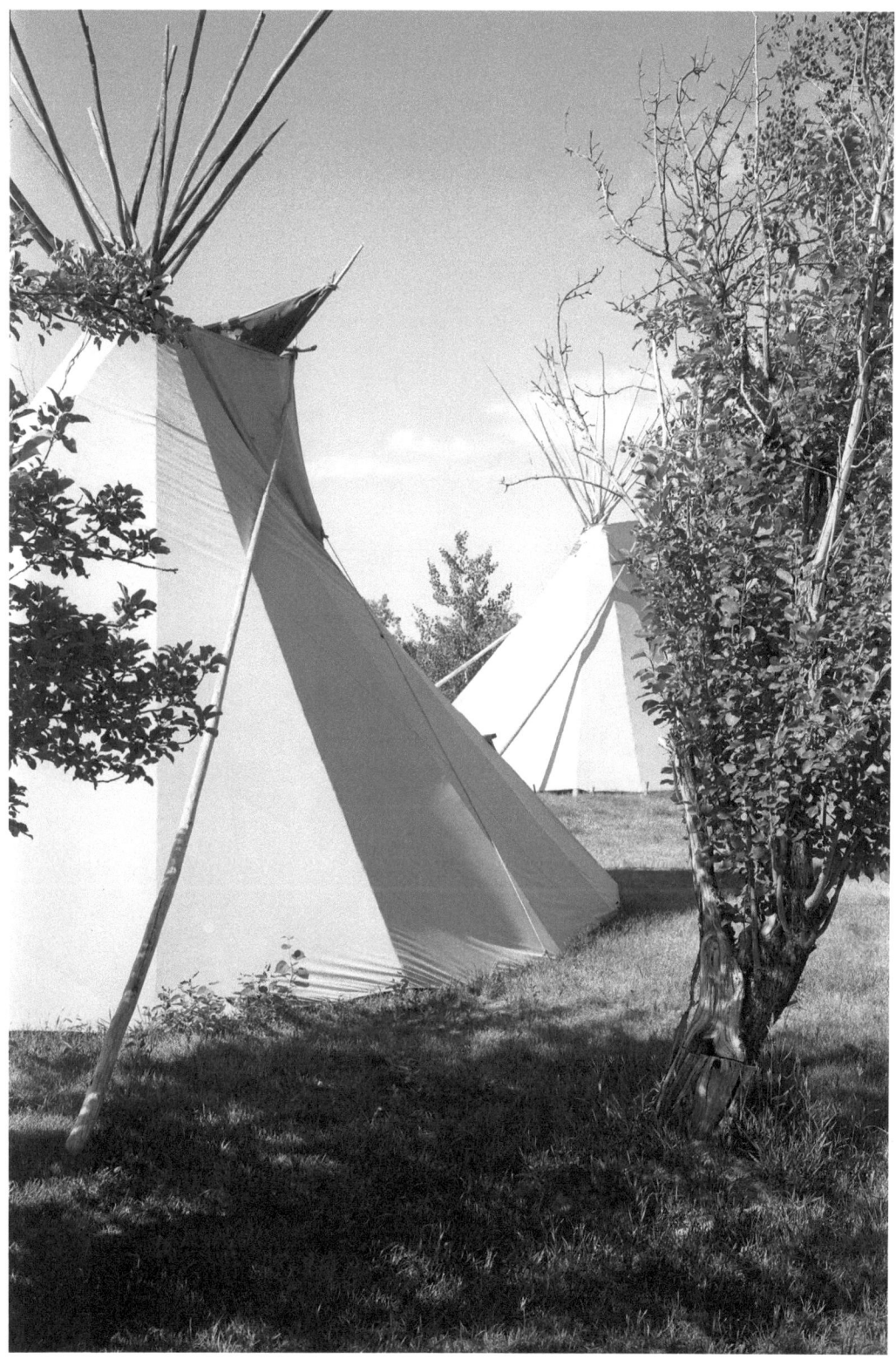

Teepee
Fort Washakie, Wyoming

Ed Lavino

Geronimo
Shoshoni, Wyoming

This tribute to Geronimo appears on the side of an abandoned bar. The mural references a famous 1887 photographic portrait of Geronimo by Ben Wittick. The expression of this Apache warrior and chief reflects his independence and fierce resistance. Modern tribal members still draw inspiration from tales of Geronimo's unconquerable spirit.

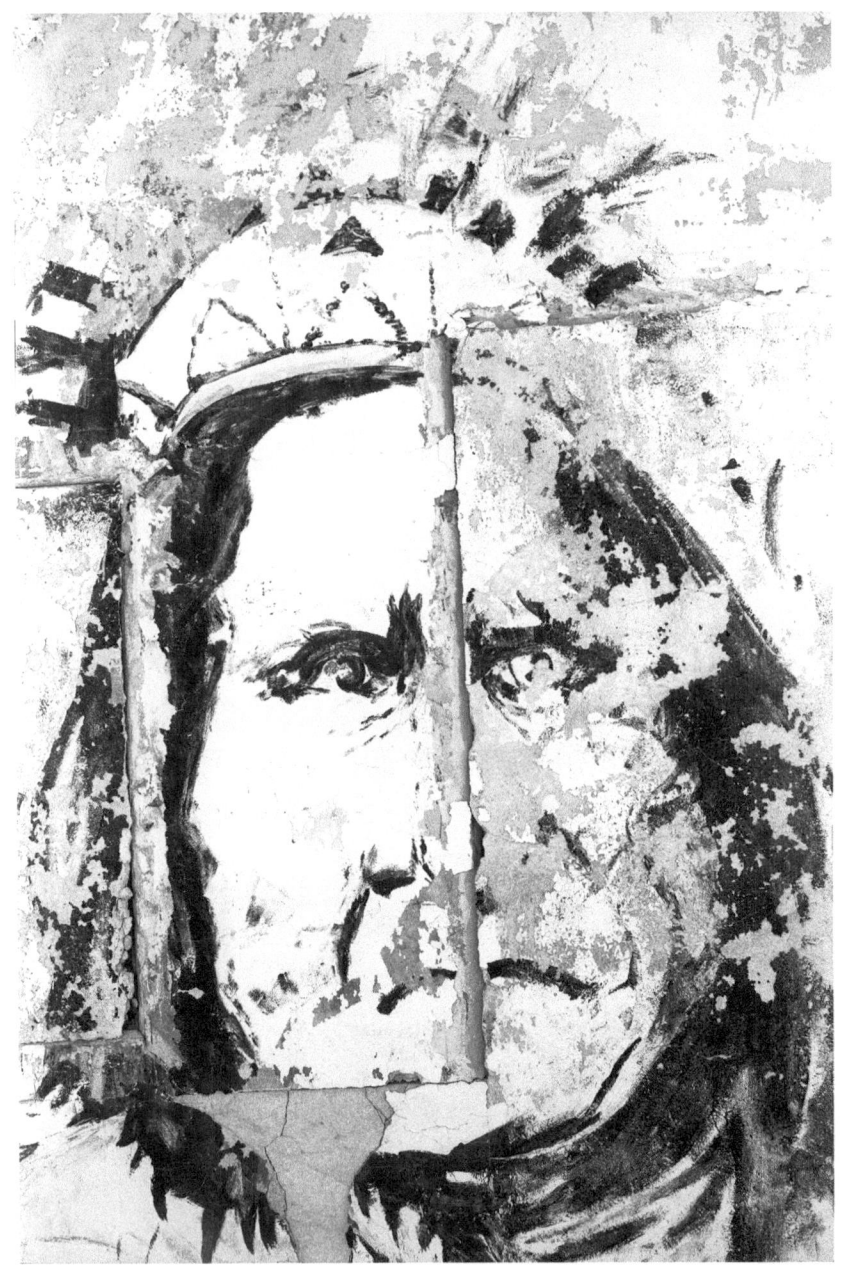

"I was born on the prairies where the wind blew free and there was nothing to break the light of the sun. I was born where there were no enclosures."
— Geronimo

Punk
Shoshoni, Wyoming

Punk (a life-long nickname) is a former cowboy, bronc rider, and oil patch worker. He was born on the Fort Peck Indian Reservation in Montana. I met Punk as he was gardening outside his house in Shoshoni. After talking with him for several enjoyable hours, I photographed him in the diffuse light of an outbuilding on his property.

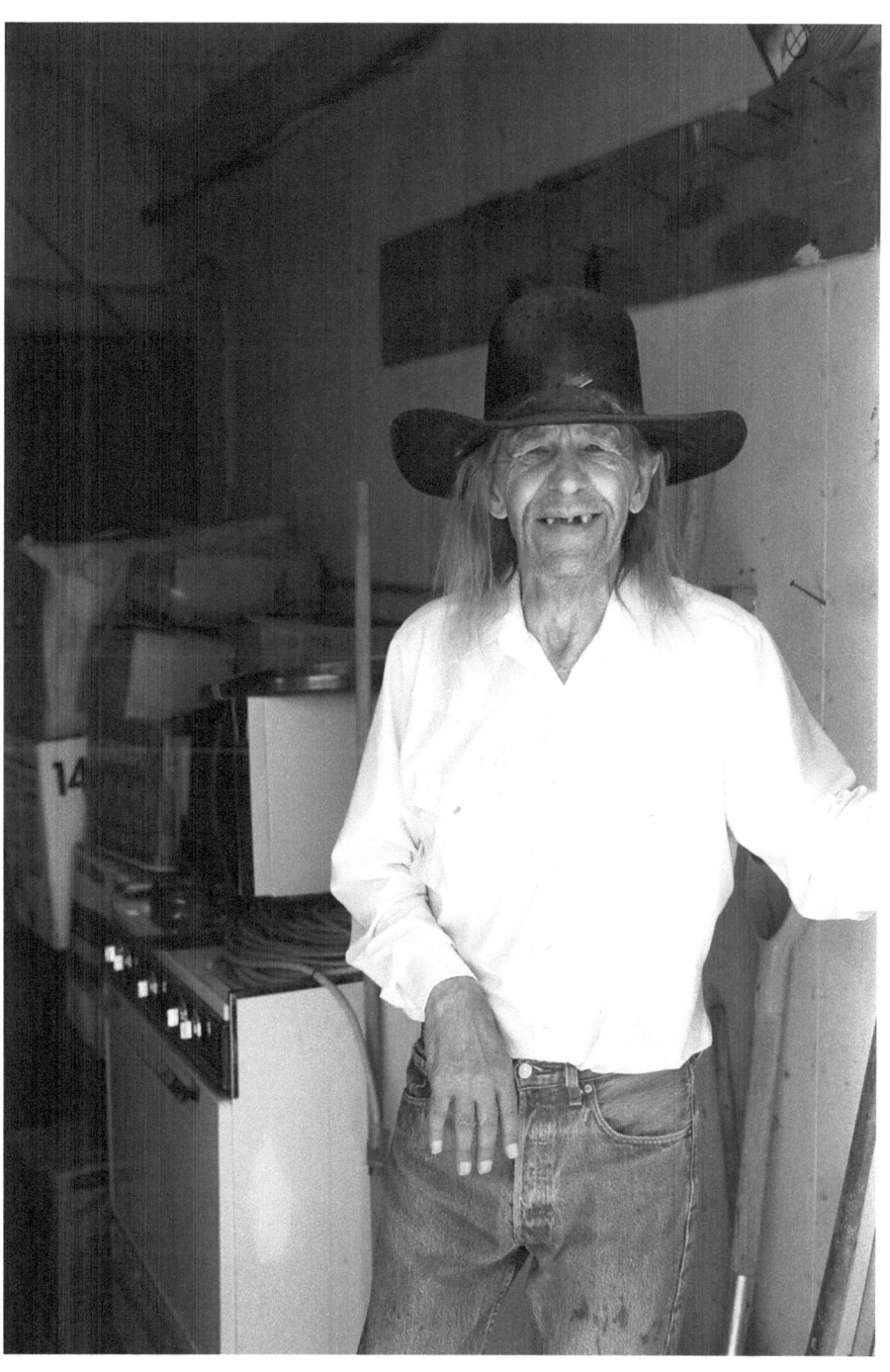

Ed Lavino

Odessa, Oyster Grass Music Festival
Kemmerer, Wyoming

I met this singer and fiddle player at the Oyster Grass Music Festival. Her strong, confident physical presence was evident in her body language and gestures. Odessa was raised and homeschooled on a ranch in California.

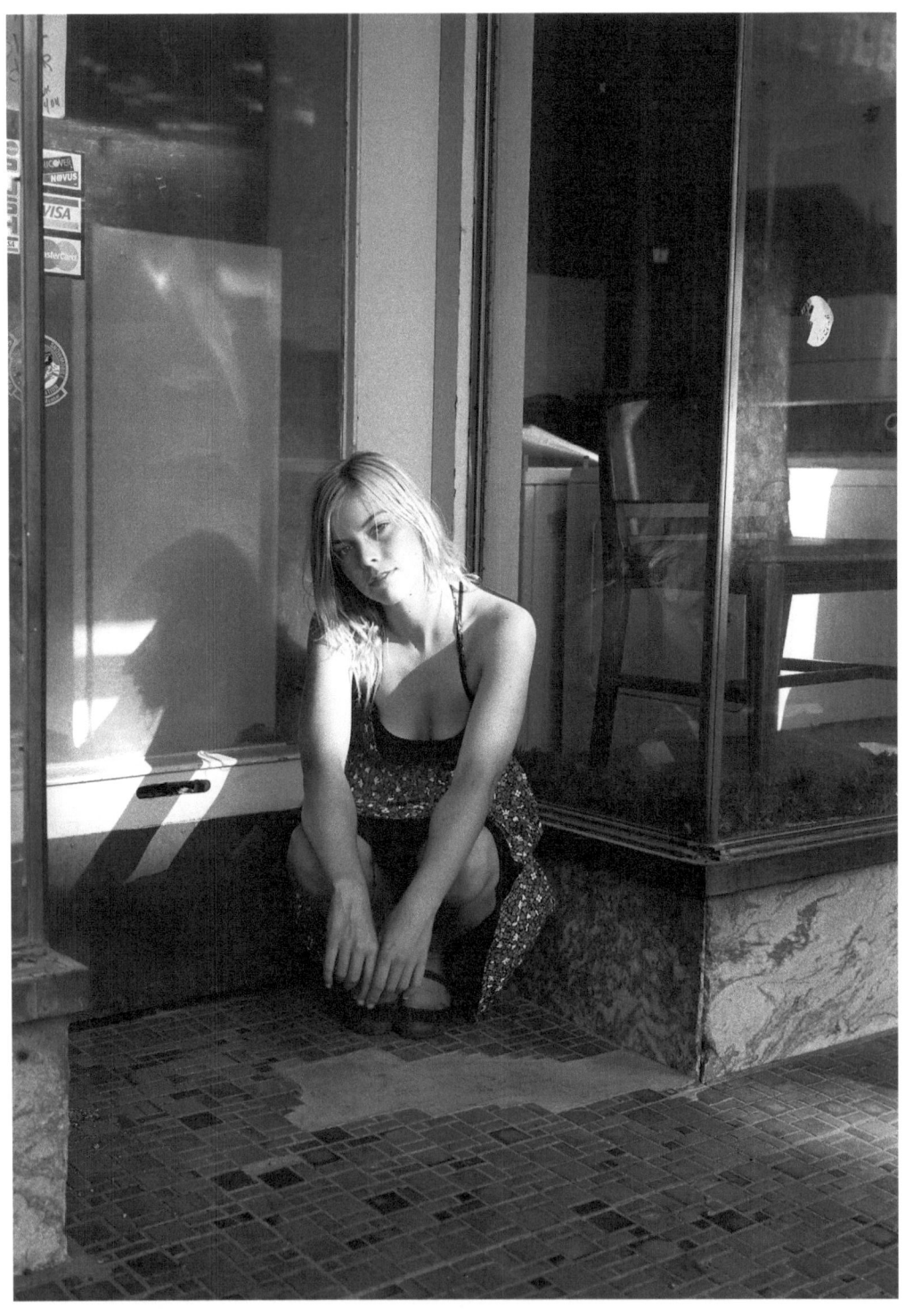

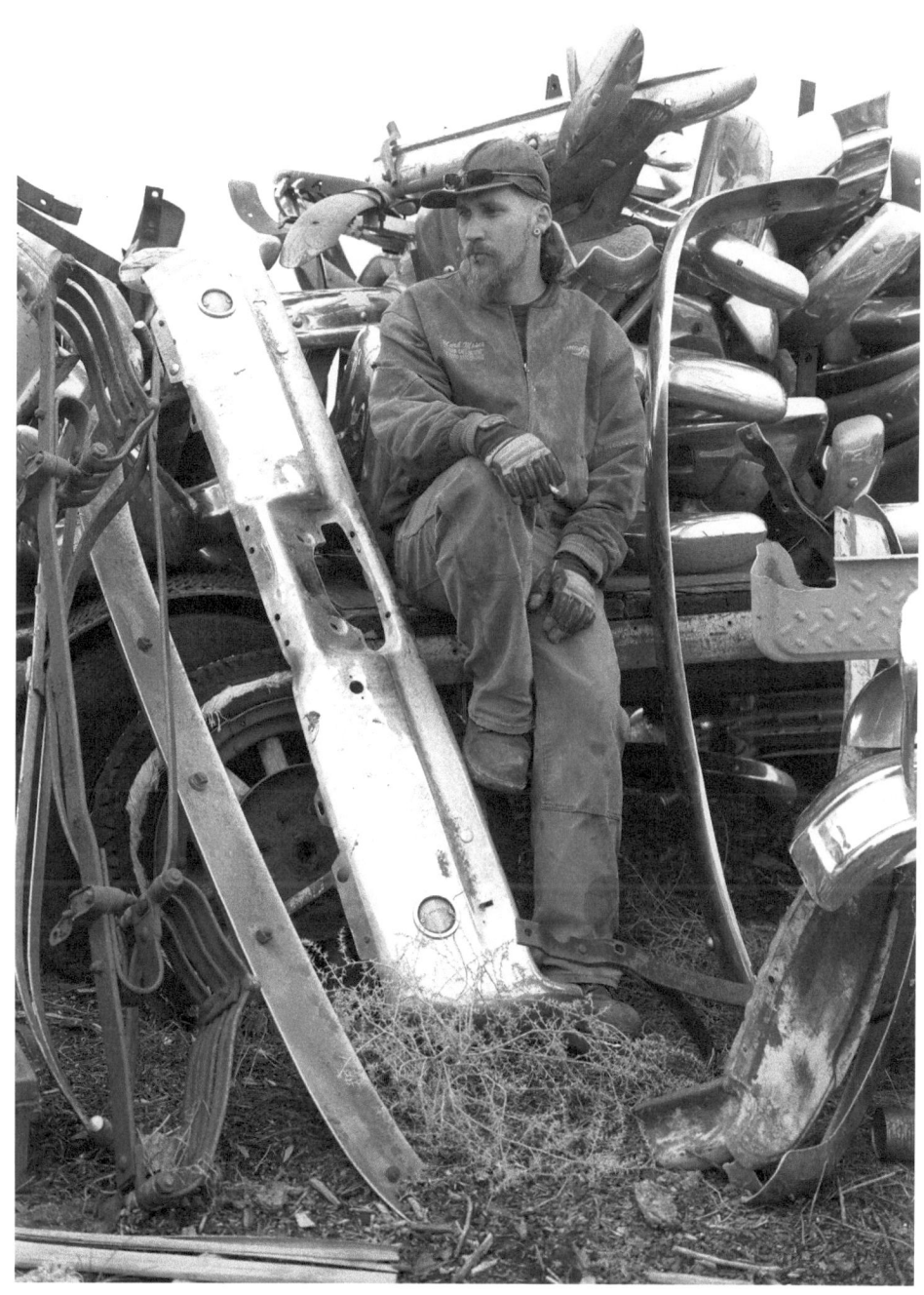

Raven
Ontario, Oregon

While on a fly fishing trip to the Owyhee River, I spotted an interesting-looking salvage yard and stopped to explore. Raven and his buddy were dismantling cars in the yard. Raven was entirely at home in his work environment, and readily agreed to be photographed. I selected a spot by a chaotic pile of bumpers, where the vertical lines accentuated his tall, thin frame.

Ed Lavino

Tubers
Moran, Wyoming

Sigma and her brother were floating the Buffalo Fork River. They were hitching back to their vehicle when I crossed paths with them on the gravel road. My inspiration in making this photograph came from a drawing I have always loved.

"The Beekeepers," by Pieter Bruegel the Elder, 1568, depicts peasants dressed in protective garb, working in the landscape. My take on this theme features tubers wearing appropriate garb, as they similarly go about their business in the landscape.

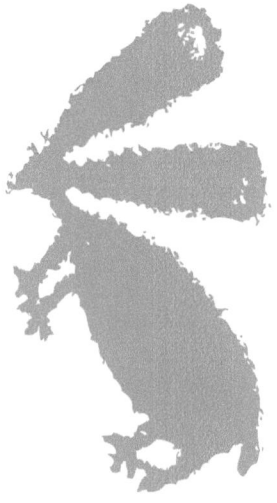

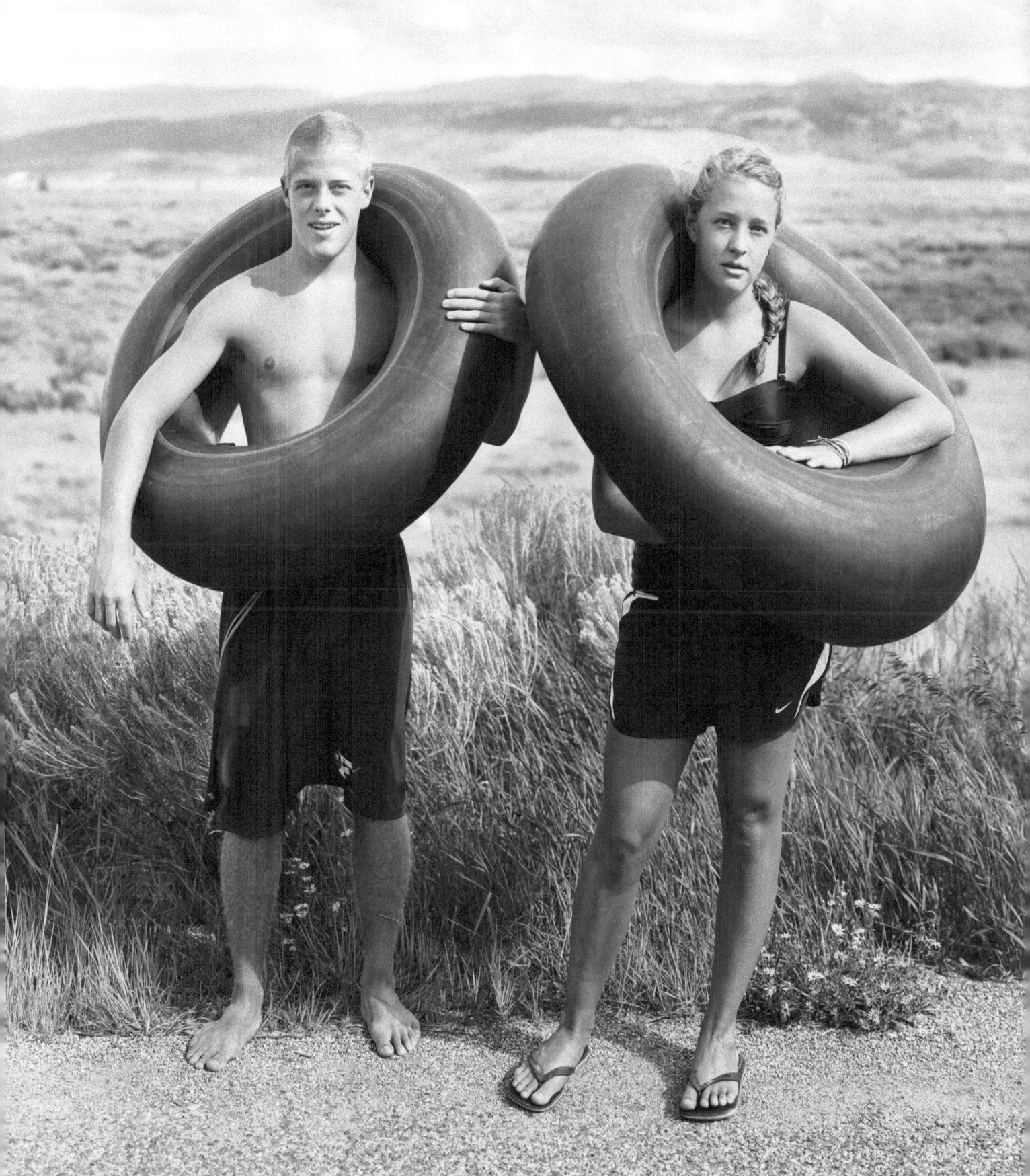

Ed Lavino

Gary
Jackson, Wyoming

Gary is a modern day mountain man on a bicycle. I observed him pushing his bike, laden with his belongings, on a bone-chilling, negative five-degree day. He told me he made his hat from the skin of a road-killed deer. The cap was stitched together with heavy cord and metal wire. This gentle, intelligent man is well read. He told me "Lonesome Dove" is his favorite western.

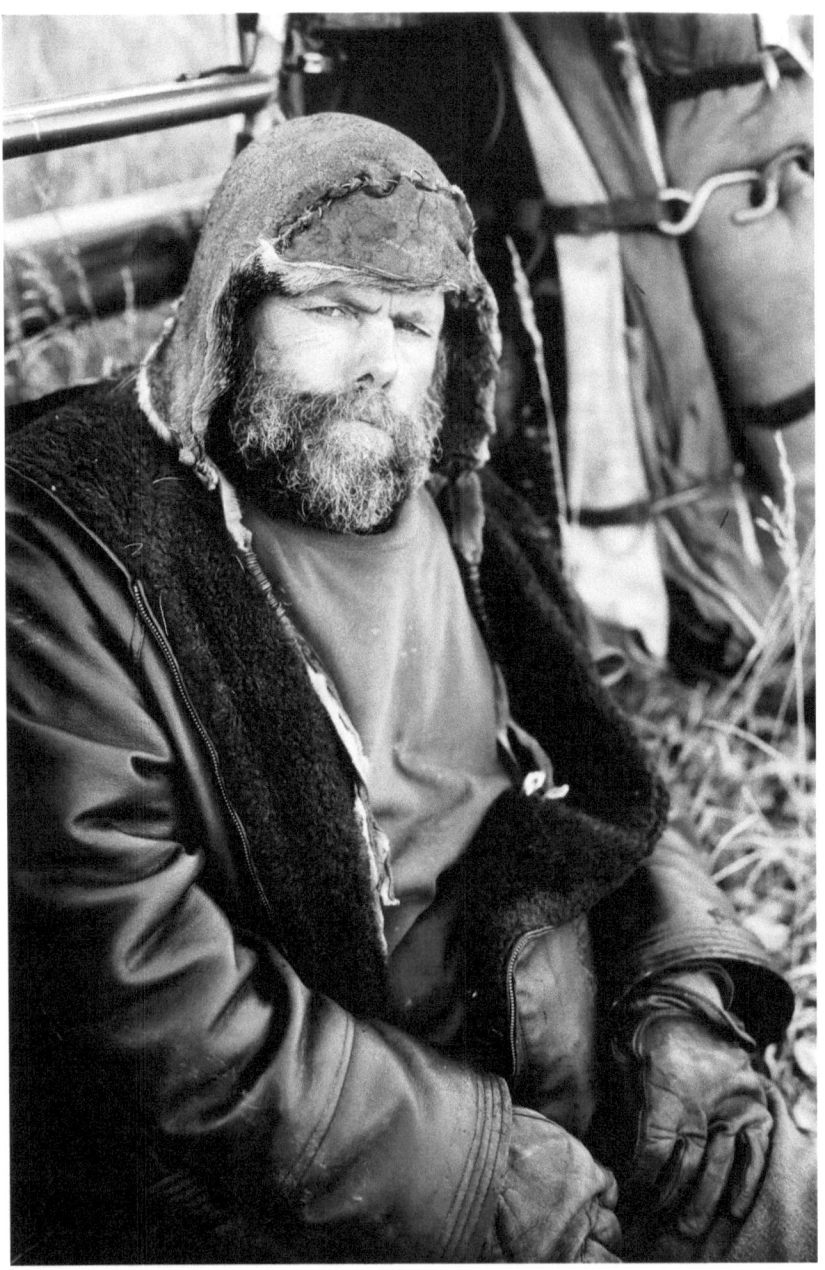

"Looking into his eyes, you seemed to see there the yet lingering images of those thousand-fold perils he had calmly confronted through life."
— Herman Melville

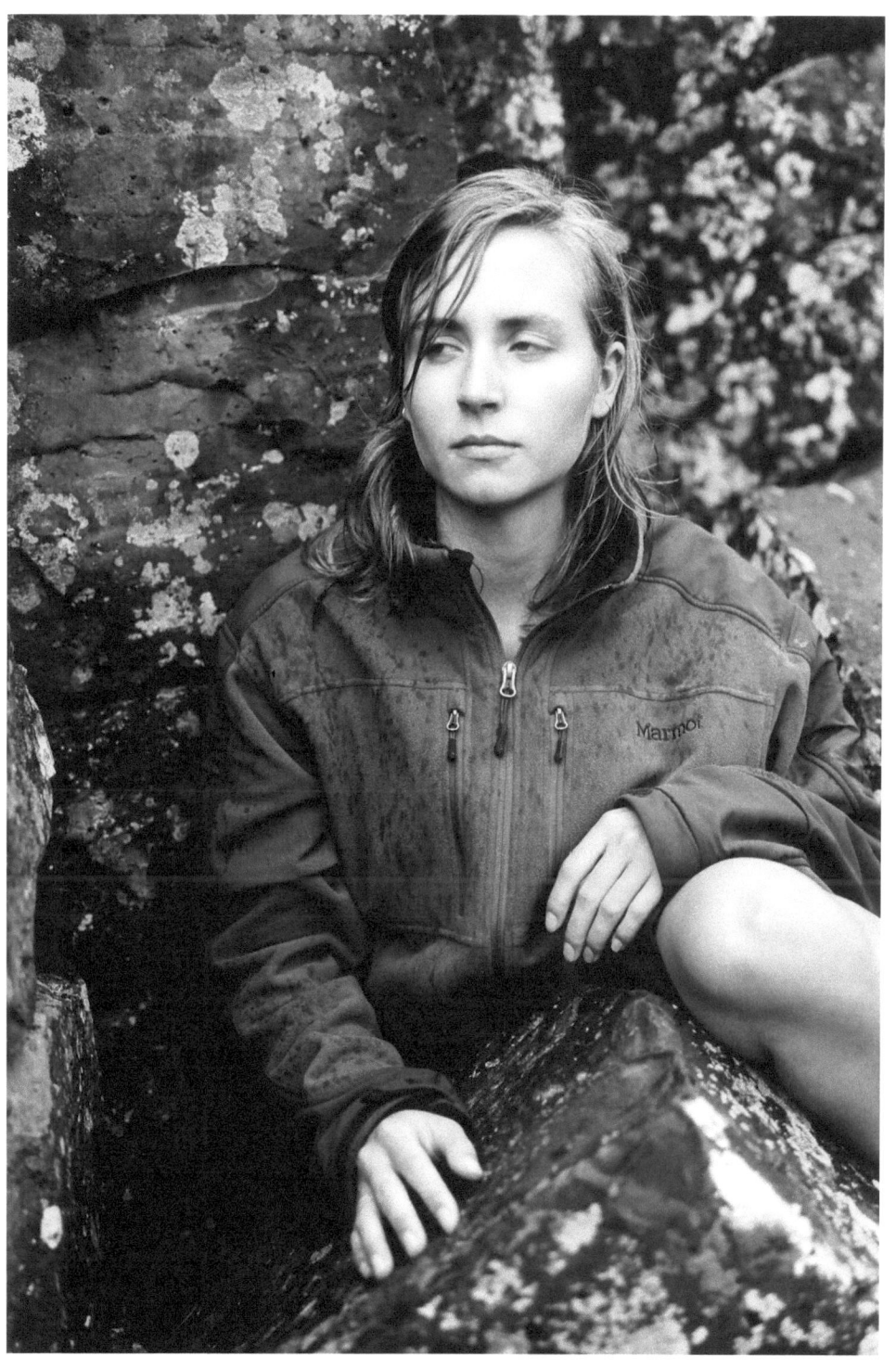

Corrie
Basalt Columns, Wyoming

Ed Lavino

"No philosopher so thoroughly comprehended us as dogs and horses."
— Herman Melville

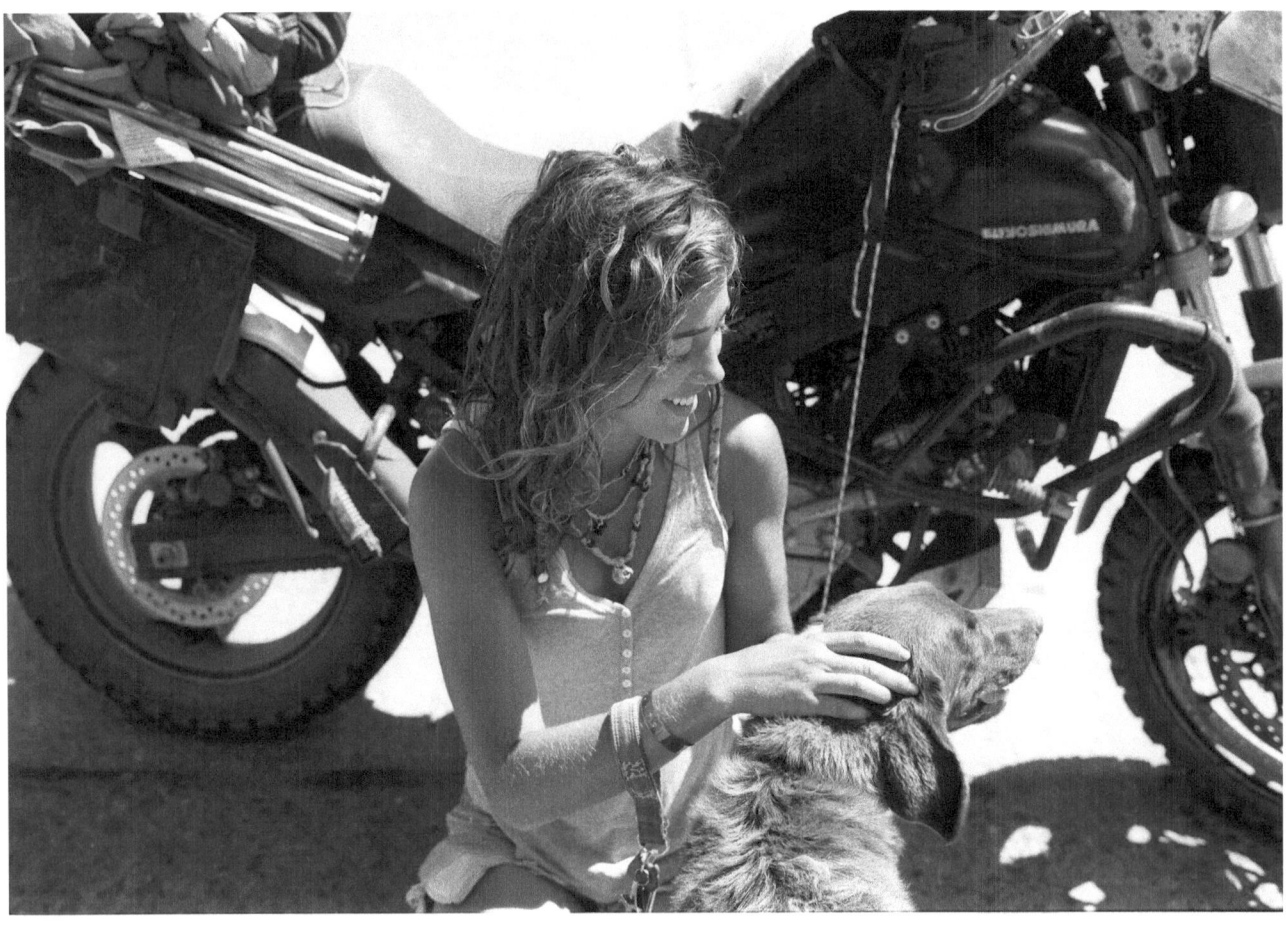

Brinley, Oyster Grass Music Festival
Kemmerer, Wyoming

Prevailing Westerlies

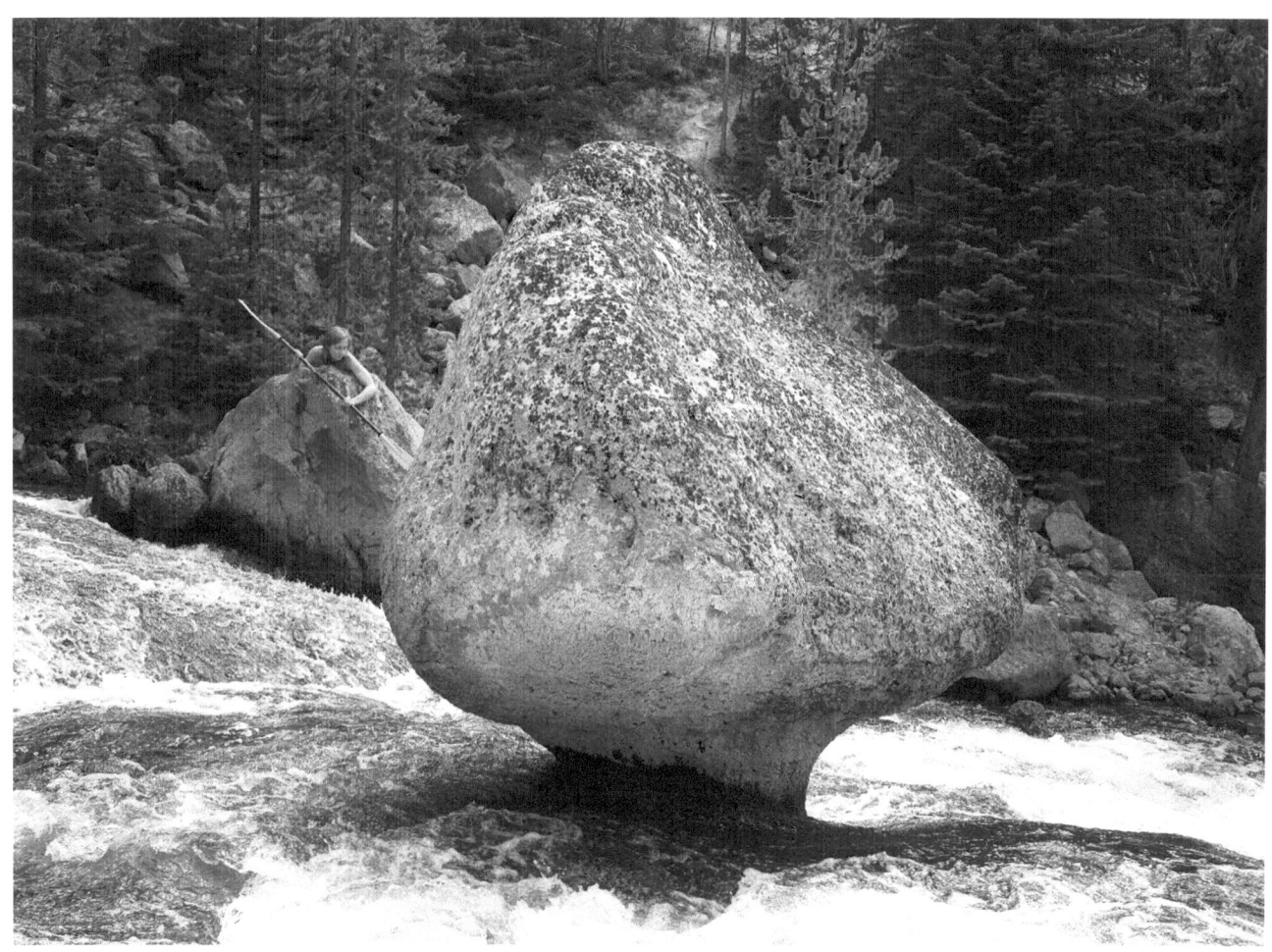

Corrie with Kayak Paddle

Ed Lavino

John
East Fork of the Wind River, Wyoming

John is a fifth generation rancher living at the headwaters of the Wind River, where the Indian reservation and the national forest meet. While making daily rounds of his ranch on horseback, John picks up antlers, horns and bones. These later find their way into his hand-carved sculptures.

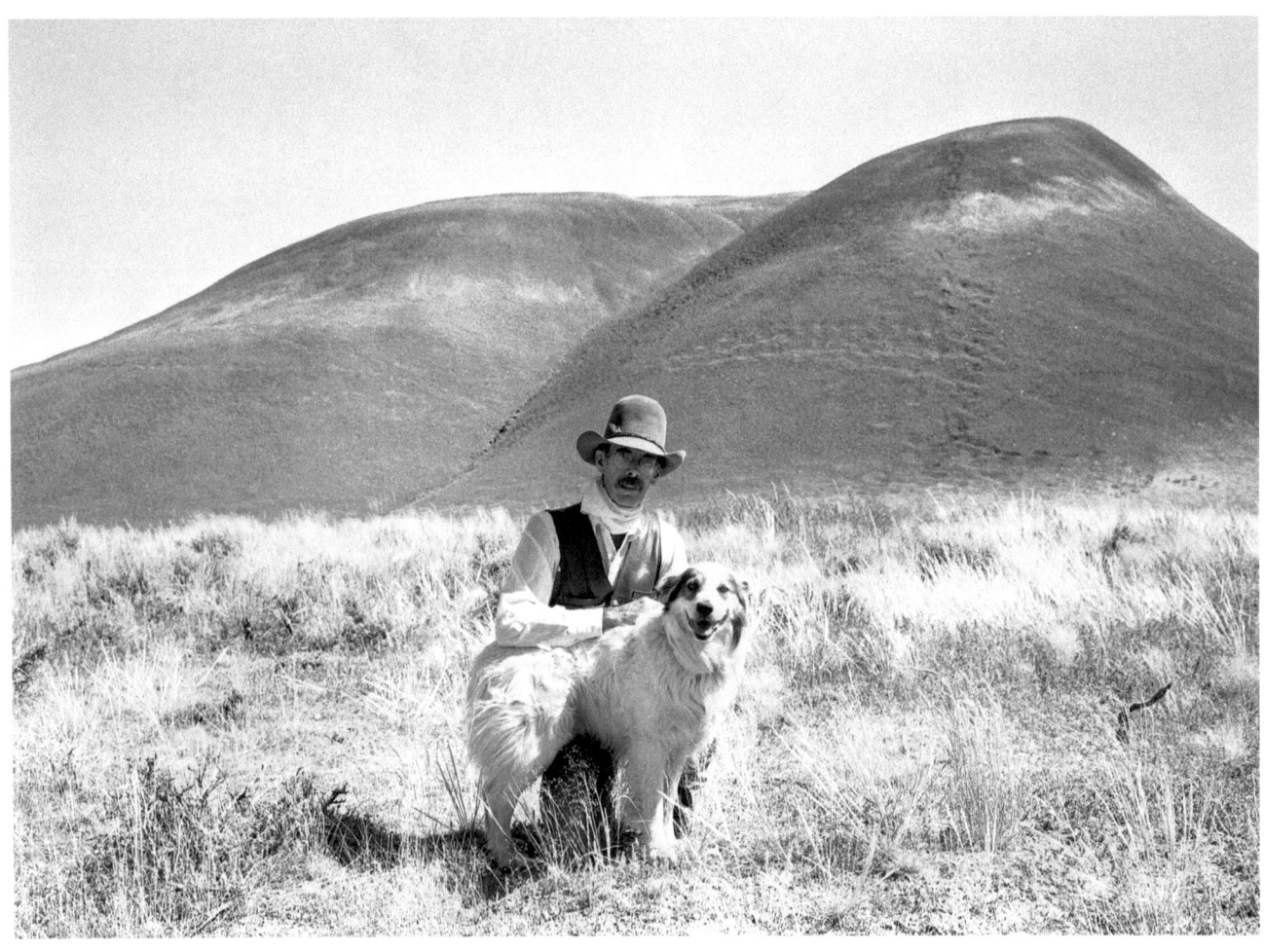

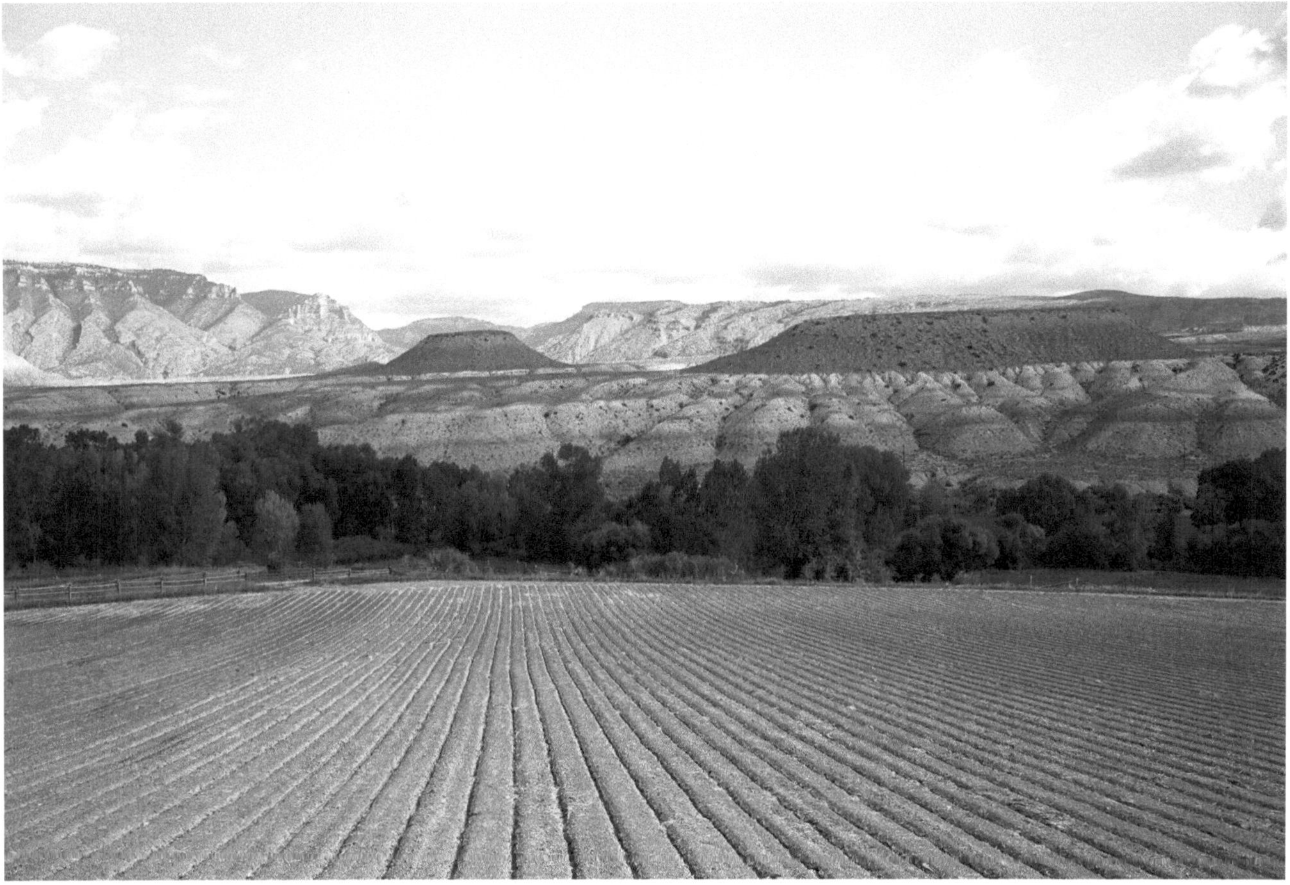

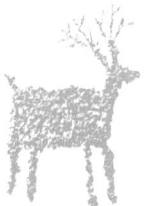

Plowed Field
Shell, Wyoming

The geometry of this landscape delineates a stark contrast between wild and tame. The foreground's parallel furrows are reassuring in their predictability. An orderly pattern describes a boundary fence at the far end of the field. Beyond that, a waving curtain of dark foliage gives way to a dramatic backdrop where wilderness reigns. Placid foothills transition to modest buttes, which yield to soaring mountains in the distance.

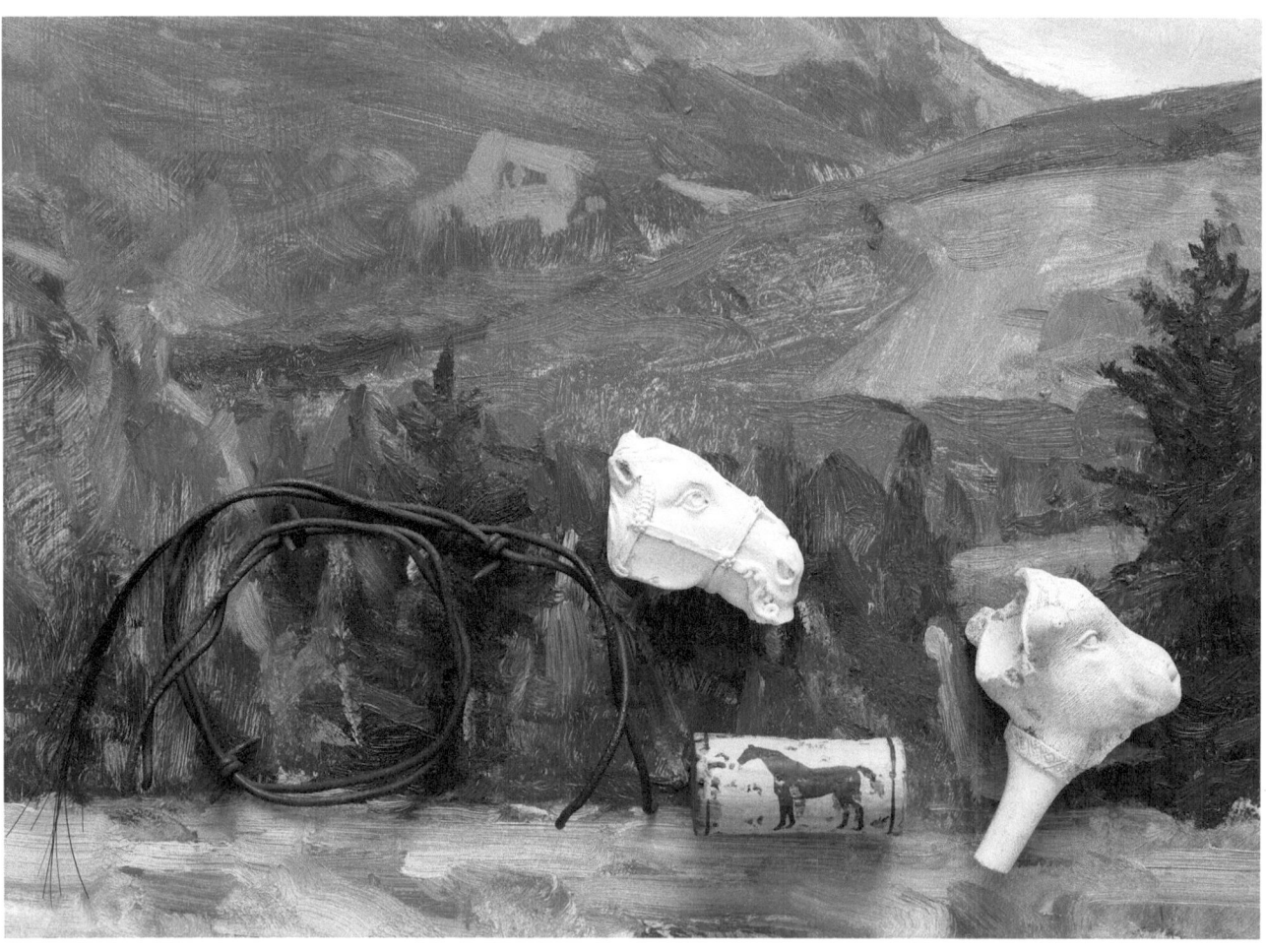

Horsehead Clay Pipe

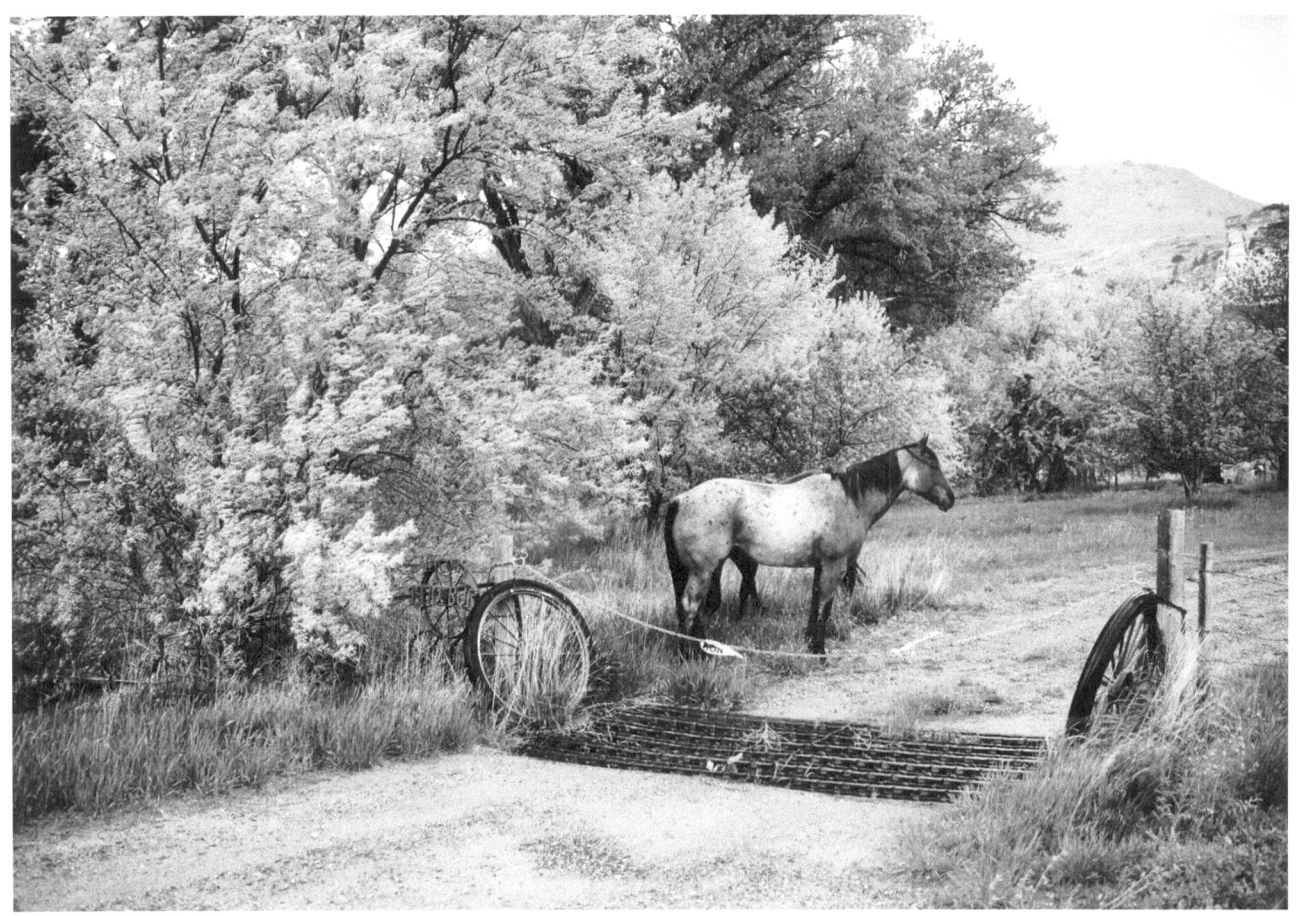

Approaching Storm
Madison Buffalo Jump, Montana

Returning from a hike to the buffalo jump cliff, I passed this ranch entrance. Strong winds, and sheets of rain were moving in. The two horses bunched together, using a tree row to break the buffeting winds.

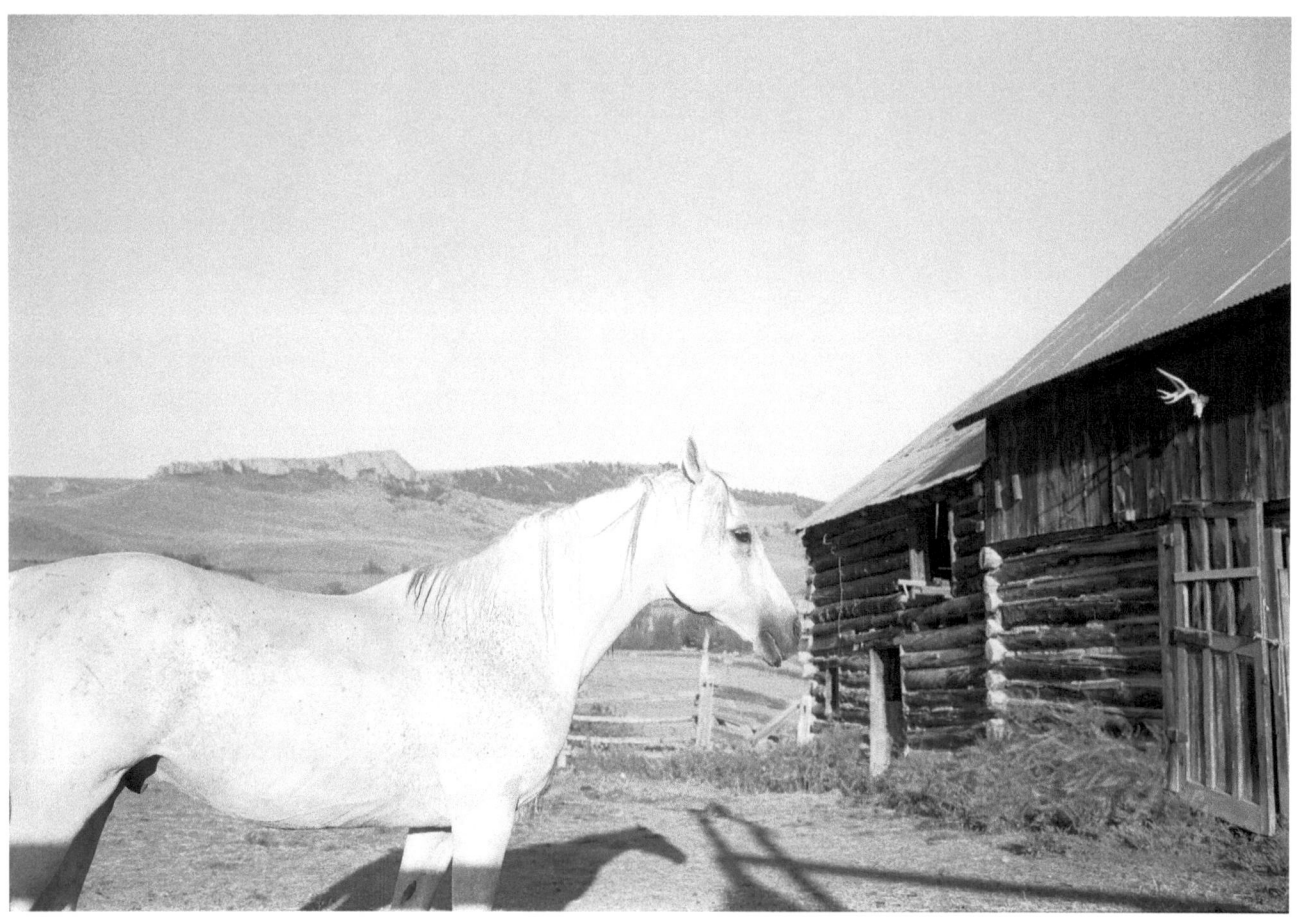

White Horse
Ohio Creek, Colorado

Prevailing Westerlies

Fish Fossil Shop
Jackson, Wyoming

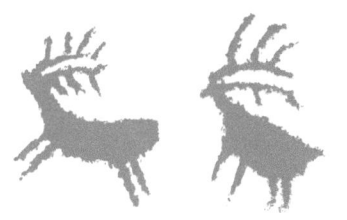

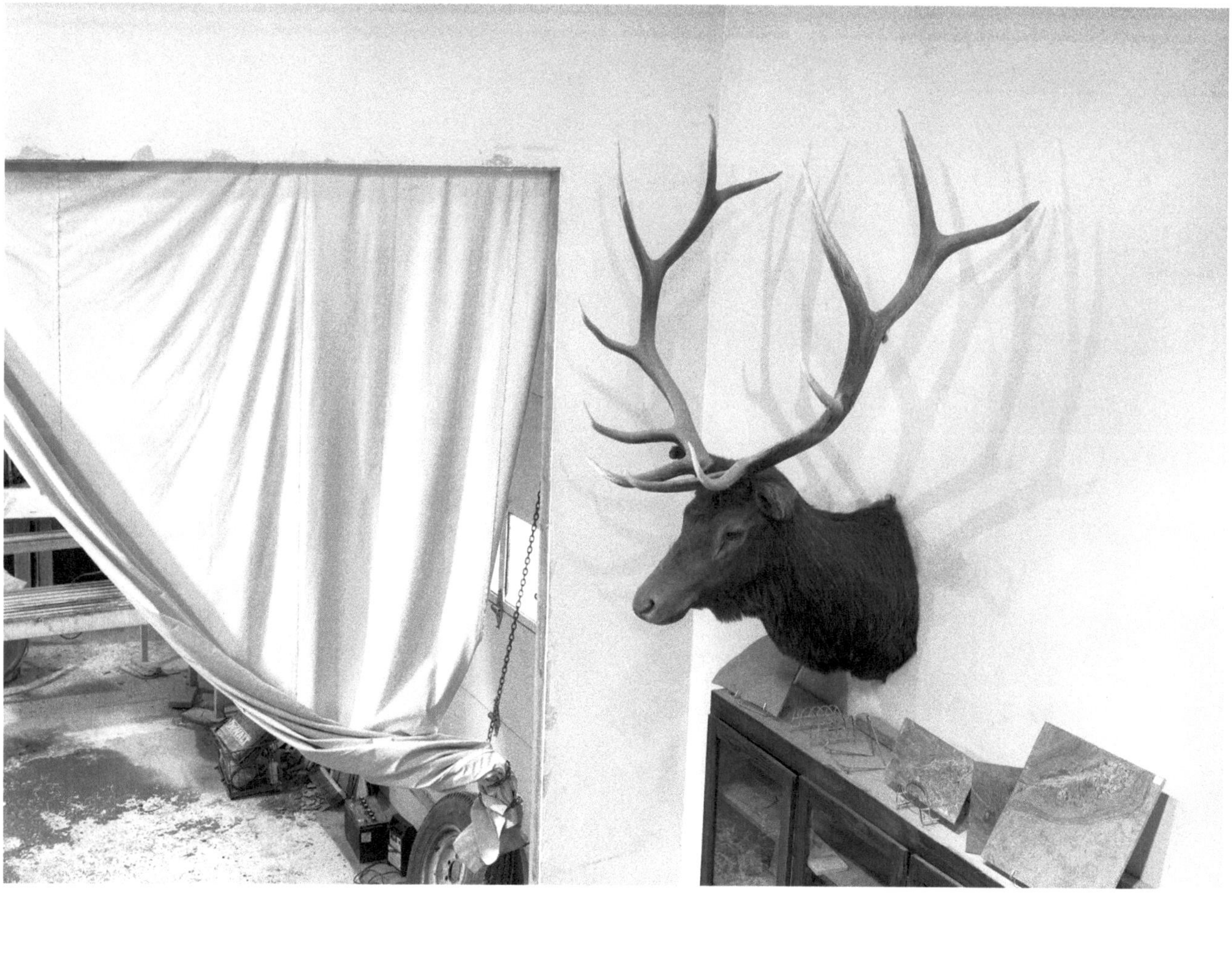

Ed Lavino

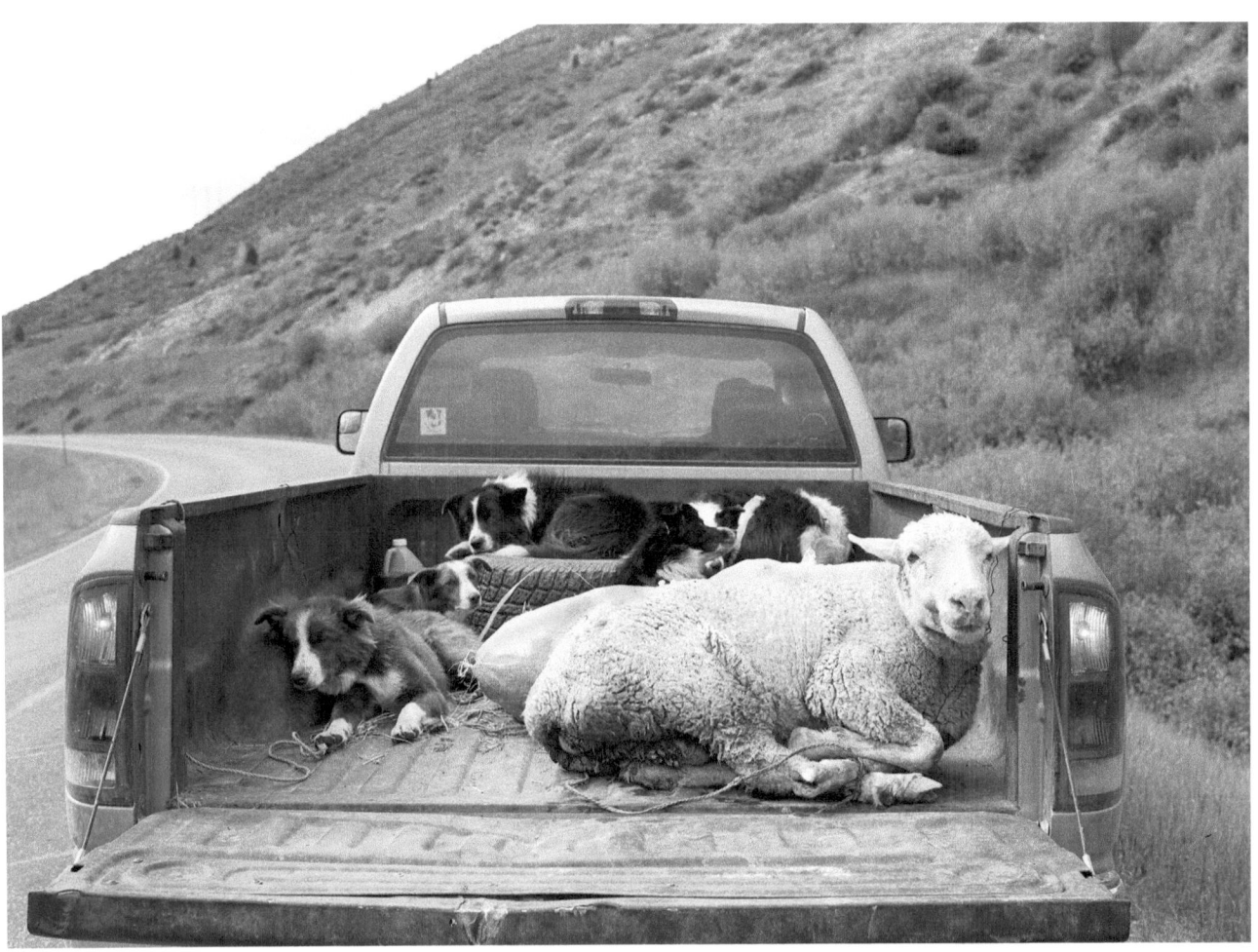

Old Ewe
Tin Cup Pass, Idaho

Five sheep dogs and an aged ewe collapse in the bed of a battered pickup truck. The Peruvian herder wired the ewe's legs to keep her still for the ride over the pass. The other herders, on horseback, were driving a white mass of sheep through the national forest to the rancher's "home place" for winter. This ewe simply could not keep up. She appears surprisingly content, sharing a ride with the spent dogs.

Ed Lavino

There is something beautifully harmonious in each of these landscapes. Some compositions inherently feel "right" and comfortable. It may be the enfolding gesture of the circular pen on Ohio Creek, or the sense of community implied within the loose ring of cattle feeding peaceably together.

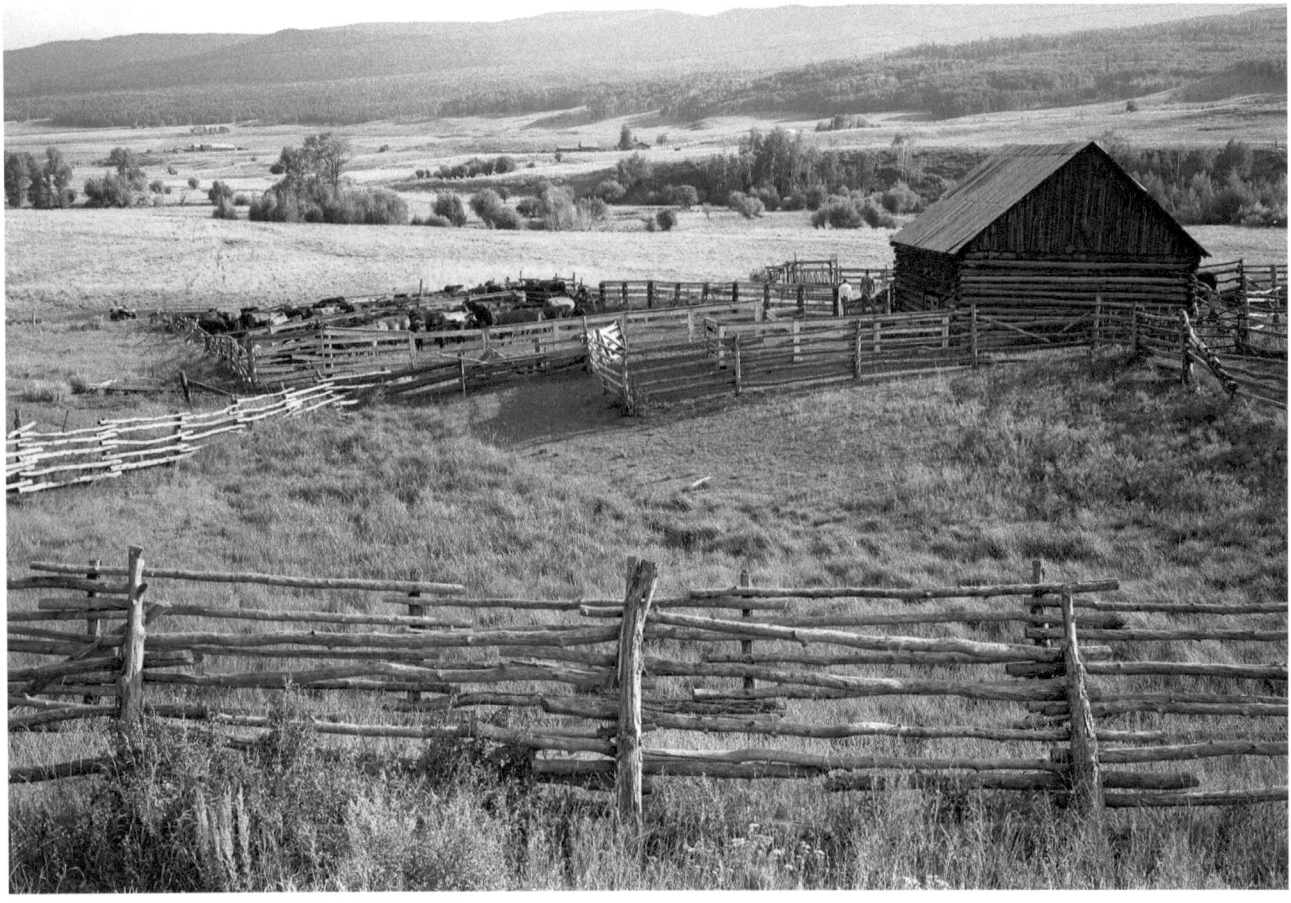

Cattle Pens
Ohio Creek, Colorado

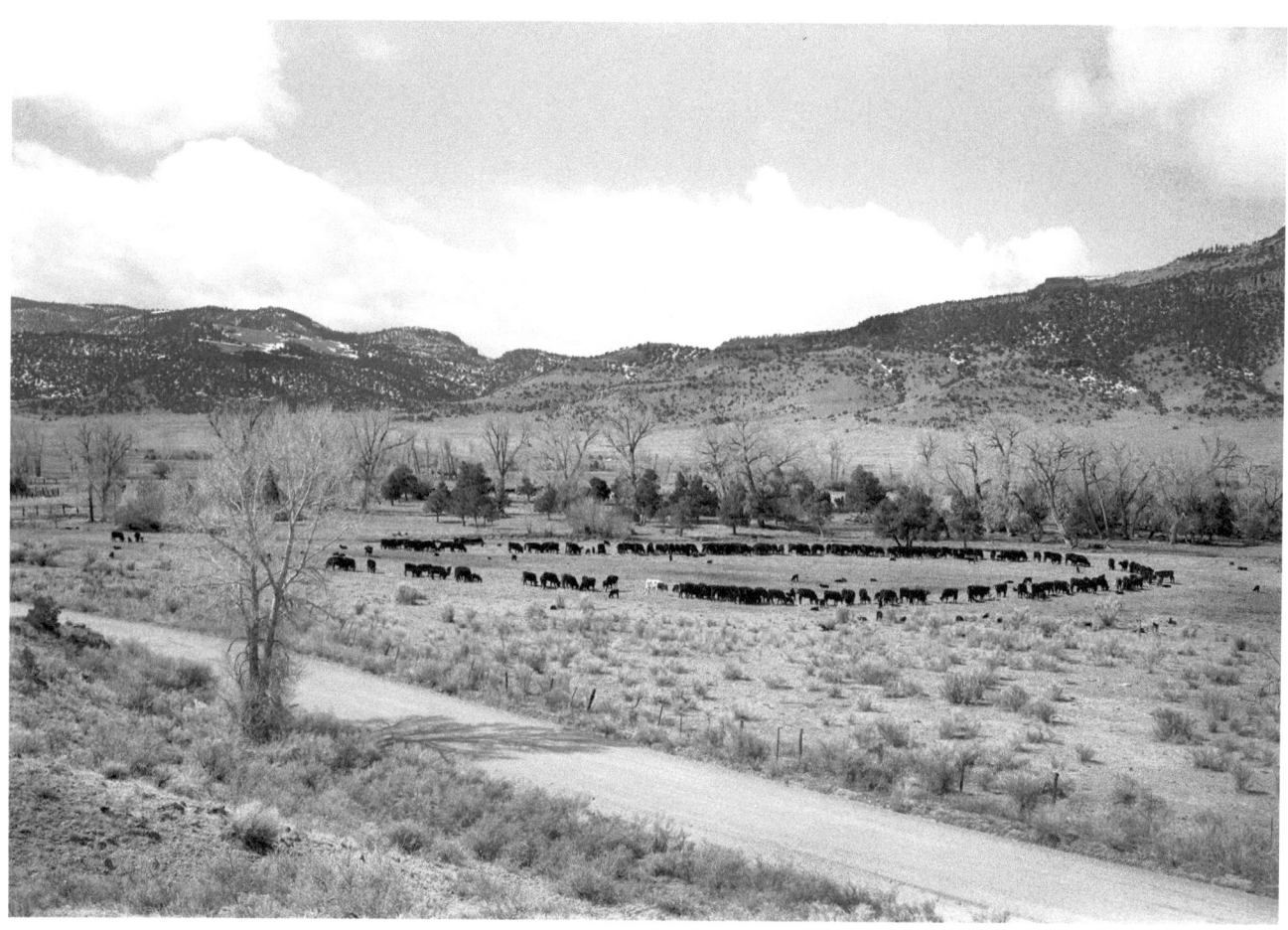

Feed Line
West Elk Loop, Colorado

Ed Lavino

Feed Line, Minus Ten Degrees
Cora, Wyoming

This photograph, taken in 1992, is significant for the record it preserves of an abundant, untainted landscape right before degradation. Sage grouse nested in the foothills, hawks soared above the irrigated hayfields, and pronghorn migrated across the flats. Sublette County, Wyoming is now inundated with oil and gas development and all that involves: a grid of new roads, noisy truck traffic, oil derricks, and noxious weeds.

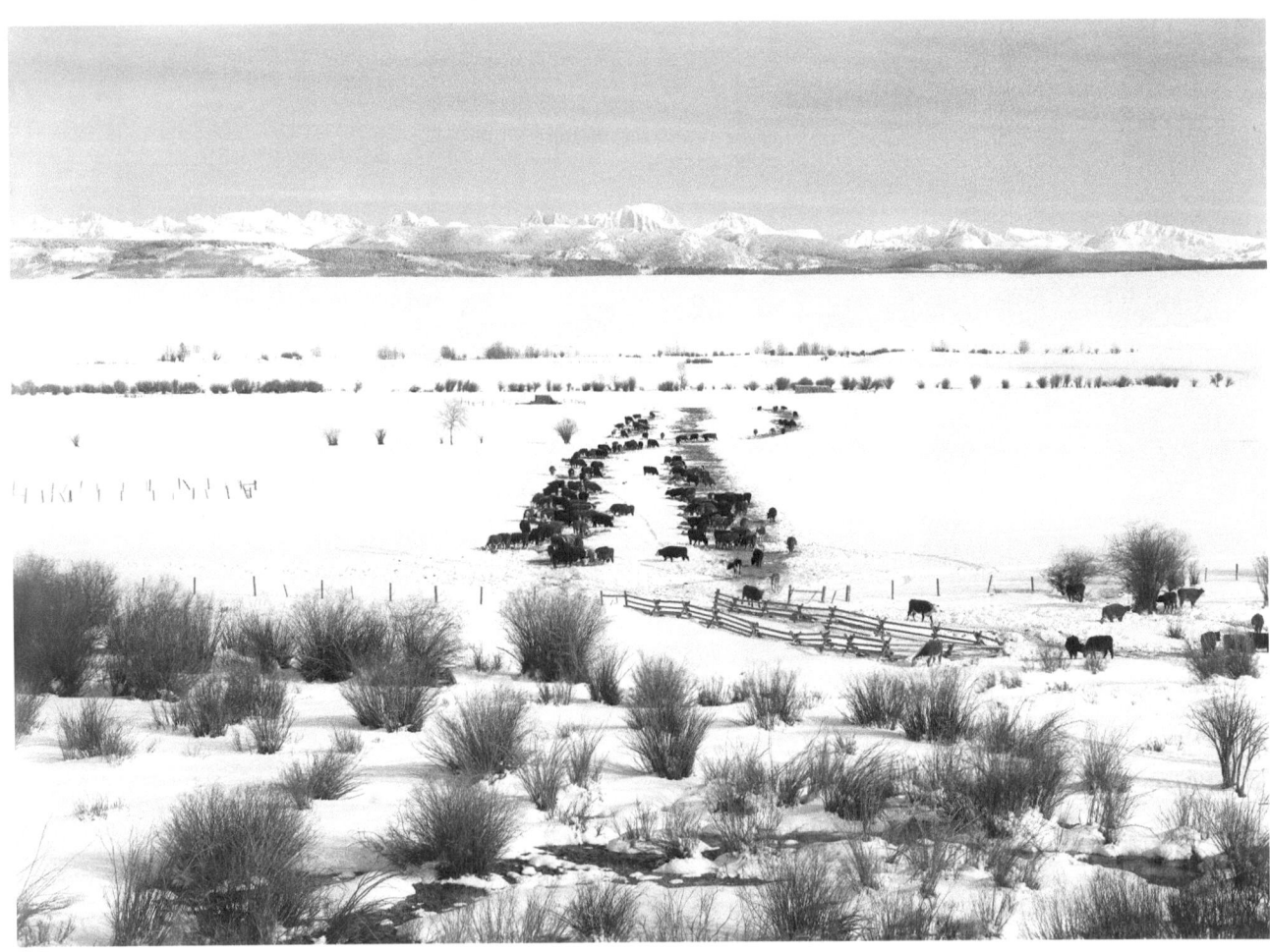

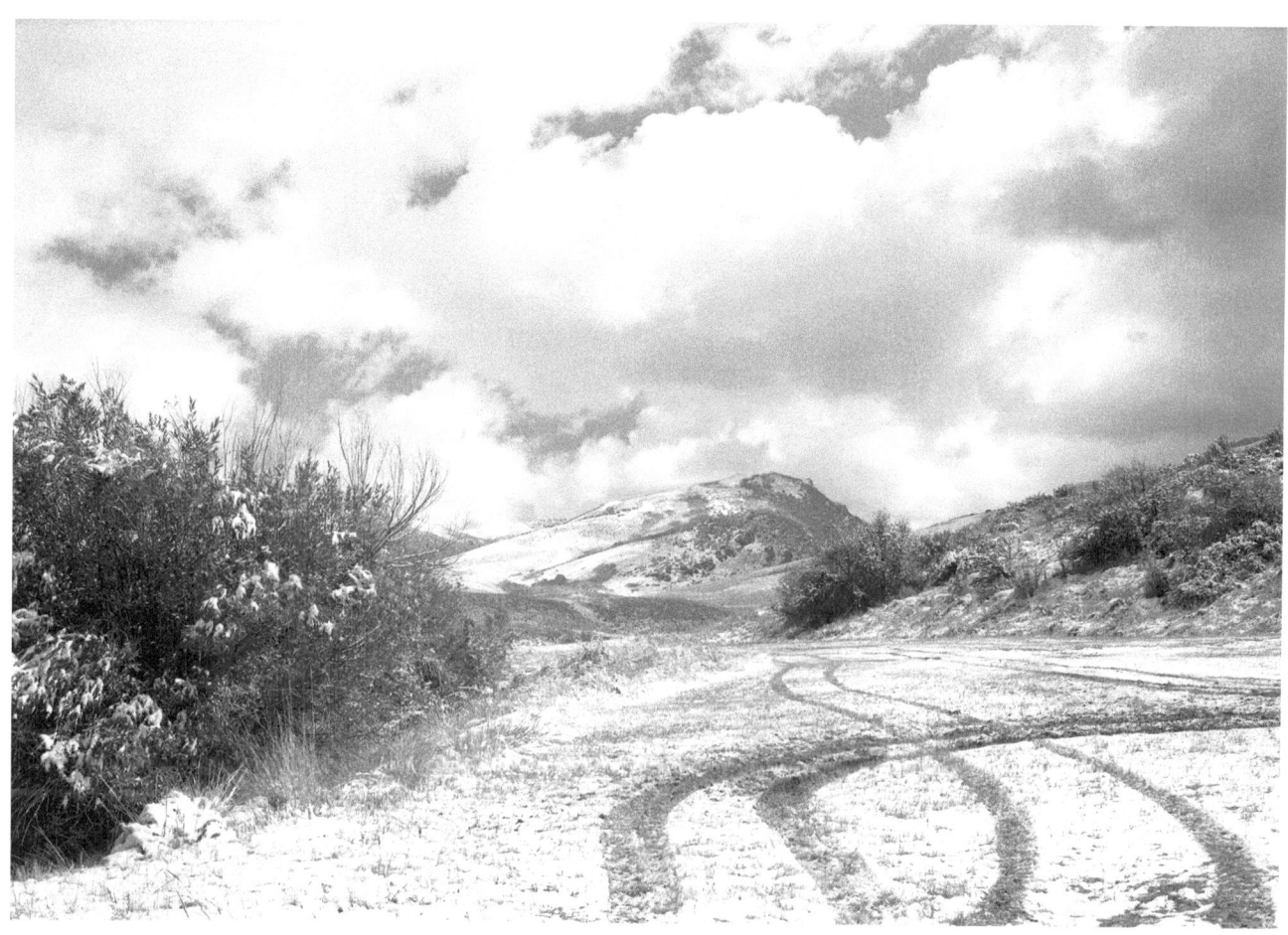

First Snow
Ruby Mountains, Nevada

The sinuous movement of the cattle feed line, and the meandering arcs created by the tire treads, reference the cycle of the seasons. Rhythms in the natural world intertwine with our comings and goings.

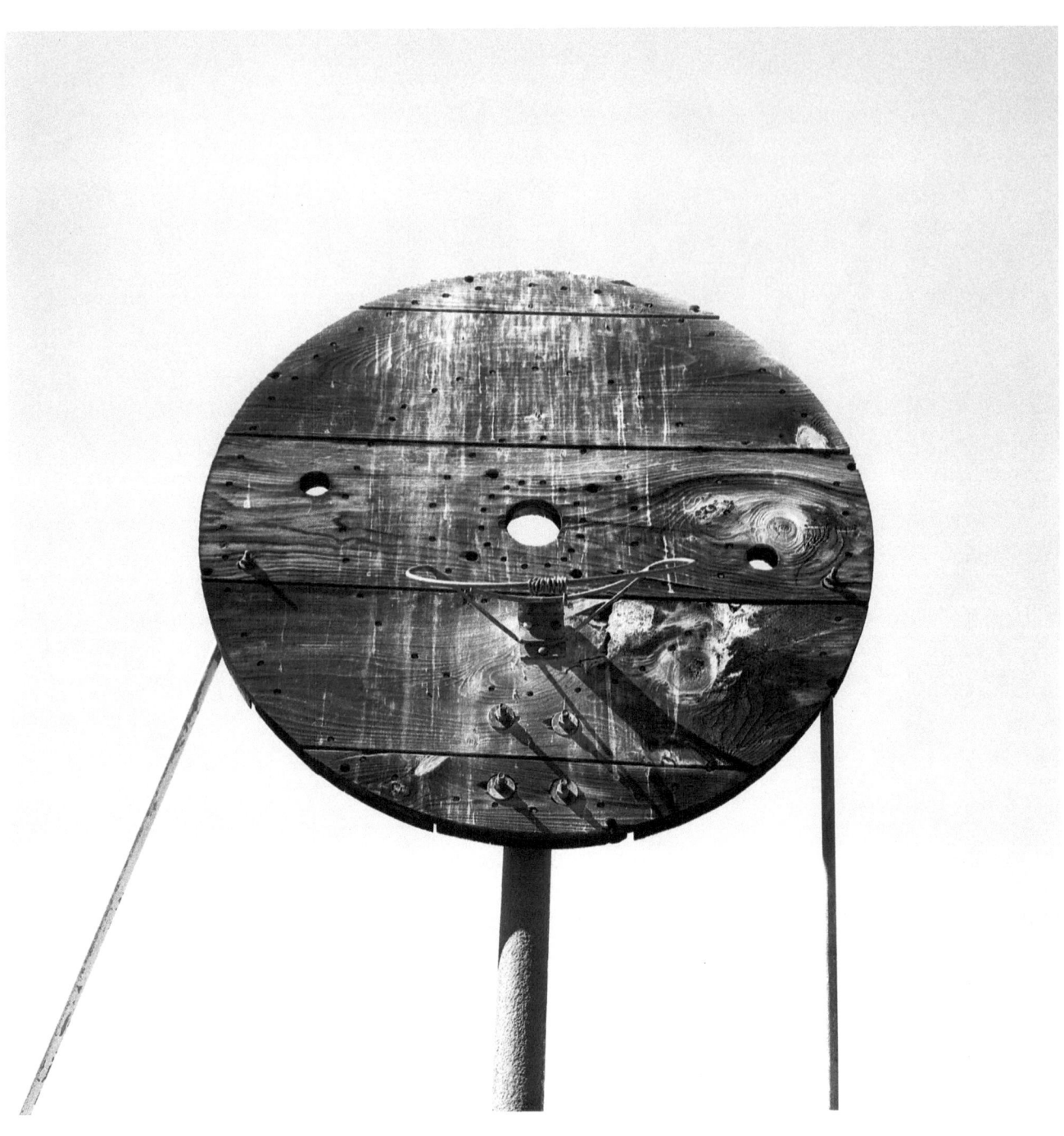

Basketball Backboard (Hawk's Rest)
Pitkin County, Colorado

Prevailing Westerlies

Road Killed Elk
Gas Hills, Wyoming

This resembles a crime scene photo. An arc of blood, a dead body, an unseen killer. This desert elk's broken body will be repurposed as nutrients for a variety of birds, mammals, and plants.

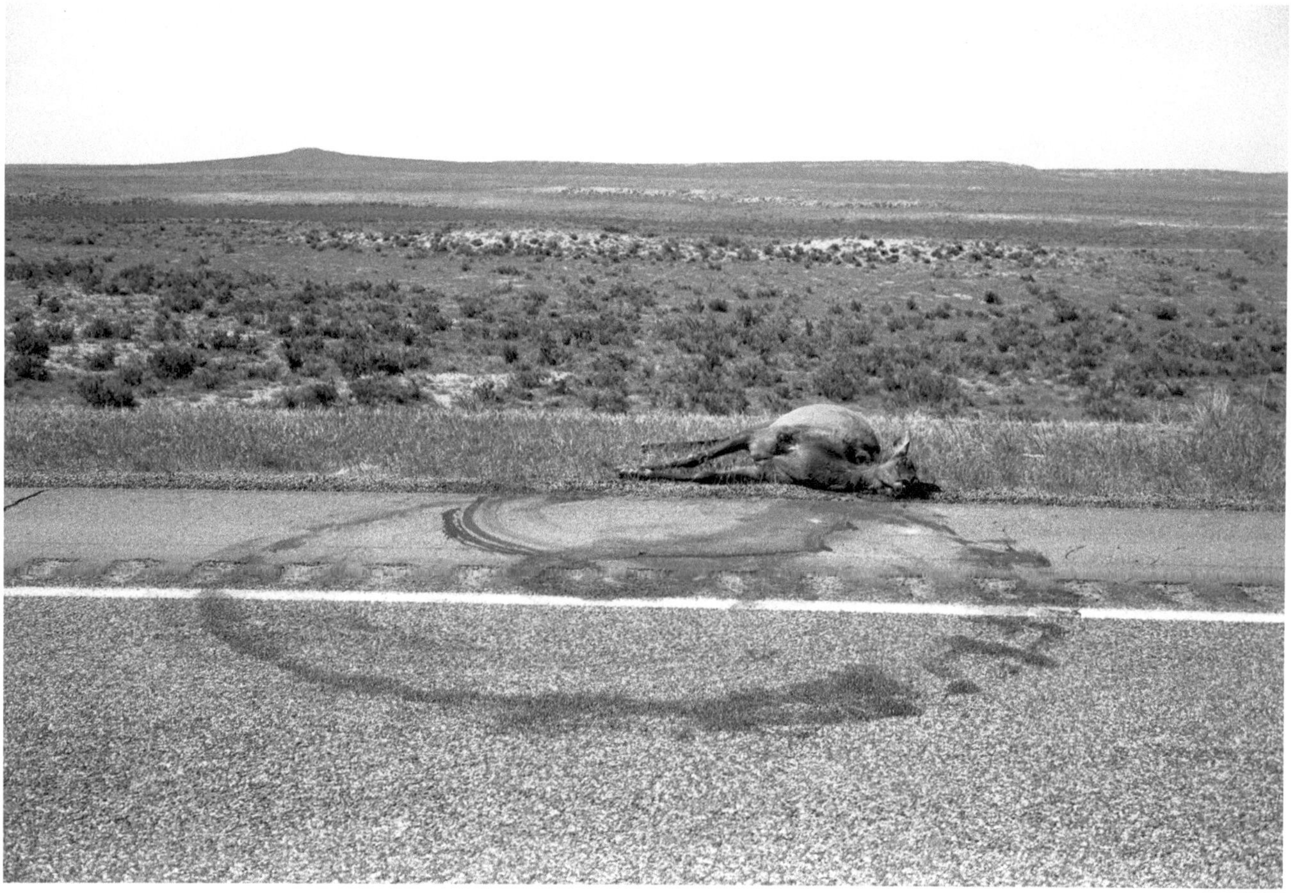

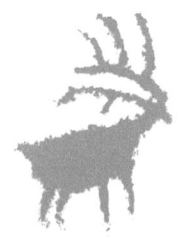

Ed Lavino

Spring claims winter's coat,
exposing the land's musculature

No more meals of bleached bones,
wolverine will feast on flesh
rising to the surface of avalanche debris

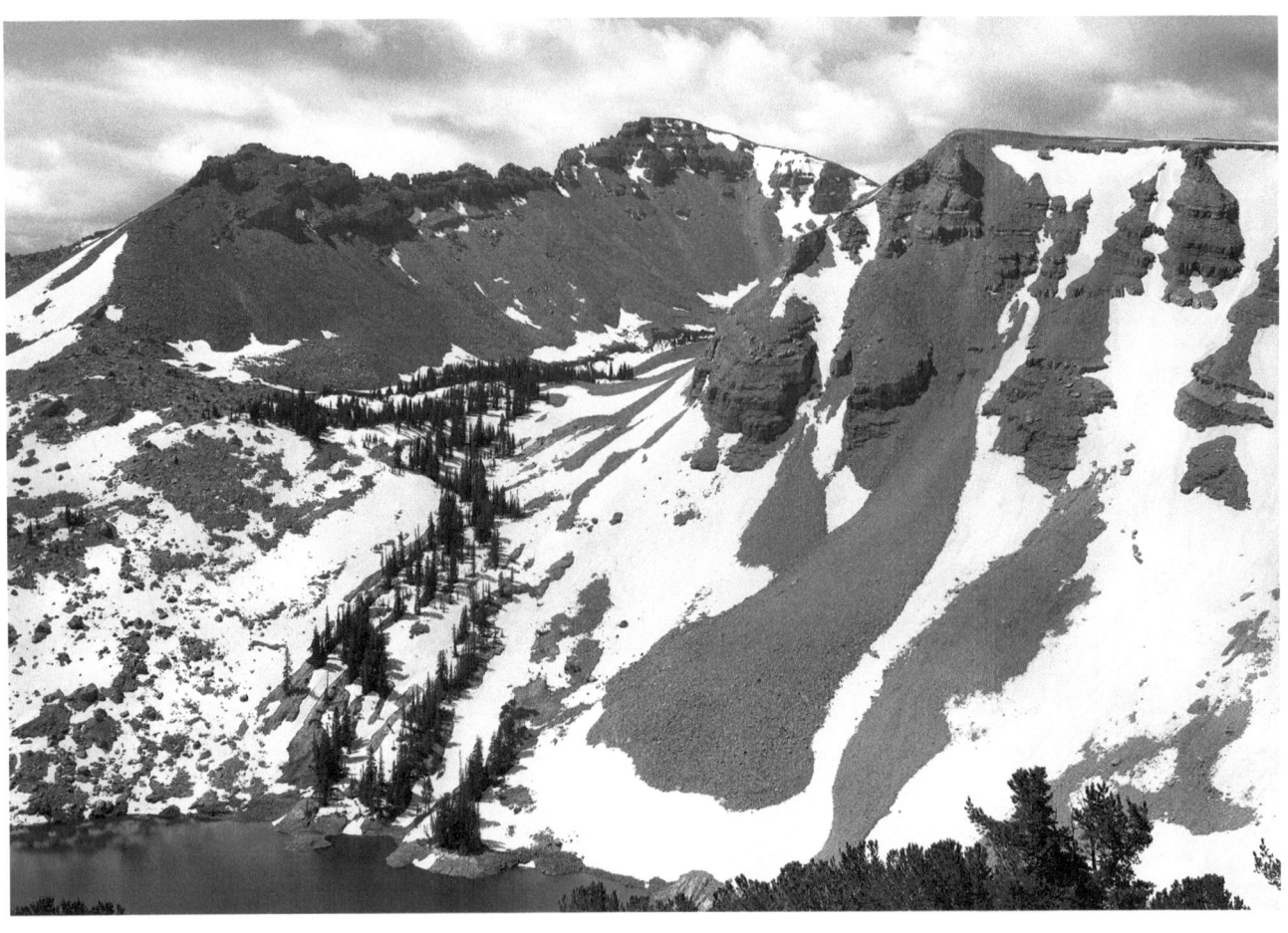

Blue Miner Lake
Bridger National Forest, Wyoming

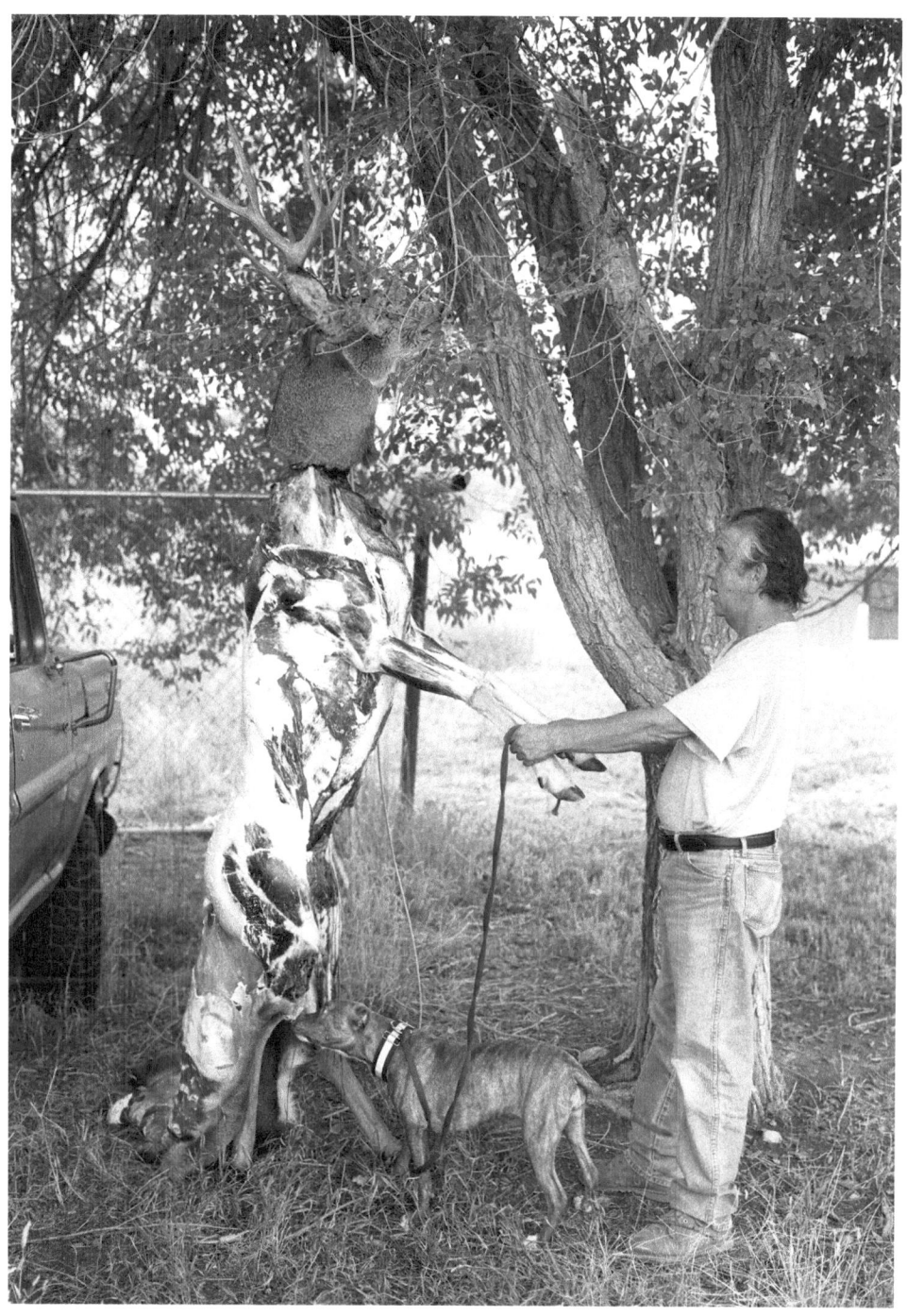

Buck
Wind River Indian Reservation, Wyoming

Frank pauses to give thanks before butchering a mule deer, harvested for winter sustenance. He appears to acknowledge the buck as a respected equal in this moment. Mule deer spend summer months at higher elevations, foraging for nutritious forbs in preparation for winter's privation. The well-fed buck's success becomes this man's steak and gloves.

Ed Lavino

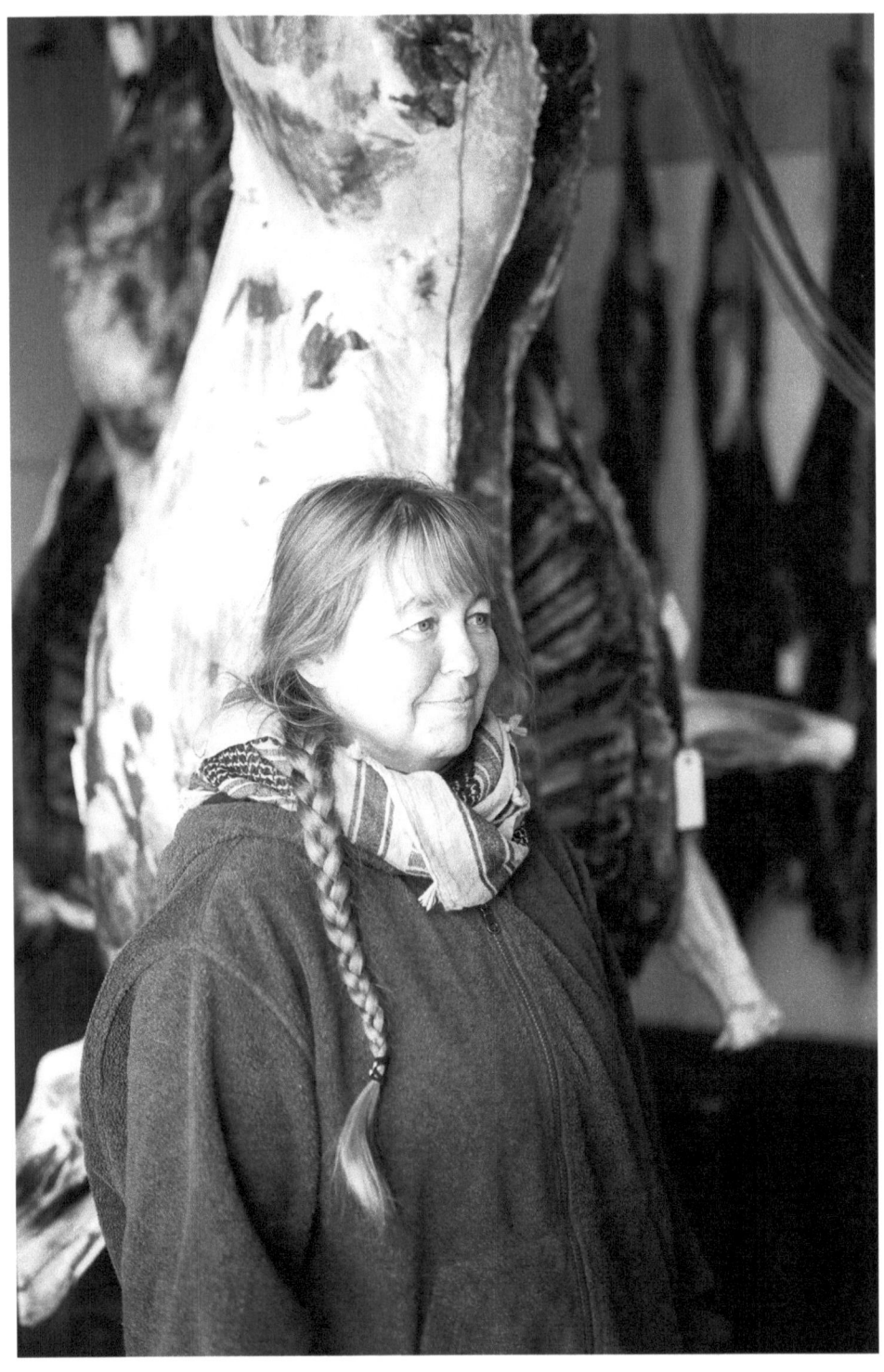

Mikki, Wind River Meats
Dubois, Wyoming

My salute to Rembrandt's *Carcass of Beef*, which hangs in the Louvre, Paris.
Rendered in oily paints 1657, Rendered in silvery emulsion 2009

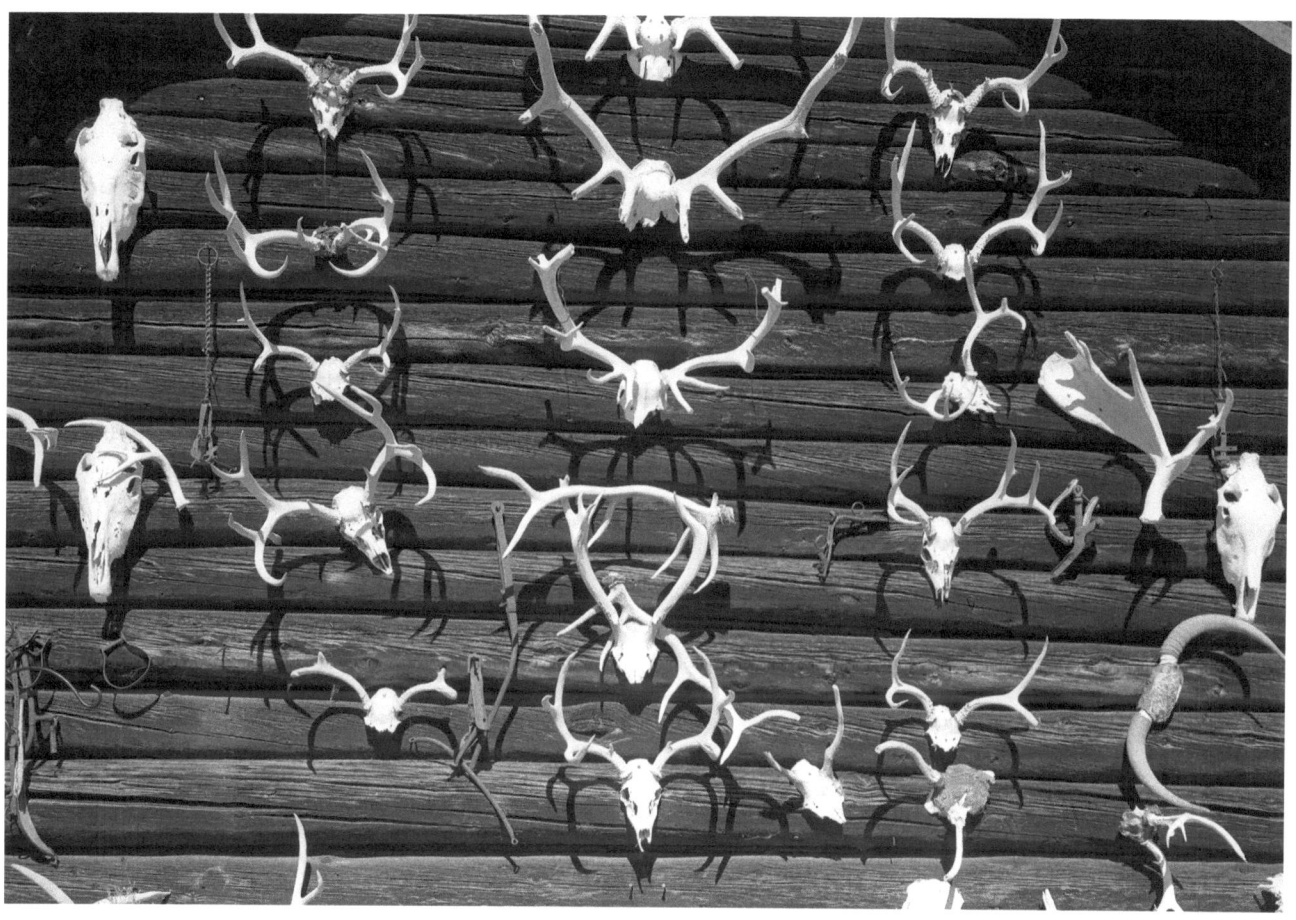

Antlers and Skulls
Pitkin County, Colorado

Ed Lavino

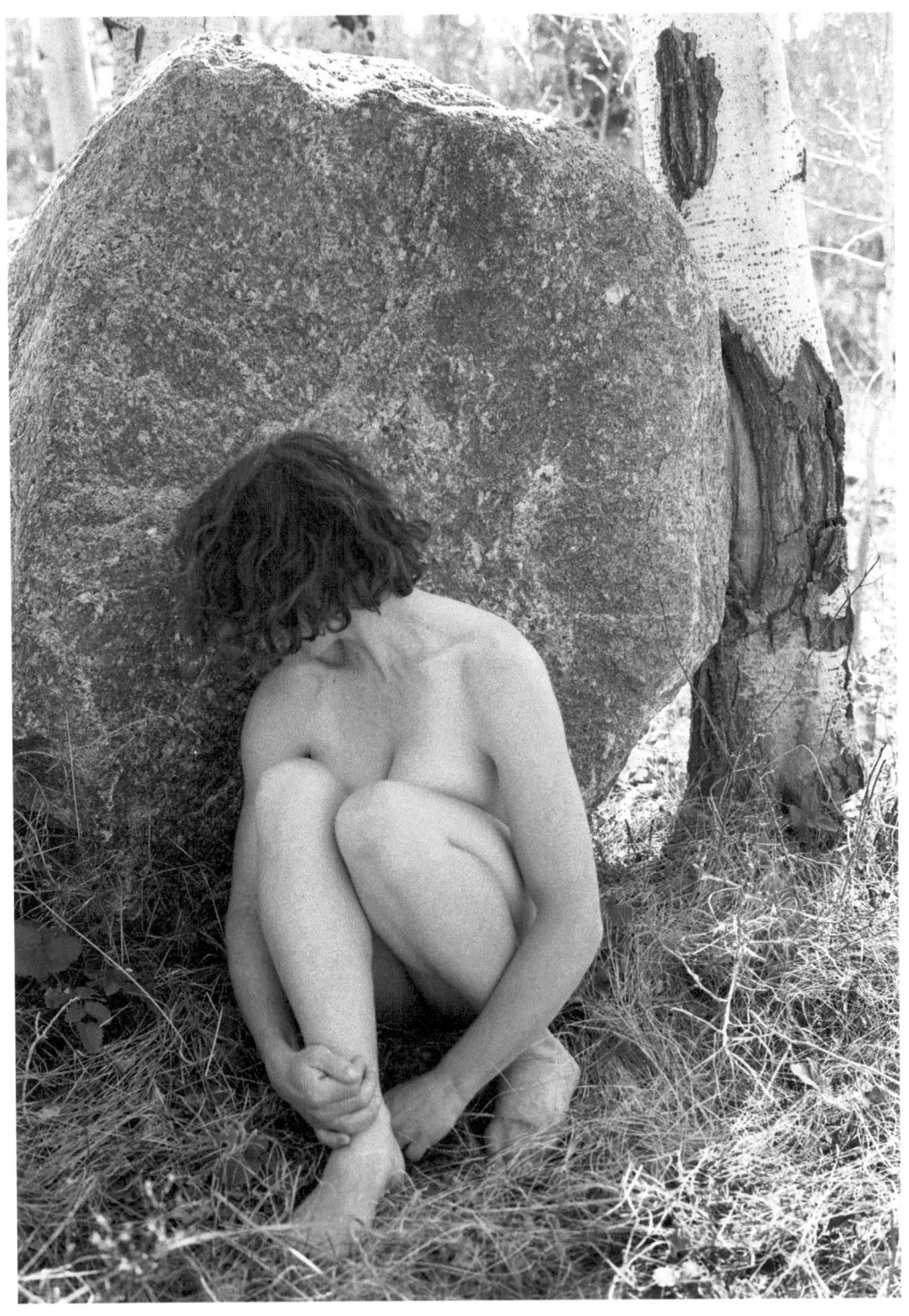

Jackie and Boulder
Fremont Lake, Wyoming

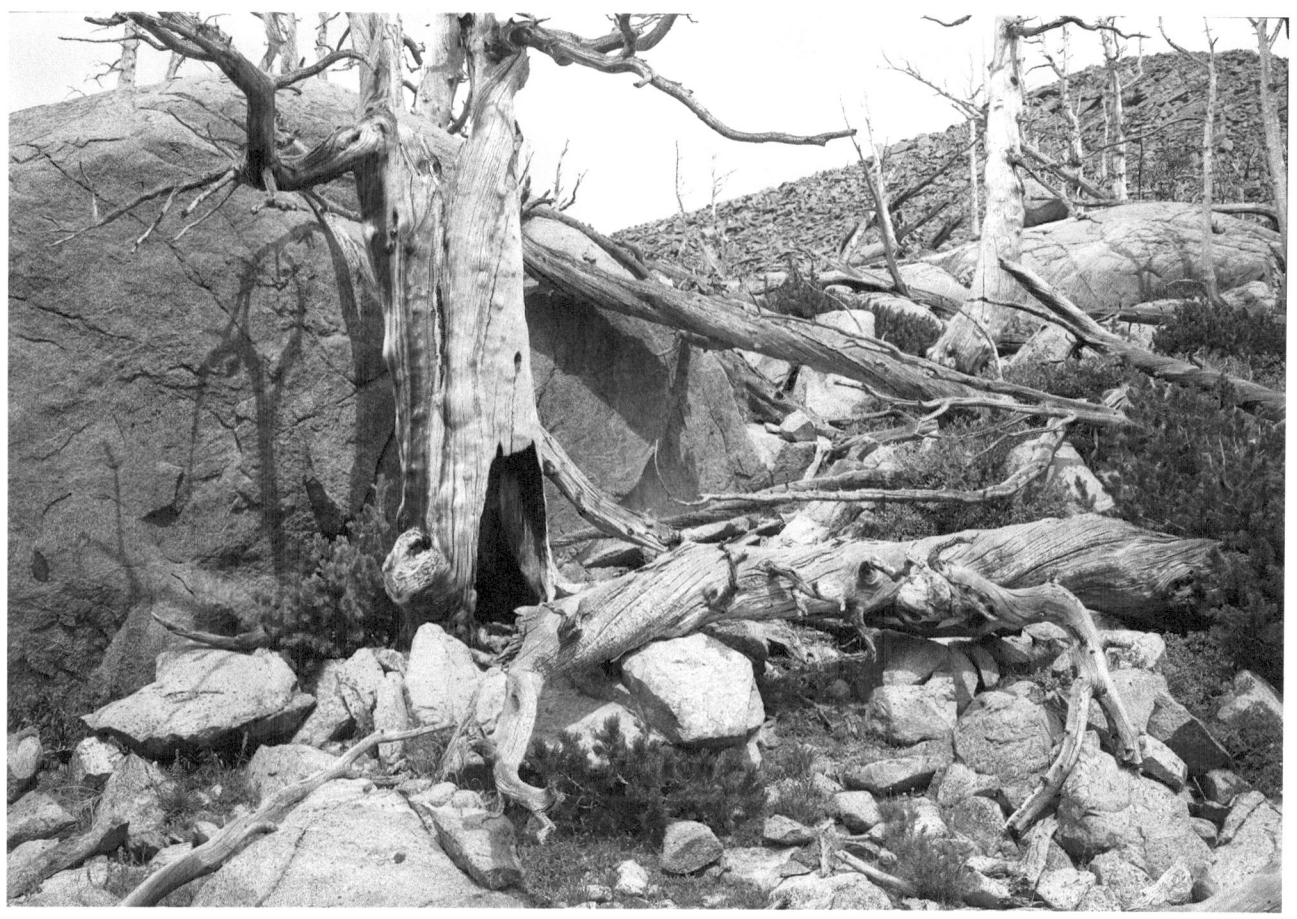

Shoshone Lake
Wind River Indian Reservation, Wyoming

A forest fire tore through this high elevation cirque, creating a natural sculpture garden of twisted, skeletal forms. The winds, over time, scoured the charred bark off the trees, leaving smooth-skinned monuments.

Ed Lavino

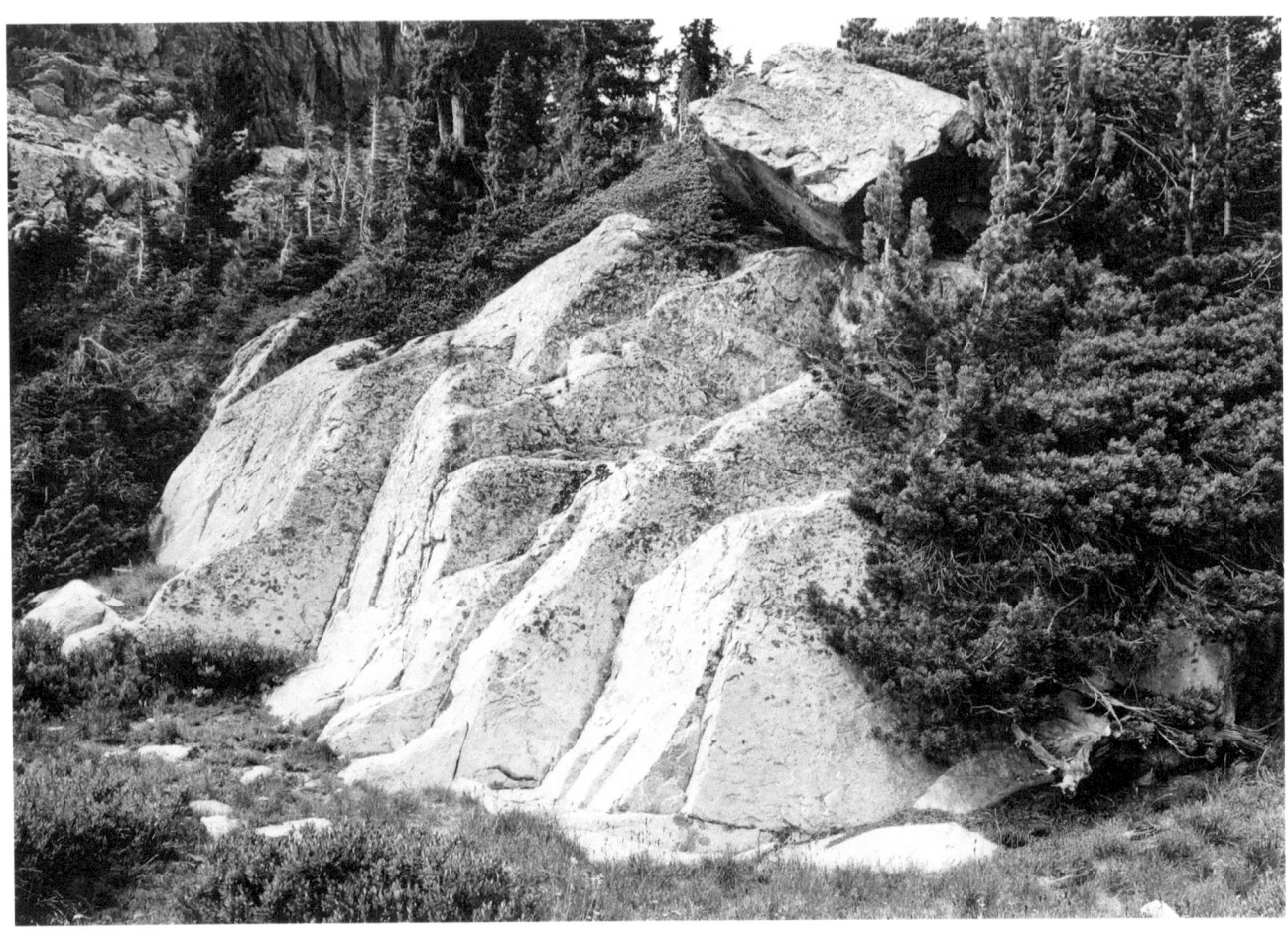

Glacial Polish
Seneca Lake, Wyoming

Prevailing Westerlies

"I took off on a journey with no destination. Riding a wave of phenomenal good luck, I chased spring, and then summer, from Texas, northwest through the mountains, making friends and losing inhibitions all along the way. By the time I reached the Tetons in August, I was tanner, and wilder, and freer than I'd been in my life; indiscriminately saying 'yes' to whatever the universe threw my way."
— Whitney

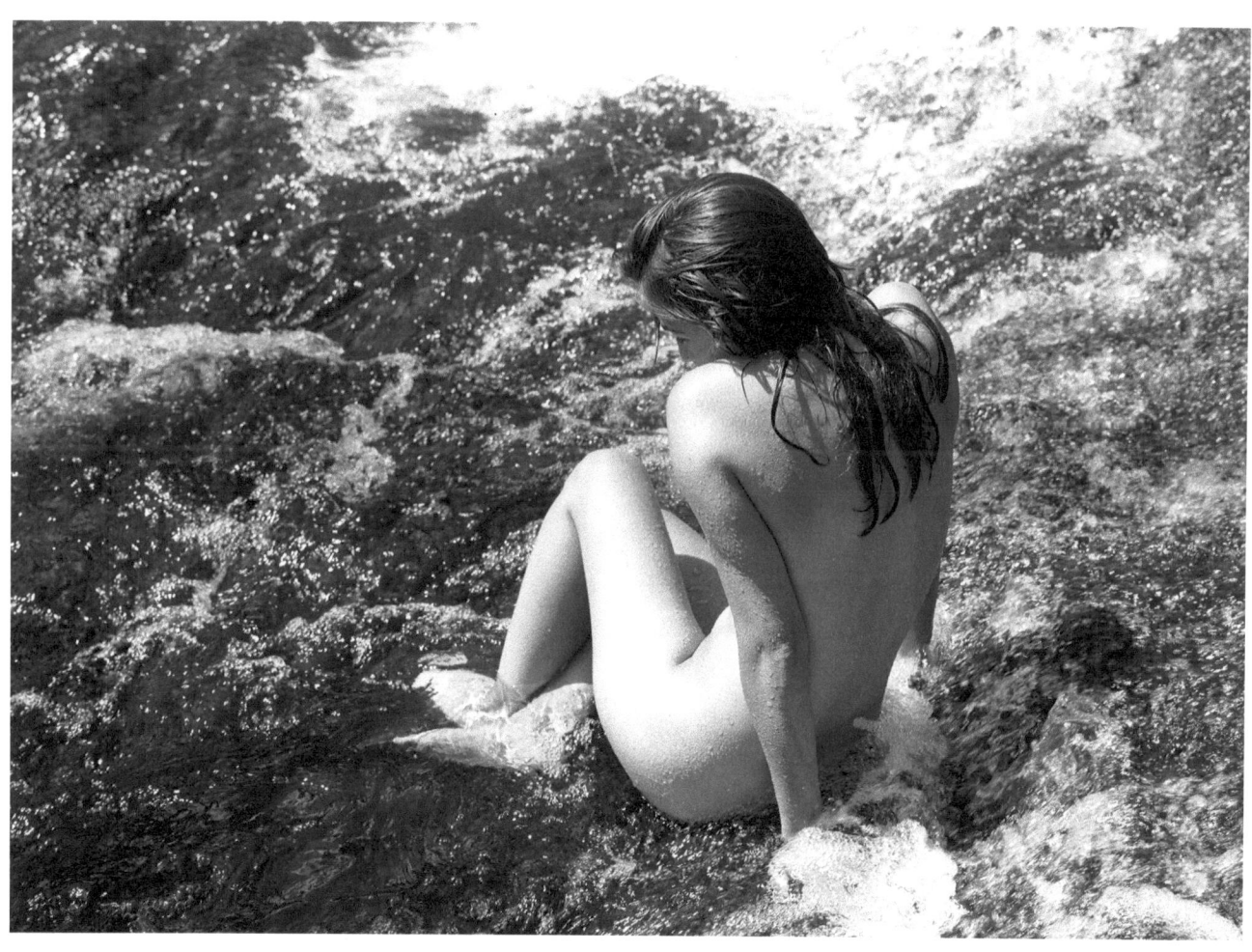

Ed Lavino

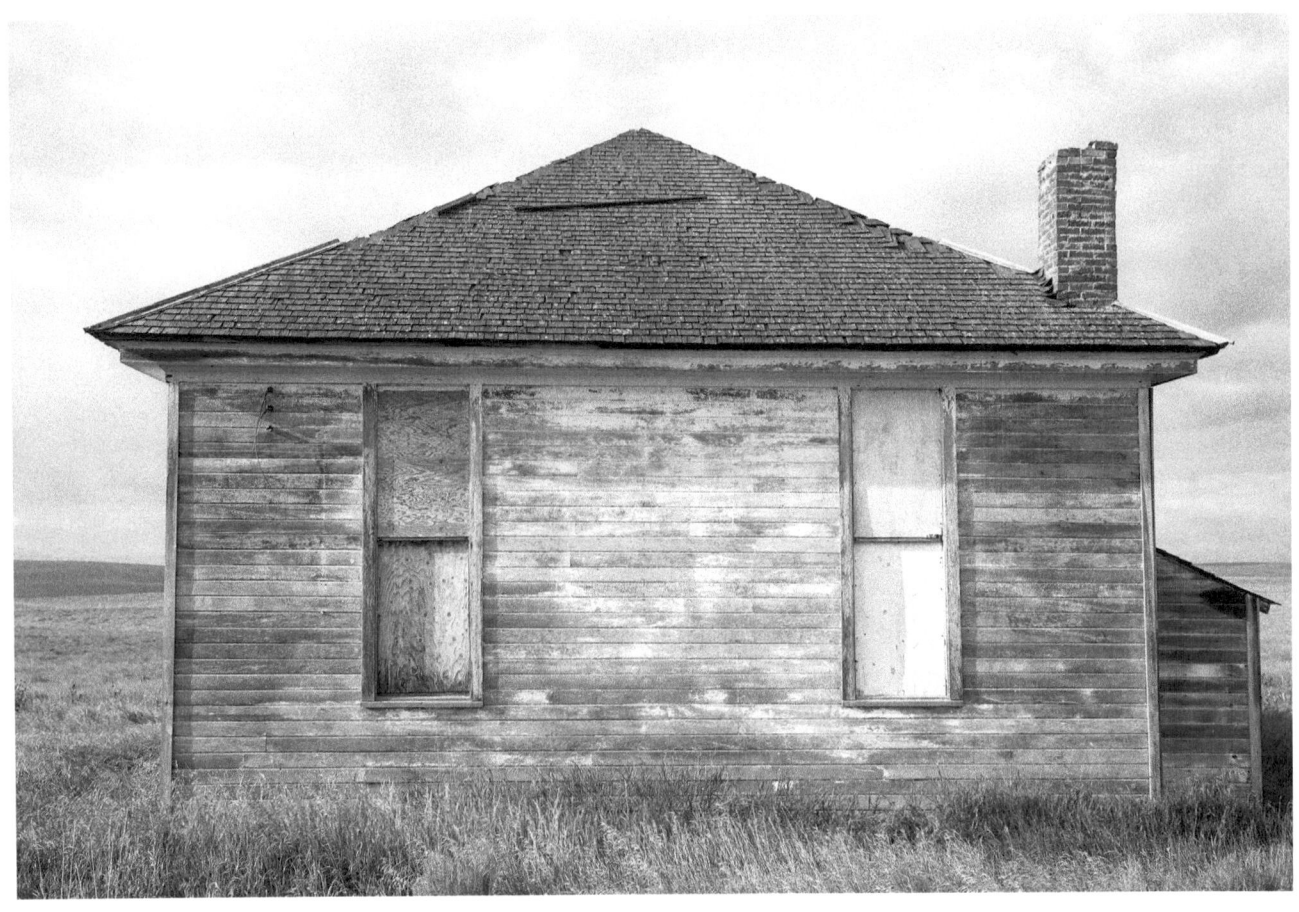

One Room Schoolhouse
Felt, Idaho

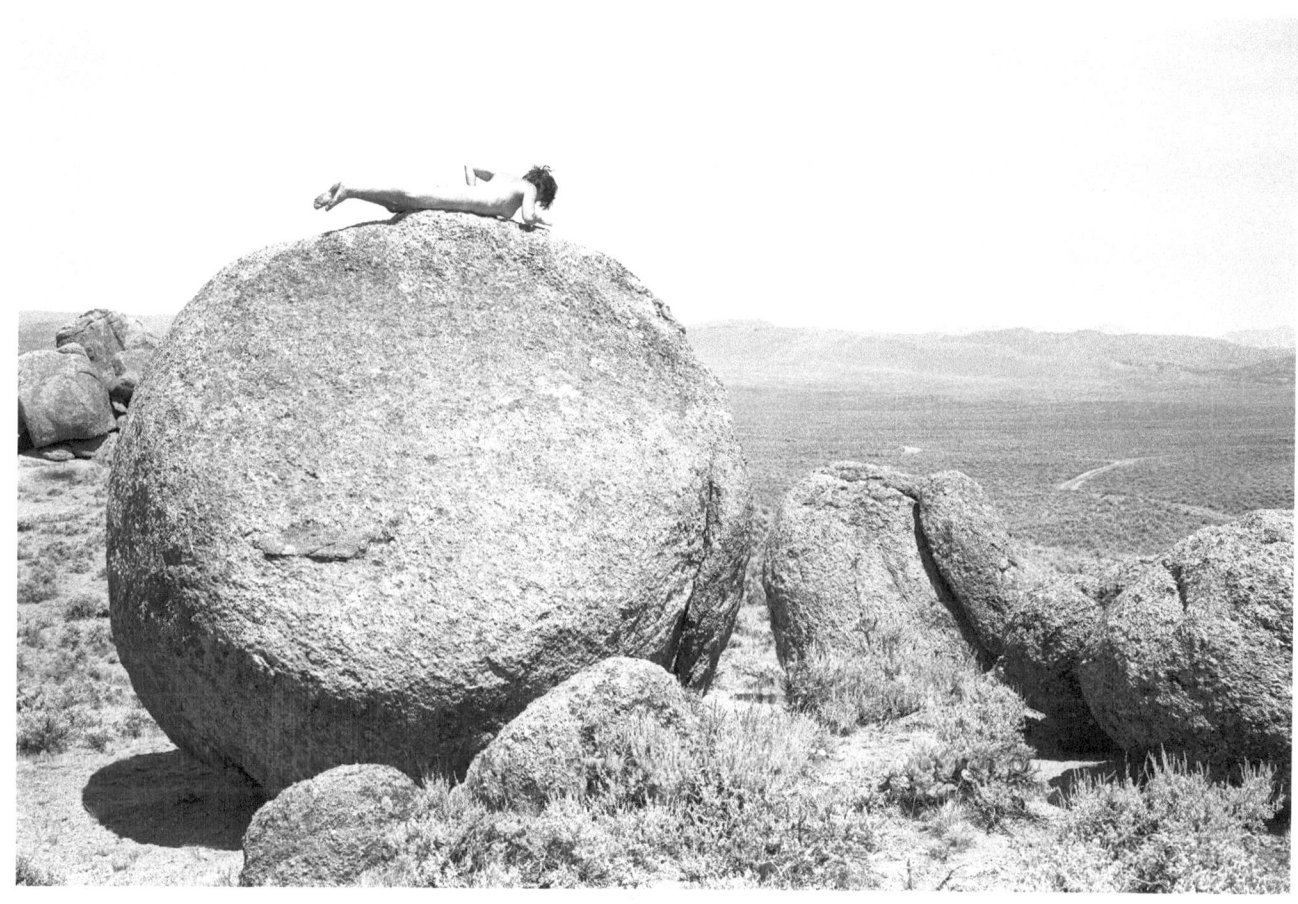

Emma
Sublette County, Wyoming

This massive glacial erratic, dubbed "Stonehenge" by local climbers, is way off the beaten path. I asked Emma to pose as if she were floating, in order to give the boulder a sense of rolling movement and instability.

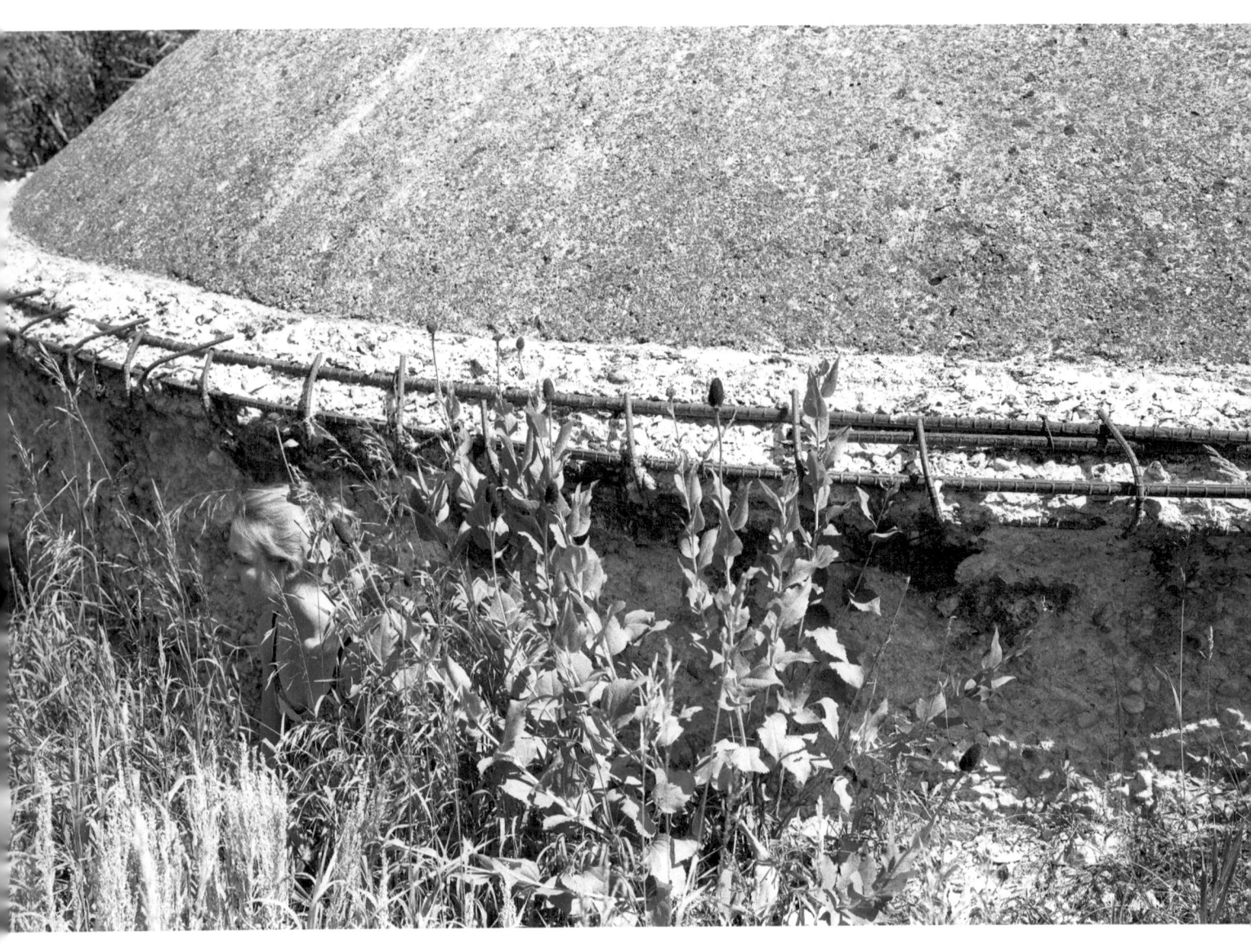

Corrie and Water Storage Tank
Victor, Idaho
(mirror images)

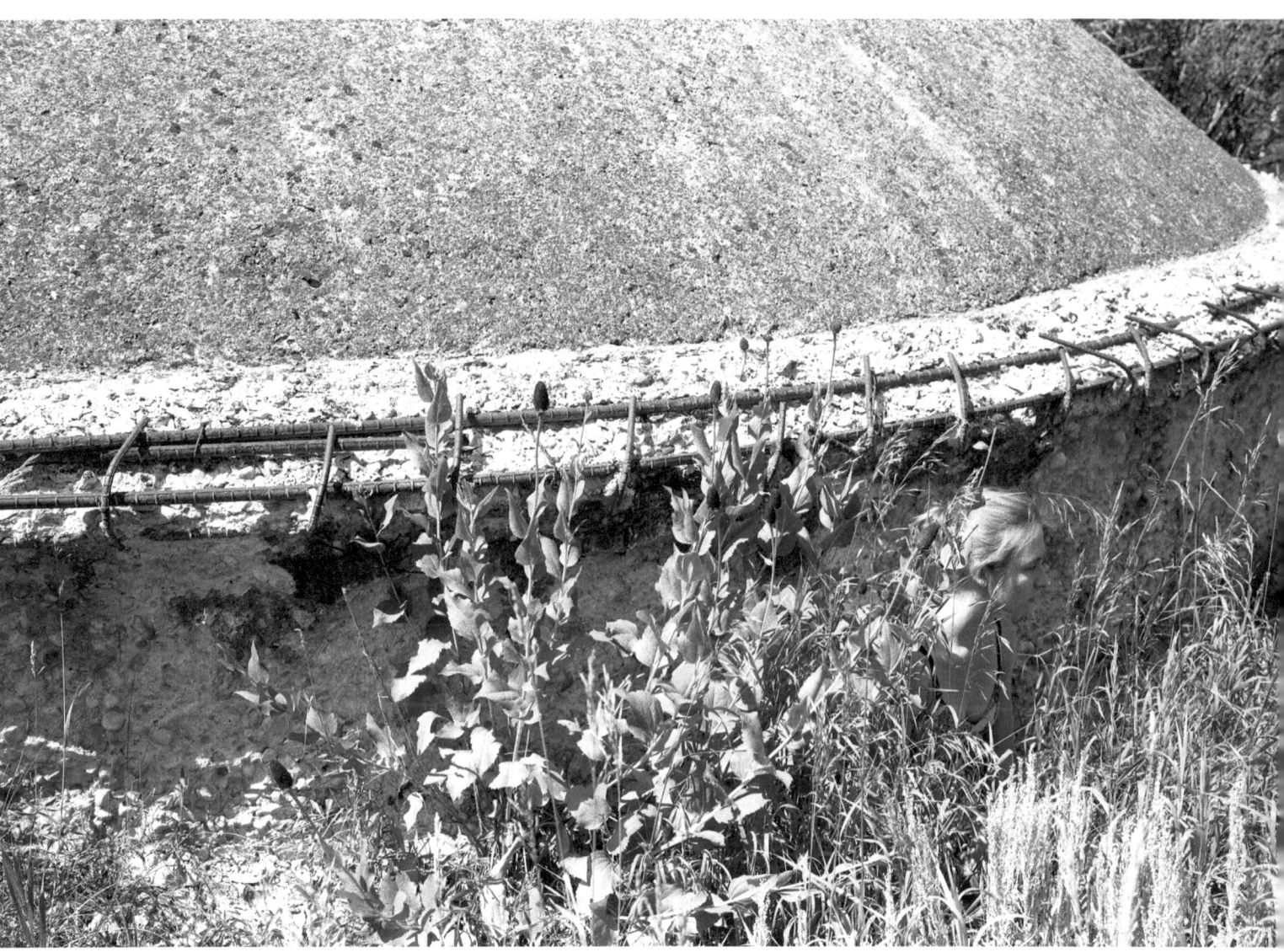

I spotted this dome-shaped, concrete water tank at a distance and was determined to investigate it. The approach was challenging. It involved climbing a steep grade, and fighting through thickets of hawthorne briars. Corrie is positioned off center, and partially obscured by foliage, making her inconspicuous. A recurring goal of mine is to photograph the figure in the landscape in such a way as to achieve integration to the point of camouflage.

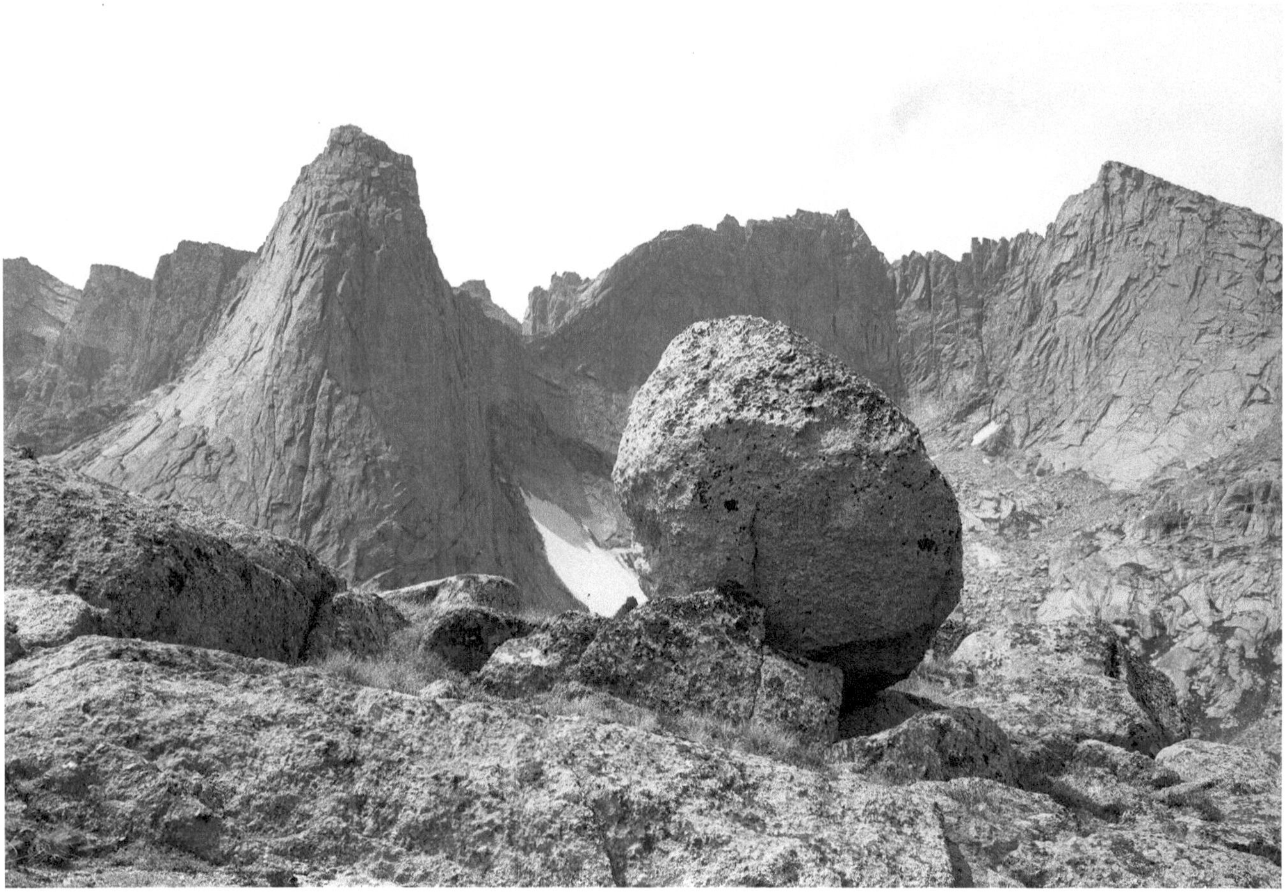

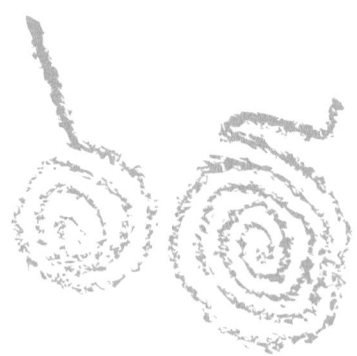

Pingora Peak
Wind River Mountains, Wyoming

In the mountains, erosional forces act as master sculptors. Wind, ice, and lichen have countered the immense upward thrust of the Rocky Mountains. Today, an elliptical boulder is stranded, teetering beneath granite buttresses.

Prevailing Westerlies

Dutch Jug, Bighorn Skull, and Driftwood

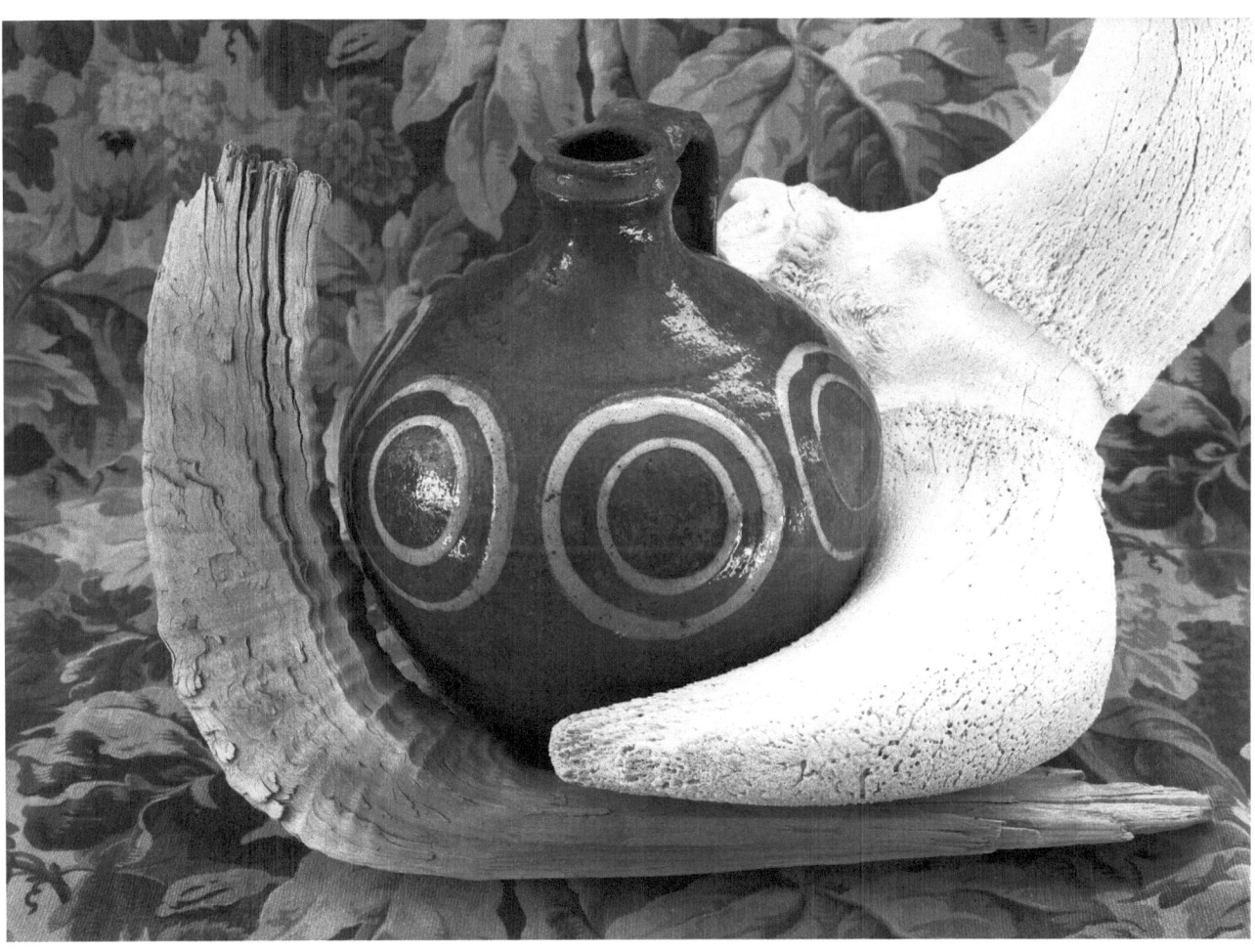

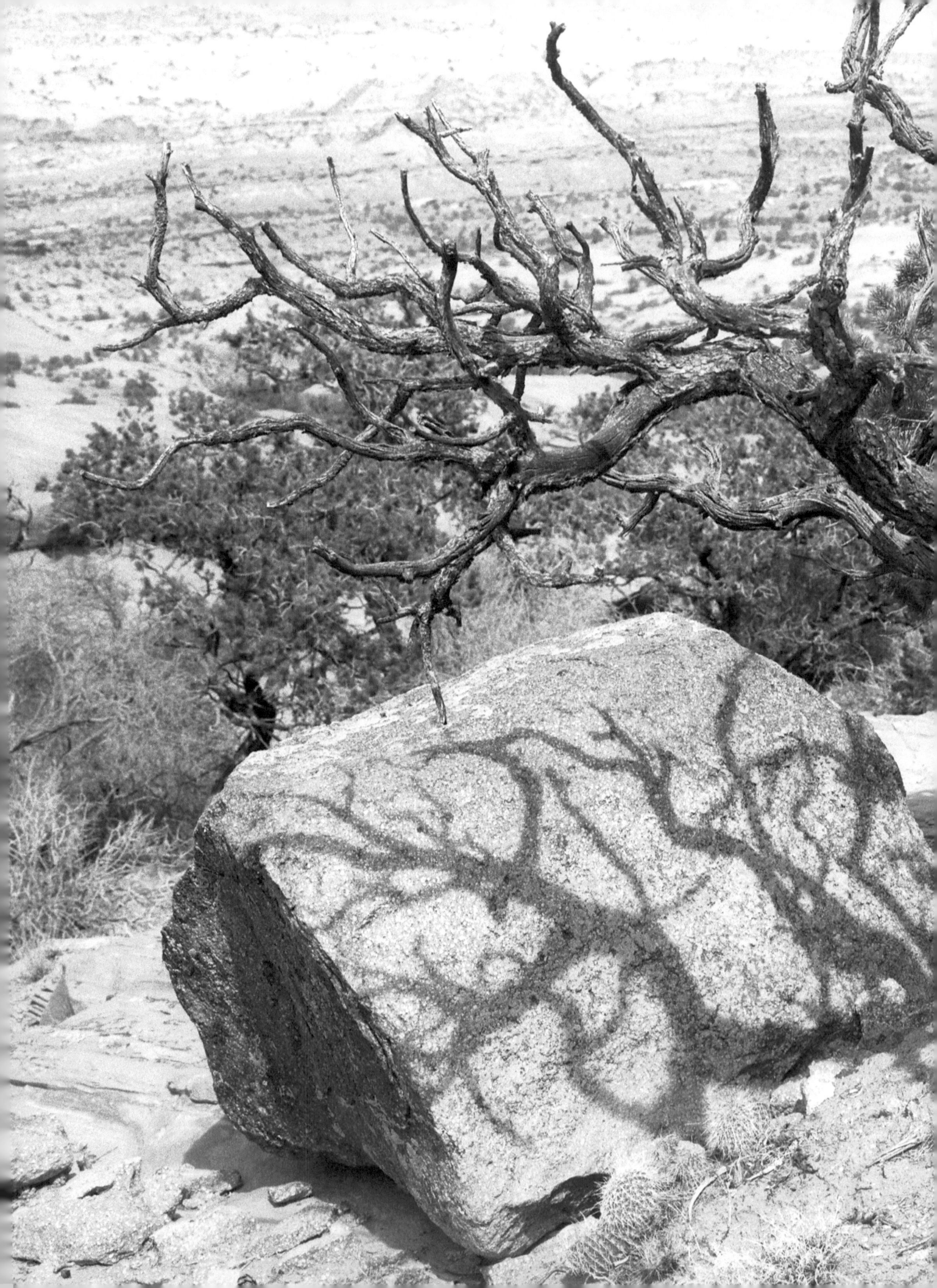

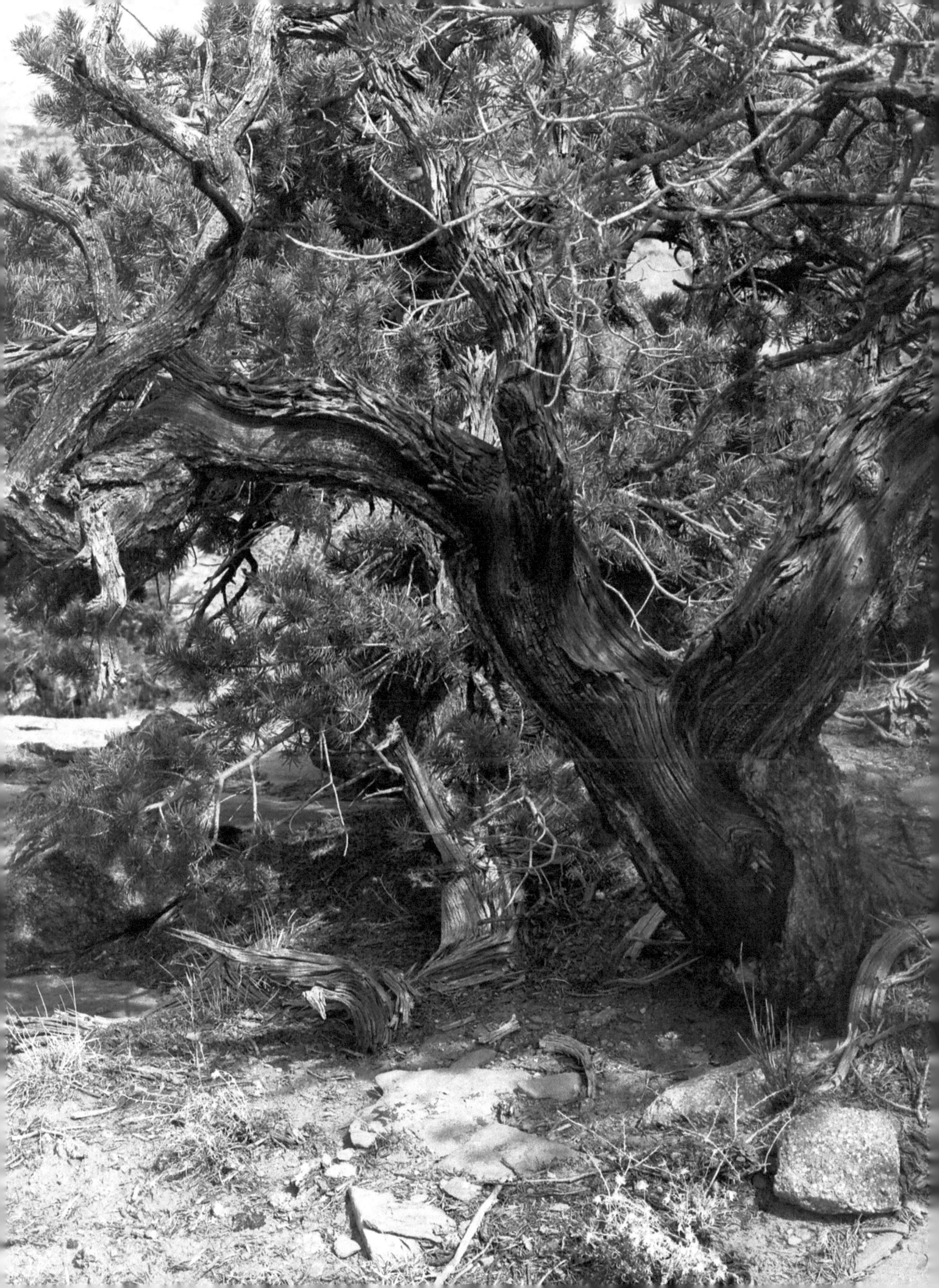

Ed Lavino

(Previous page) Shadow Cast on Boulder
Southern Utah

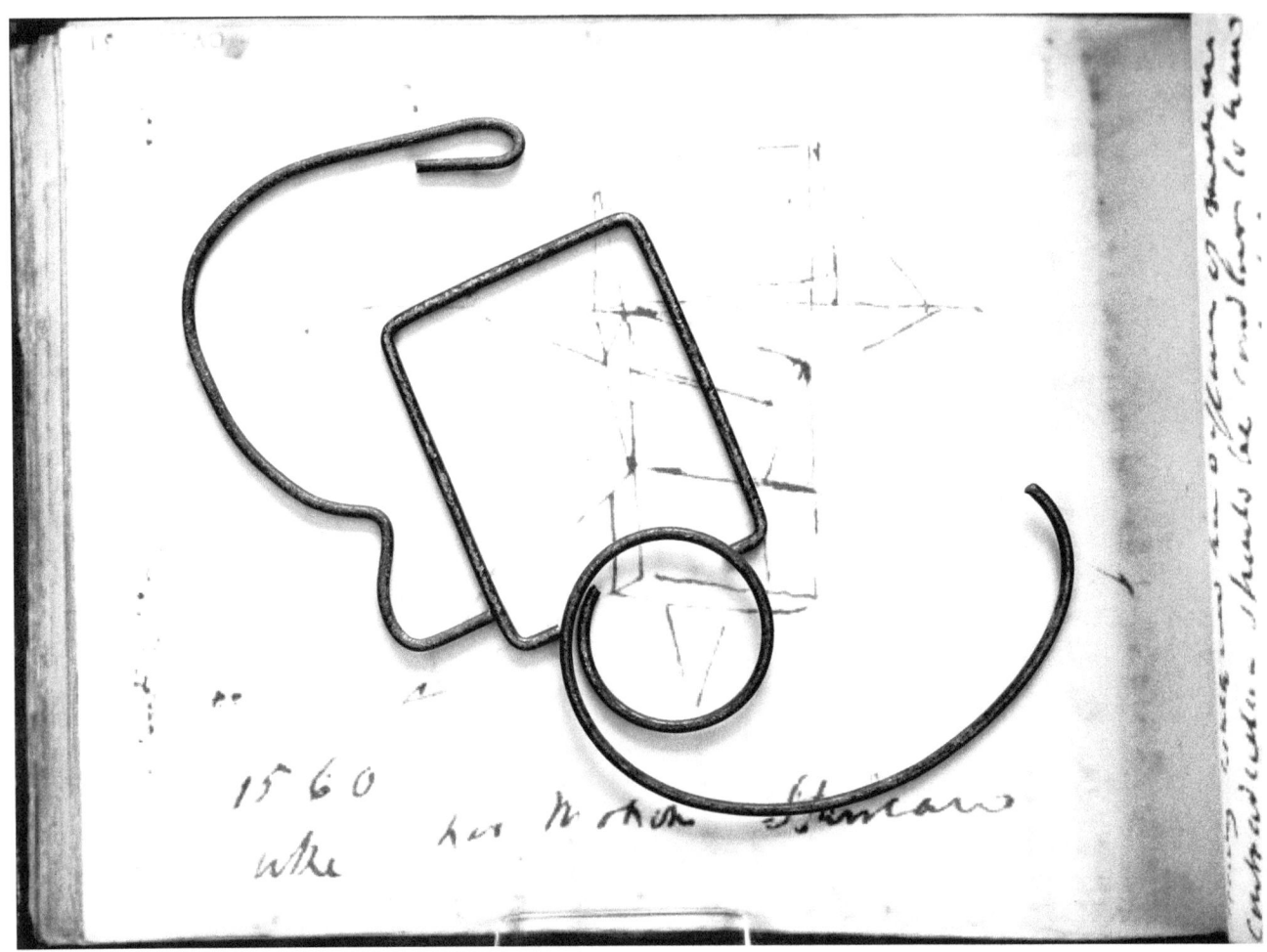

A Study of Static Motion

When out walking, I keep an eye out for compelling, found objects. I store them in boxes, and at times they end up being exactly what's needed to express a particular idea. The three scraps of shaped wire in this image were found in different locations and collected over a period of years. They make sense together, and seem to offer a visual solution to an abstract problem.

Prevailing Westerlies

The boulder's course prescribed by gravity.
The promise of repose is halted.
Meanwhile, a shaded lizard rests, free from care,
oblivious to silent stalkers gliding above.
Sanctuary from today's blistering sun trumps threats of tomorrow's fall.

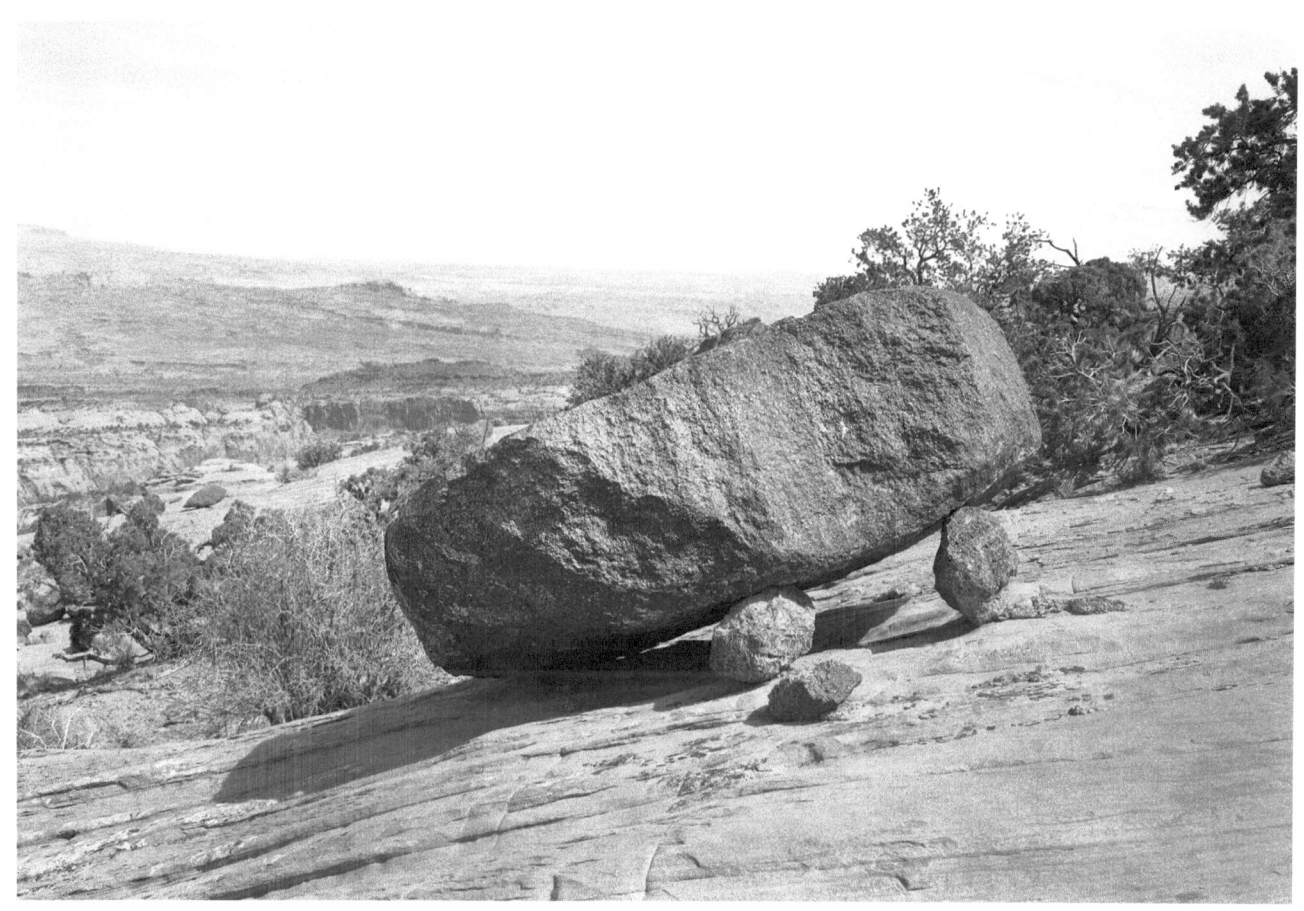

Tilted Boulder
Glen Canyon Wilderness, Utah

The sense of arriving in an otherworldly realm was underscored by the extreme isolation of this spot. I was on an extended backpacking trip with a friend whose goal was to see "no one else's footprints for the entire time." We were off trail, and gained access by scrambling through a slot canyon. The remoteness and lack of water make it an unlikely destination for most humans.

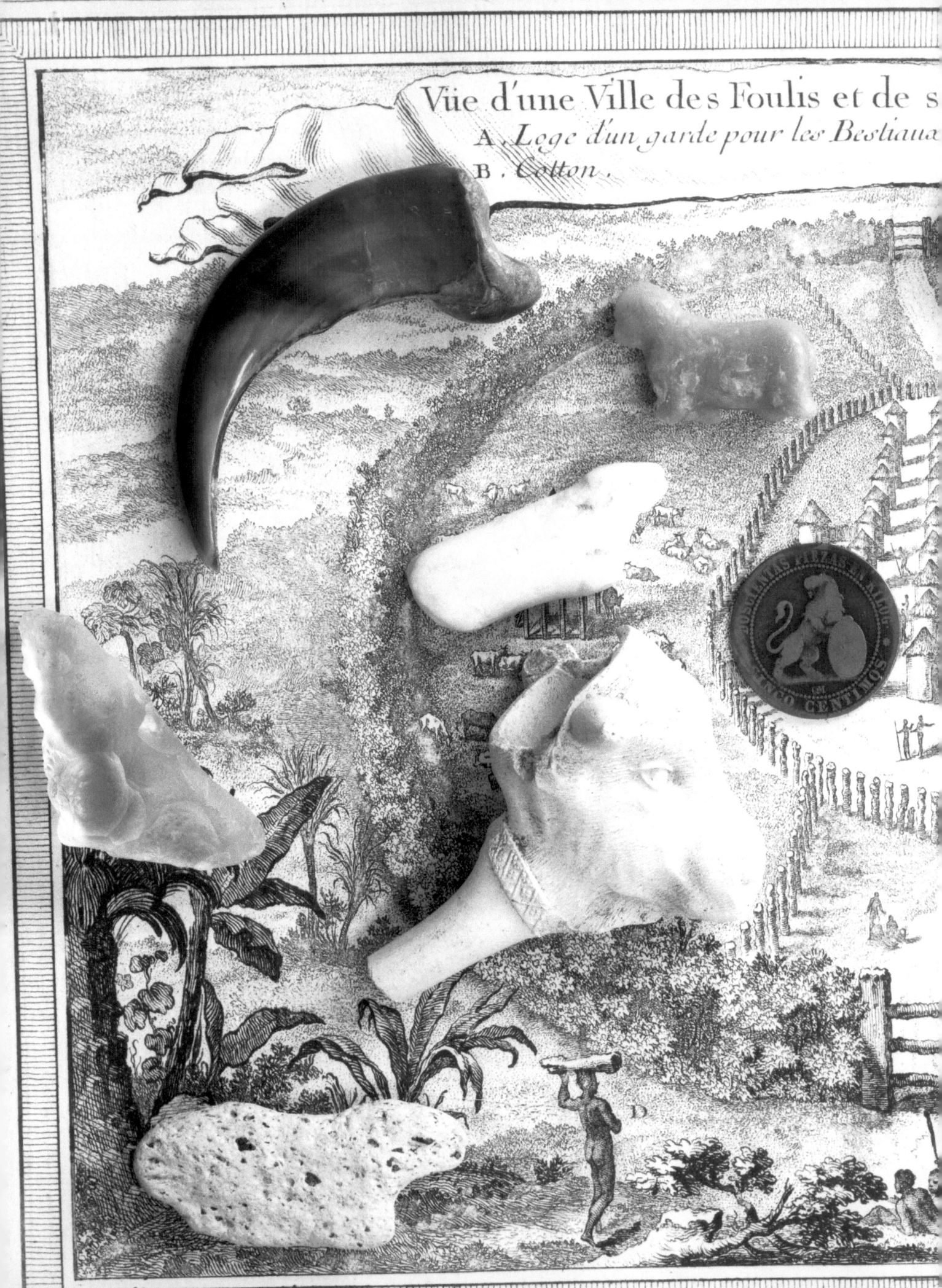

Vüe d'une Ville des Foulis et de s
A . Loge d'un garde pour les Bestiaua
B . Cotton .

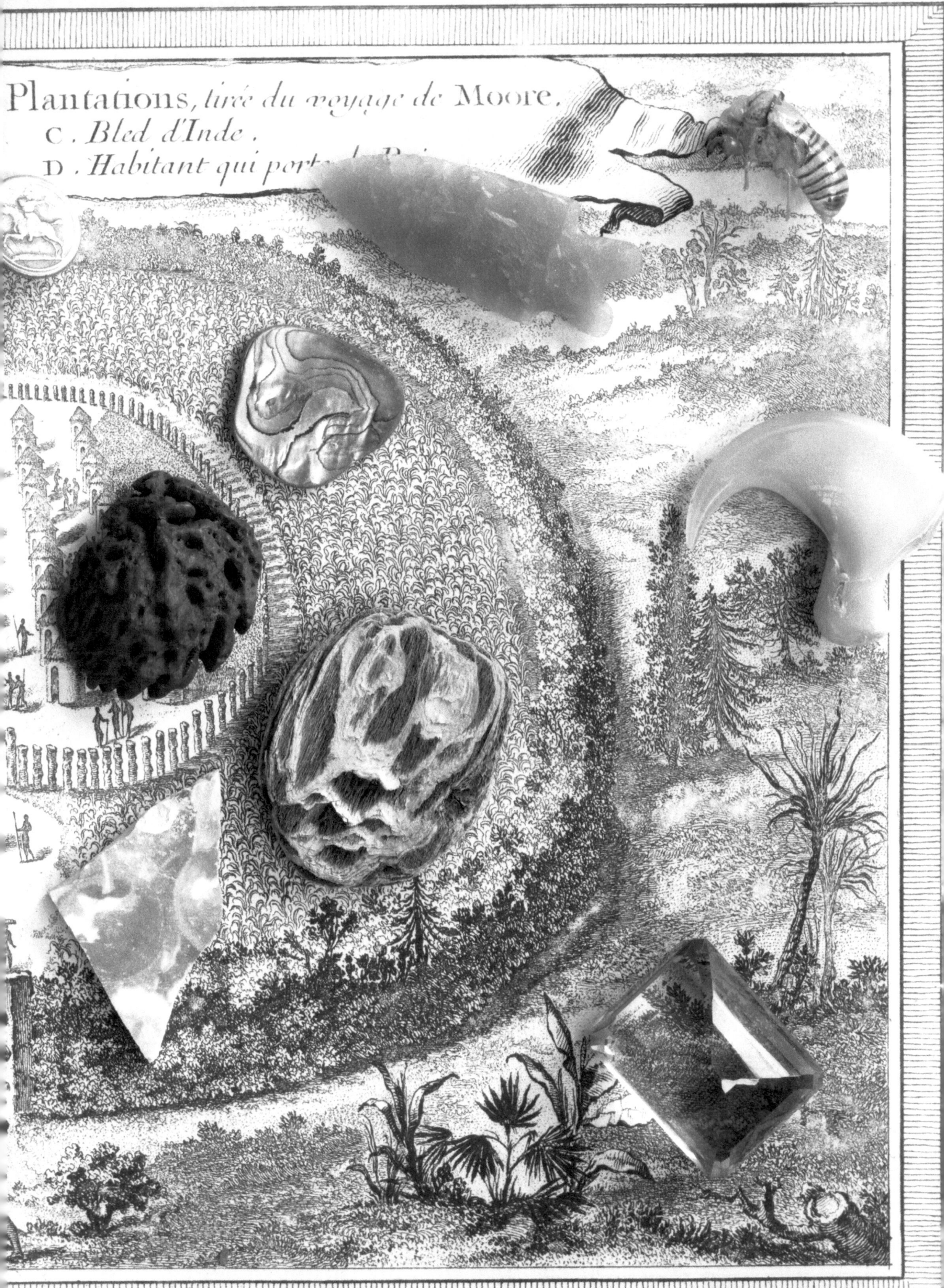

Plantations, *tiré du voyage de Moore.*
C. *Bled d'Inde.*
D. *Habitant qui porte...*

Ed Lavino

(Previous page) Colonization

Shielded from the lion, in a compound ringed with thorns,
hopeful crops are sown.

Harvest takes flight, leaving with the crown,
beyond guard, beyond regard.

Tribes are paid with the story of a crown of thorns,
casting a shadow blacker than the lion's maw.

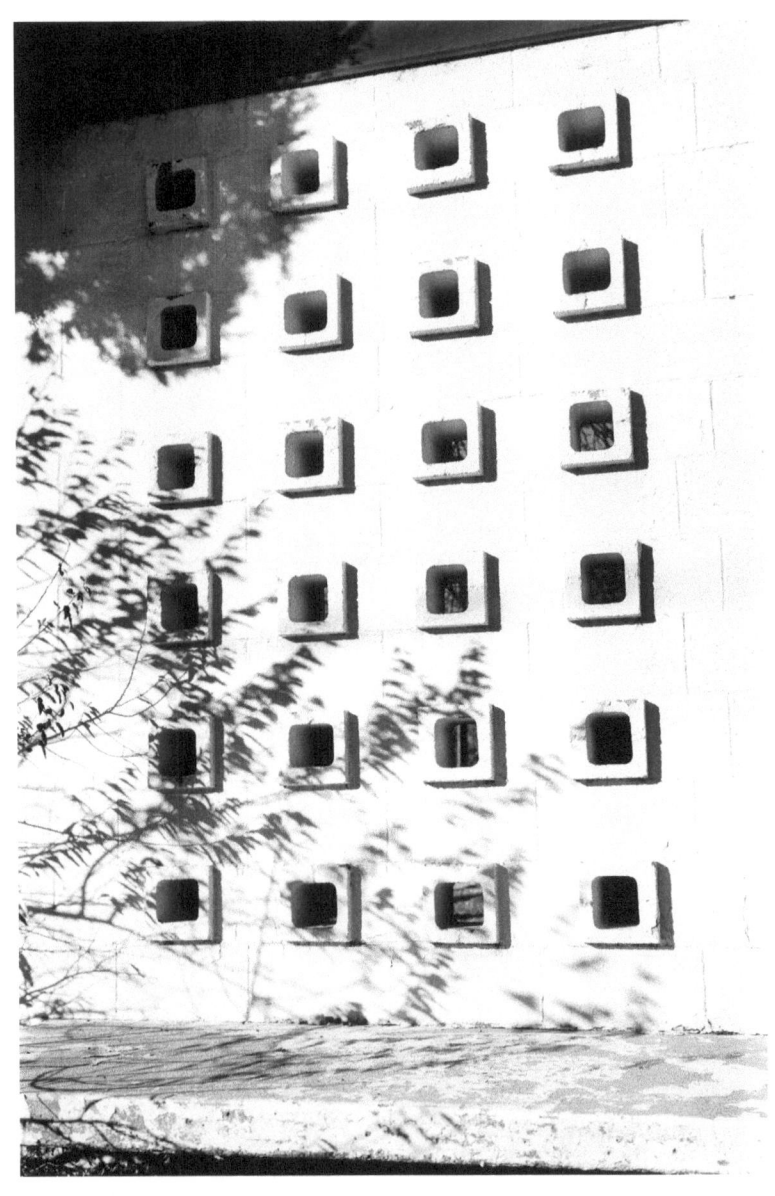

Concrete Block Wall, Casper, Wyoming

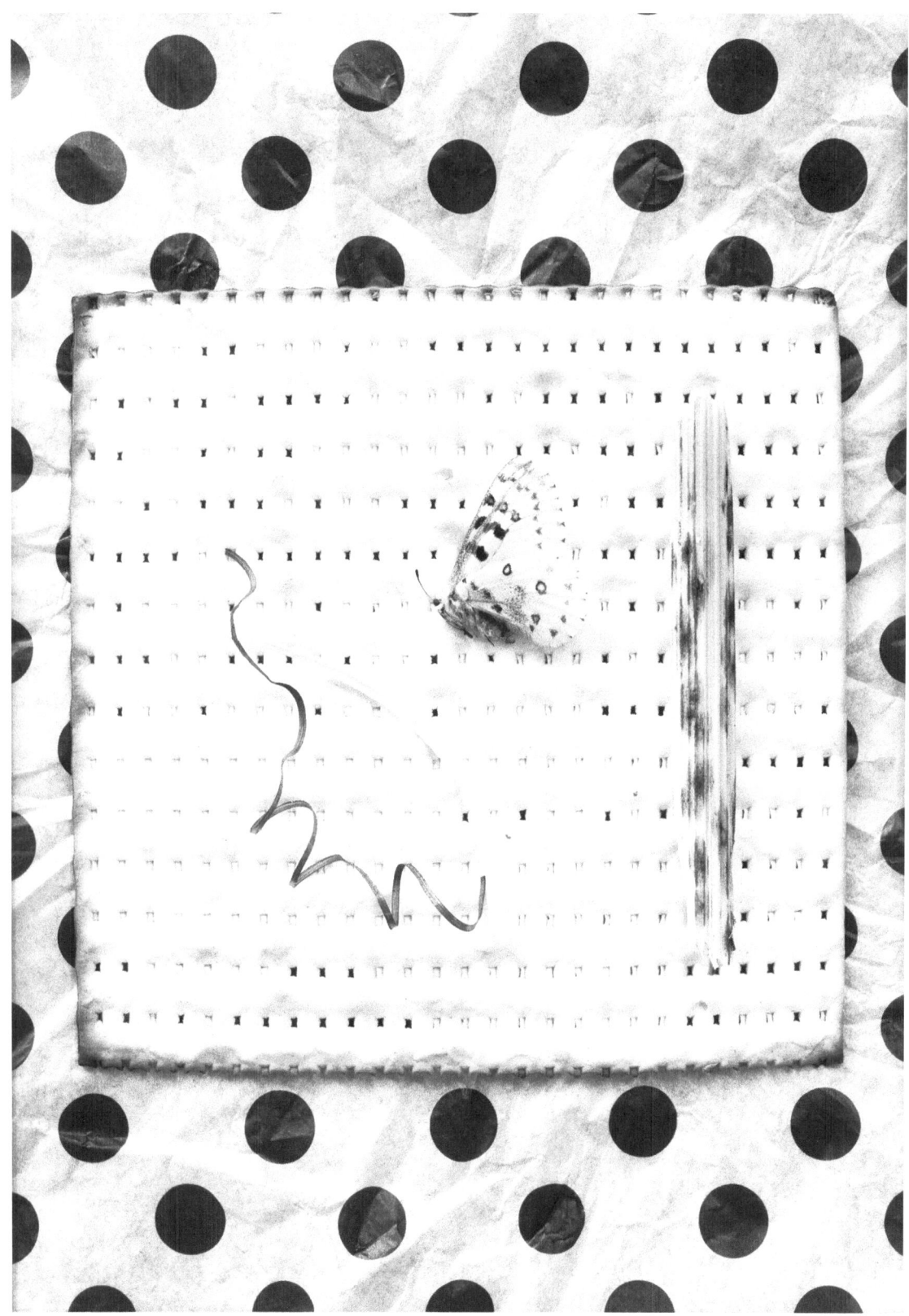

Matzo and Metal Shaving

Ed Lavino

Wyoming Baroque
Kemmerer, Wyoming

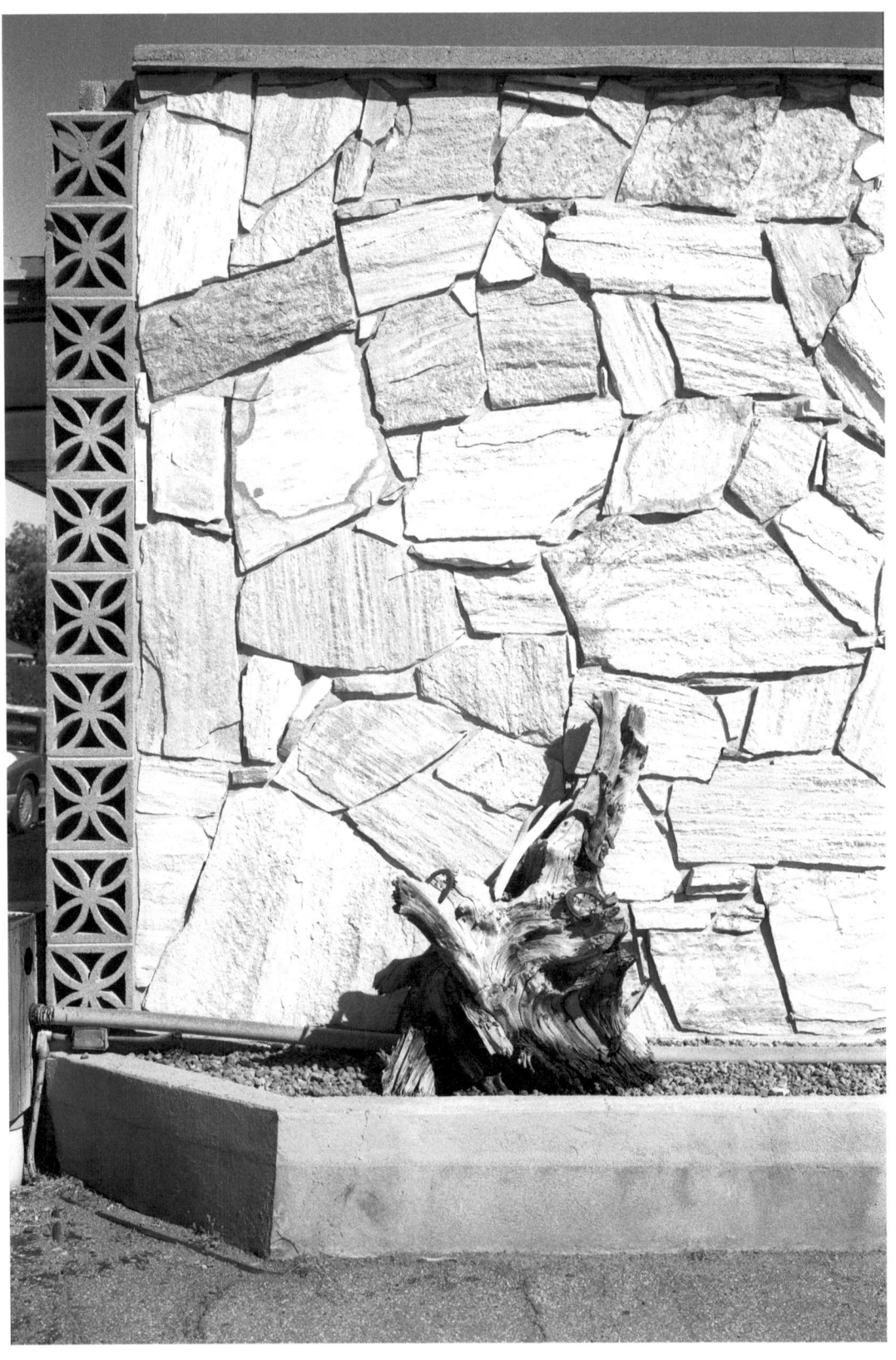

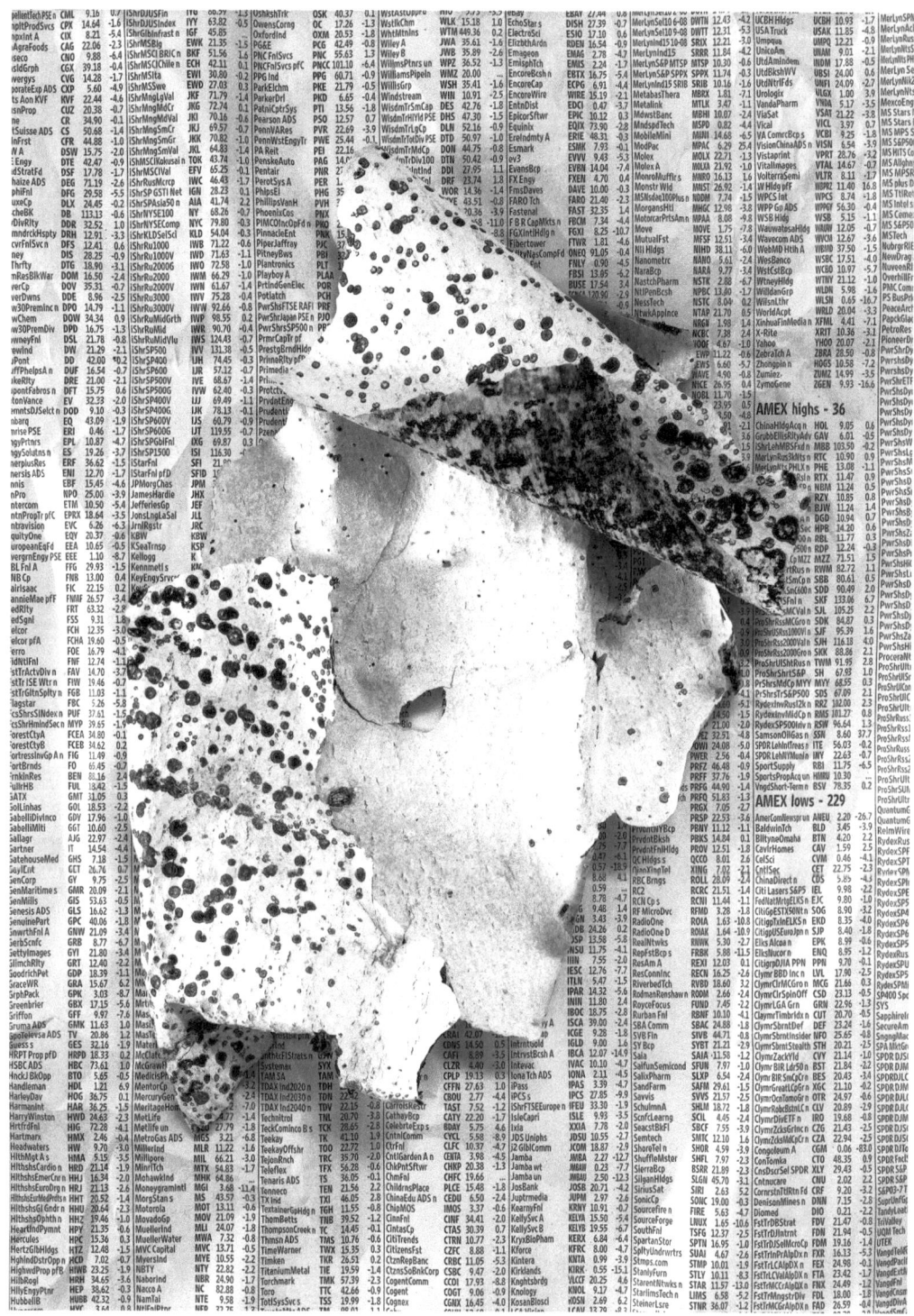

Aspen and Wall Street Journal

The Wall Street Journal's predictable, tidy rows belie storms of whim and passion beneath the ink. In contrast, Aspen bark's rogue, random beauty disguises pure precision dictated by DNA.

Ed Lavino

Sylvan Springs
Yellowstone National Park, Wyoming

This spot is extremely difficult to access. The excursion involves fording the Gibbon River, wading a brackish marsh, and swatting voracious deer flies, all while keeping an eye out for grizzlies. Just outside the frame of this photo, beyond a chalky grotto, the bleached skull and antlers of a bull elk speak to the difficulty of wintering on this high plateau.

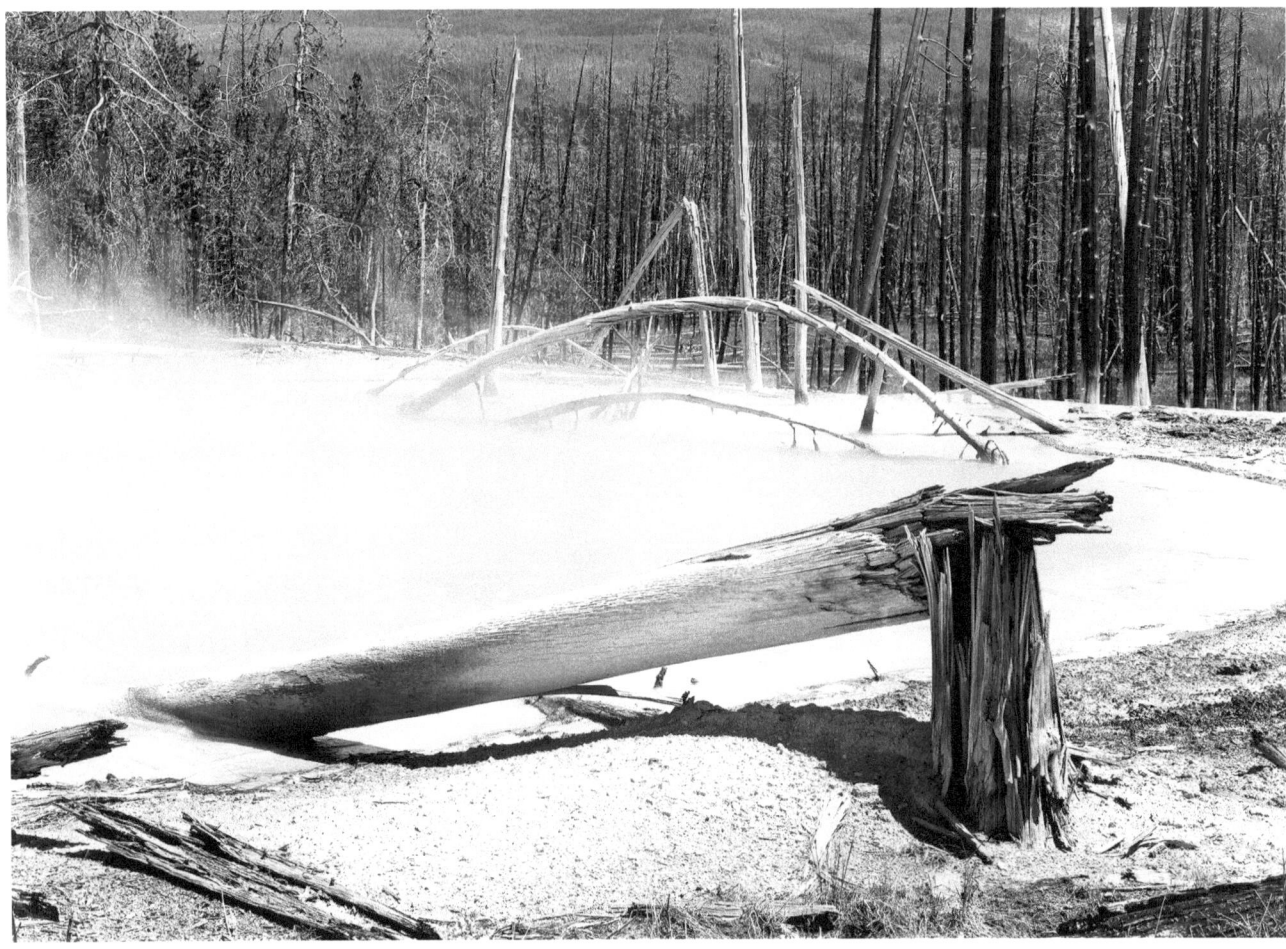

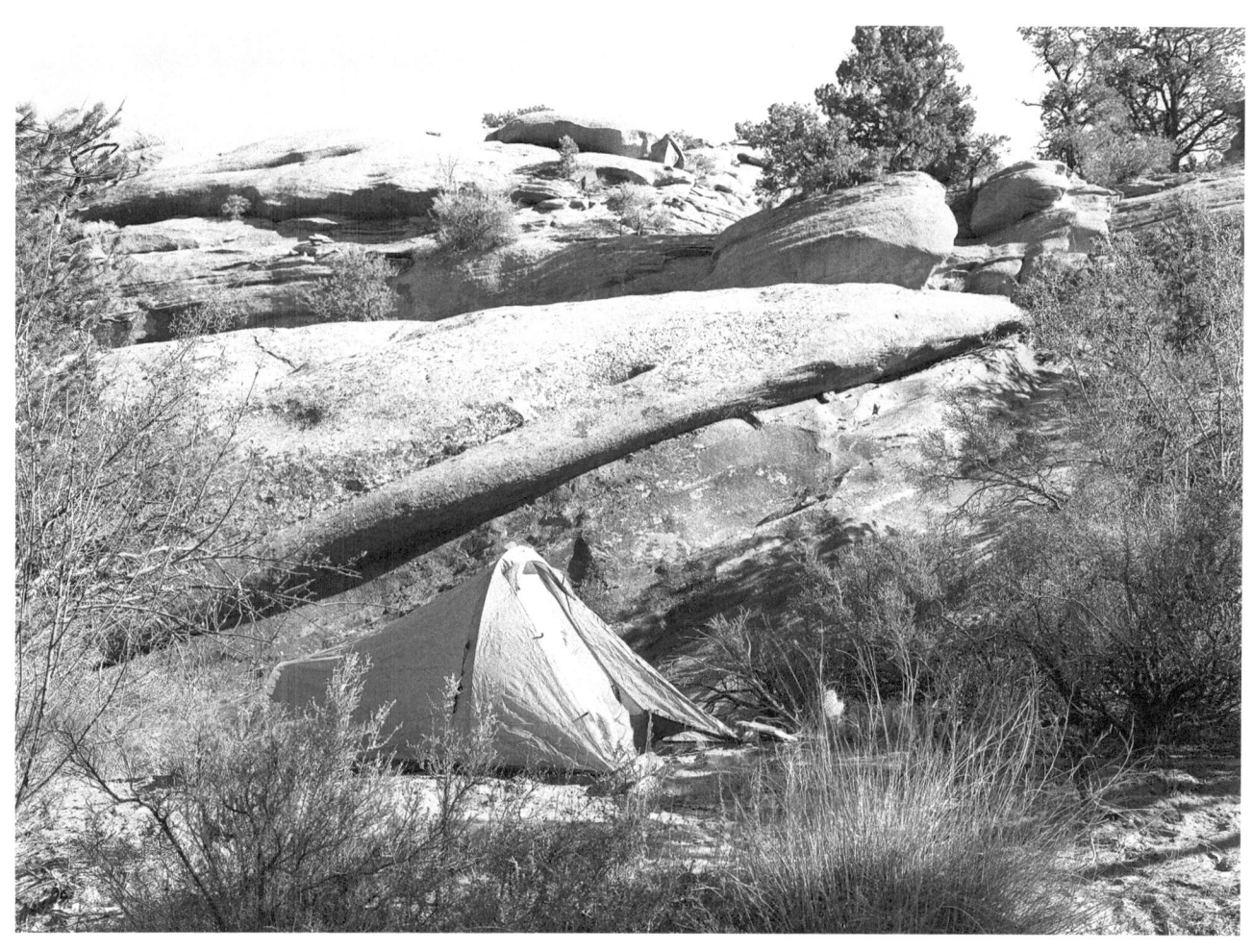

One Man Tent
Glen Canyon Wilderness, Utah

"It is not down on any map; true places never are."
— Herman Melville, Moby Dick

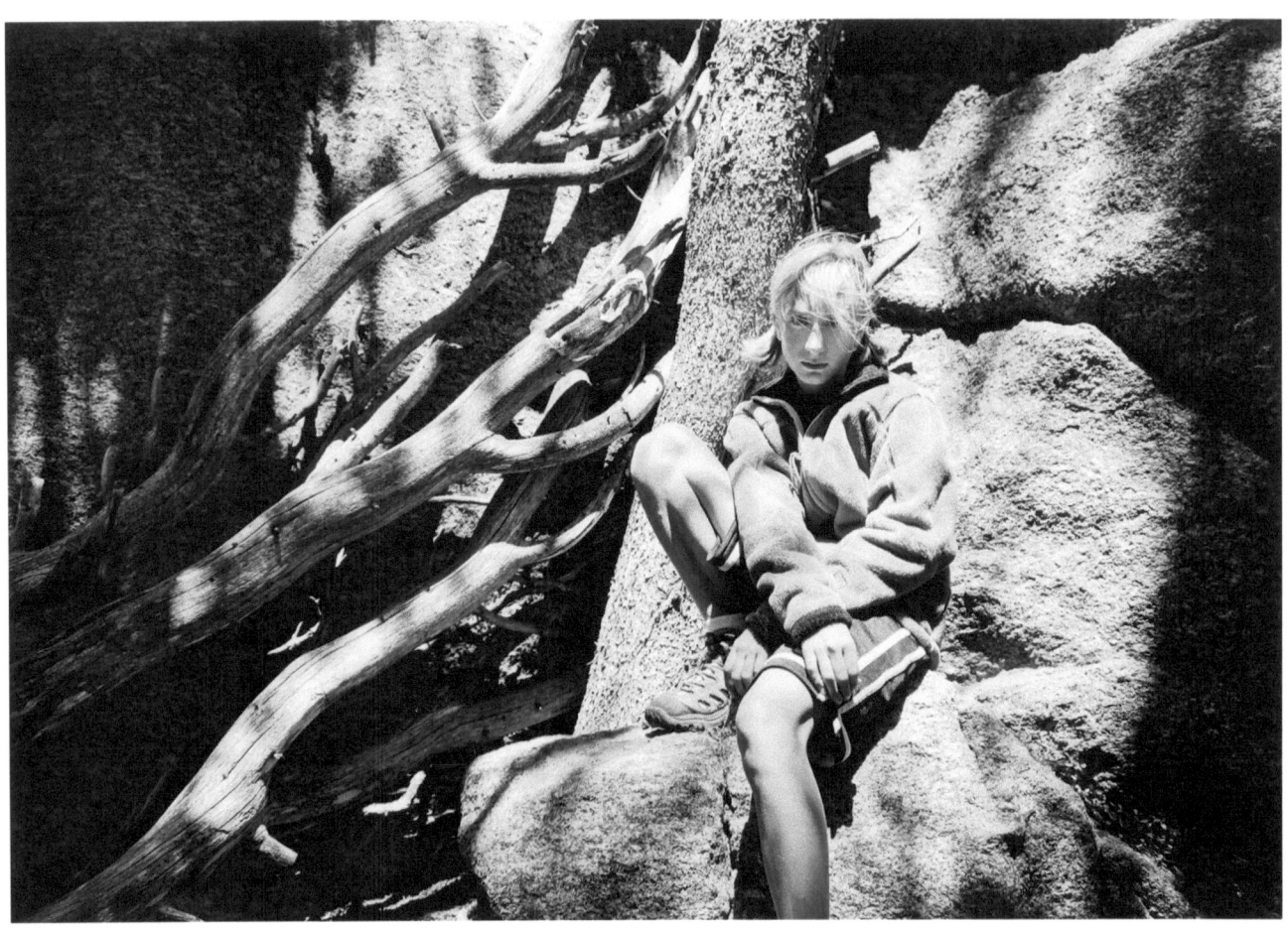

Hillary
Haystack Mountain, Wyoming

My daughter was a reluctant model for this image. We were on a family backpacking trip in the Wind River Range, coming down off the shoulder of Haystack Mountain, when I came upon this complex array of sunlit rock and pine trunks. It was too good to pass up, even though it delayed our much-anticipated dinner back at camp.

Prevailing Westerlies

Corrie's off-balance posture, and the angles of the downed timber, emphasize the instability of the bank as it reacts to shifting forces.

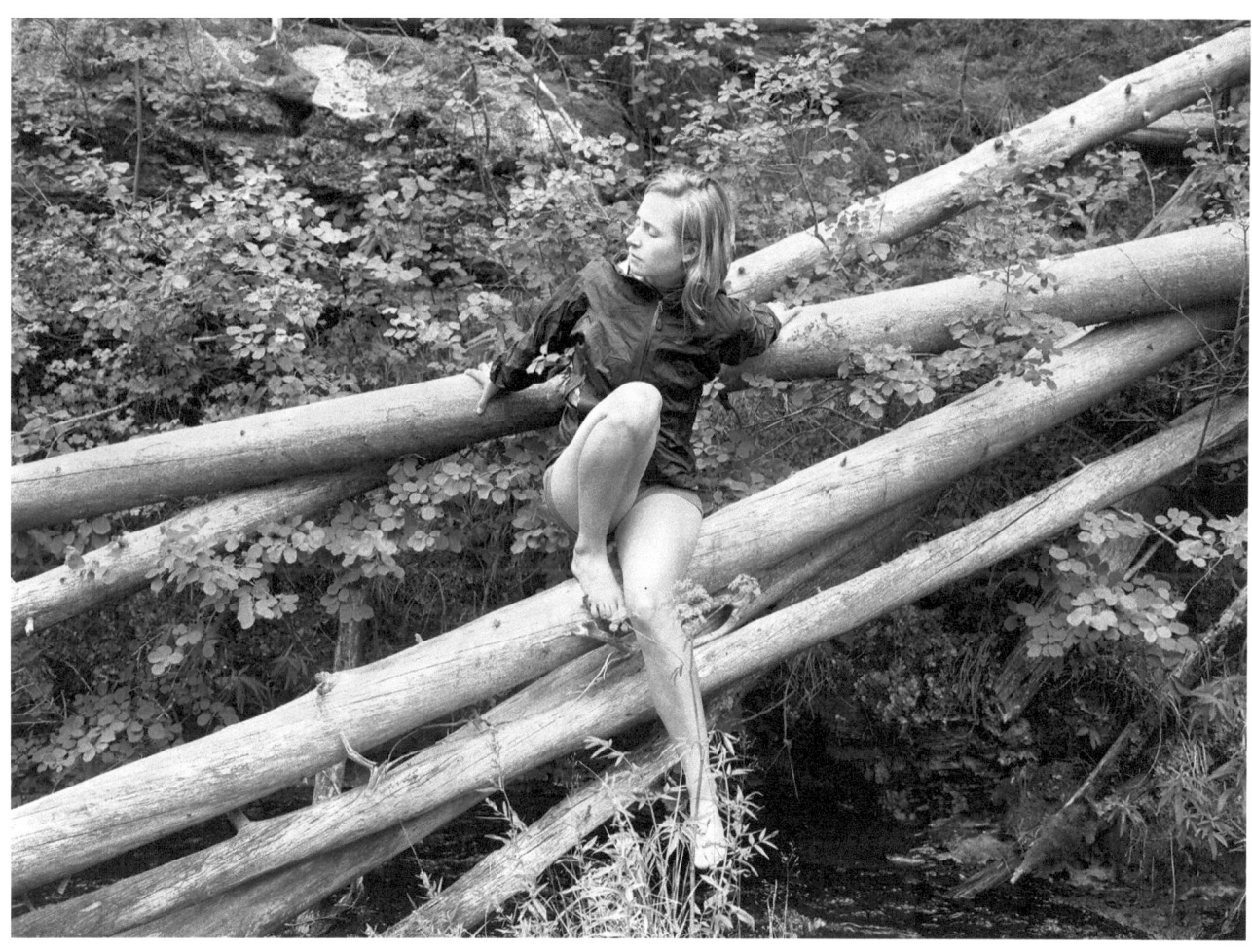

Ed Lavino

Darwin and Elk Antler
Whiskey Basin, Wyoming

In the grip of a frigid north wind, Darwin finds shelter on the leeward side of a Douglas fir.

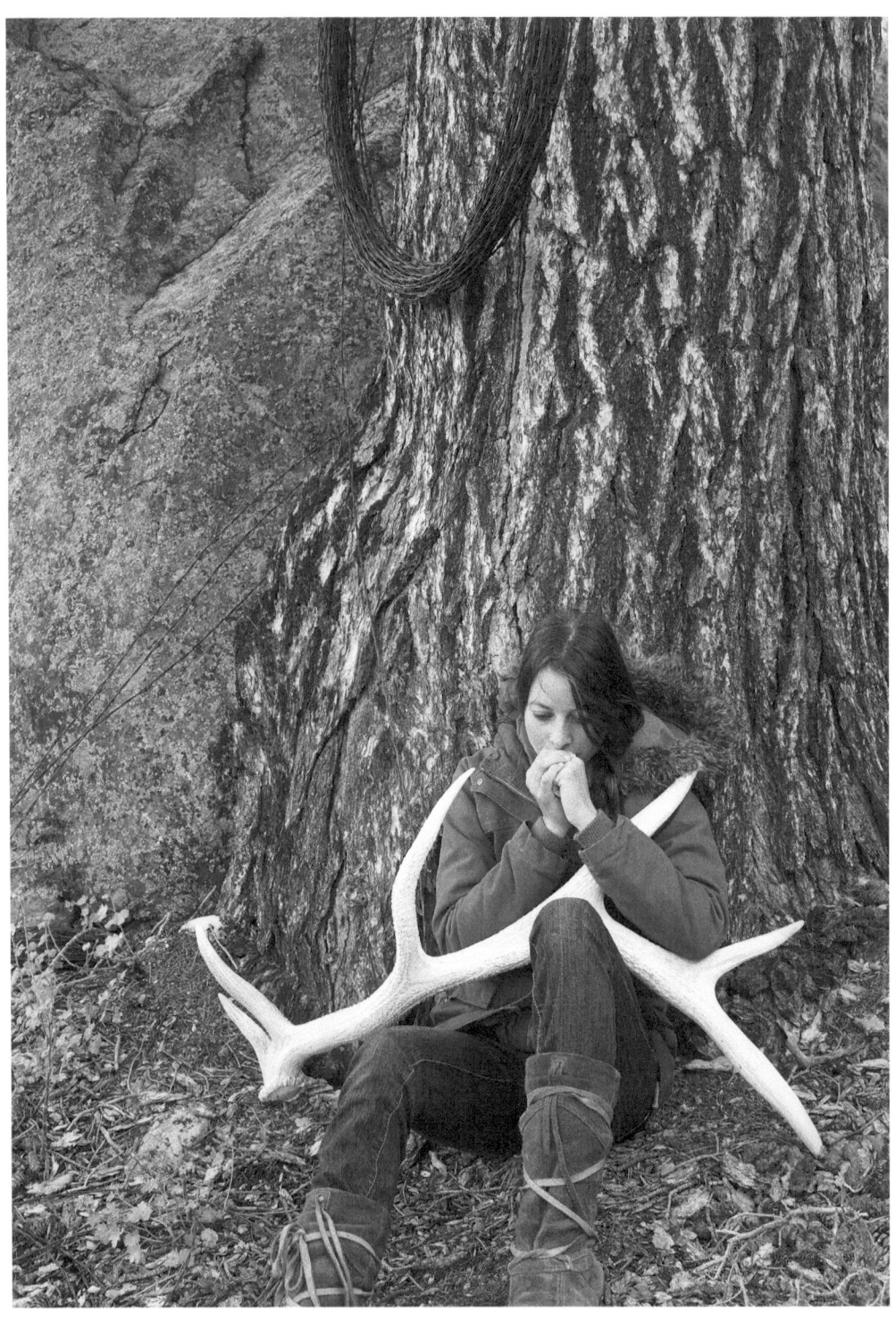

Prevailing Westerlies

Aspens at the Rim
Hoback Canyon, Wyoming

Public lands offer wide-open range and healthy habitat. Whether assuring the presence of livestock, wildlife, or both, it is a valuable commodity. Animals bring diversity and richness to the landscape, contributing to ecological, economic, and aesthetic well-being.

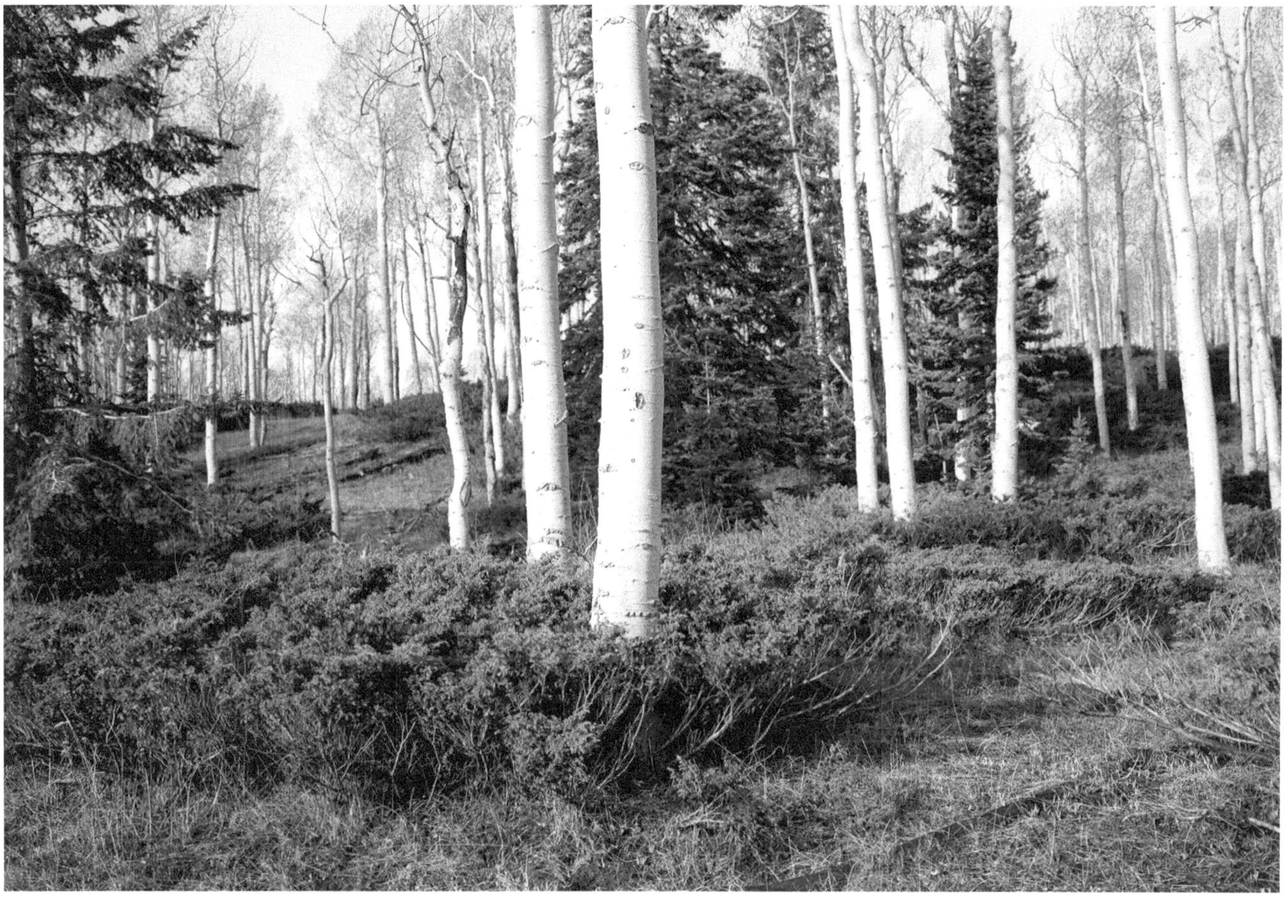

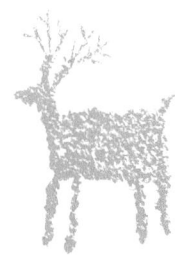

Ed Lavino

Red Onion, Gravy Boat, Banded Iron

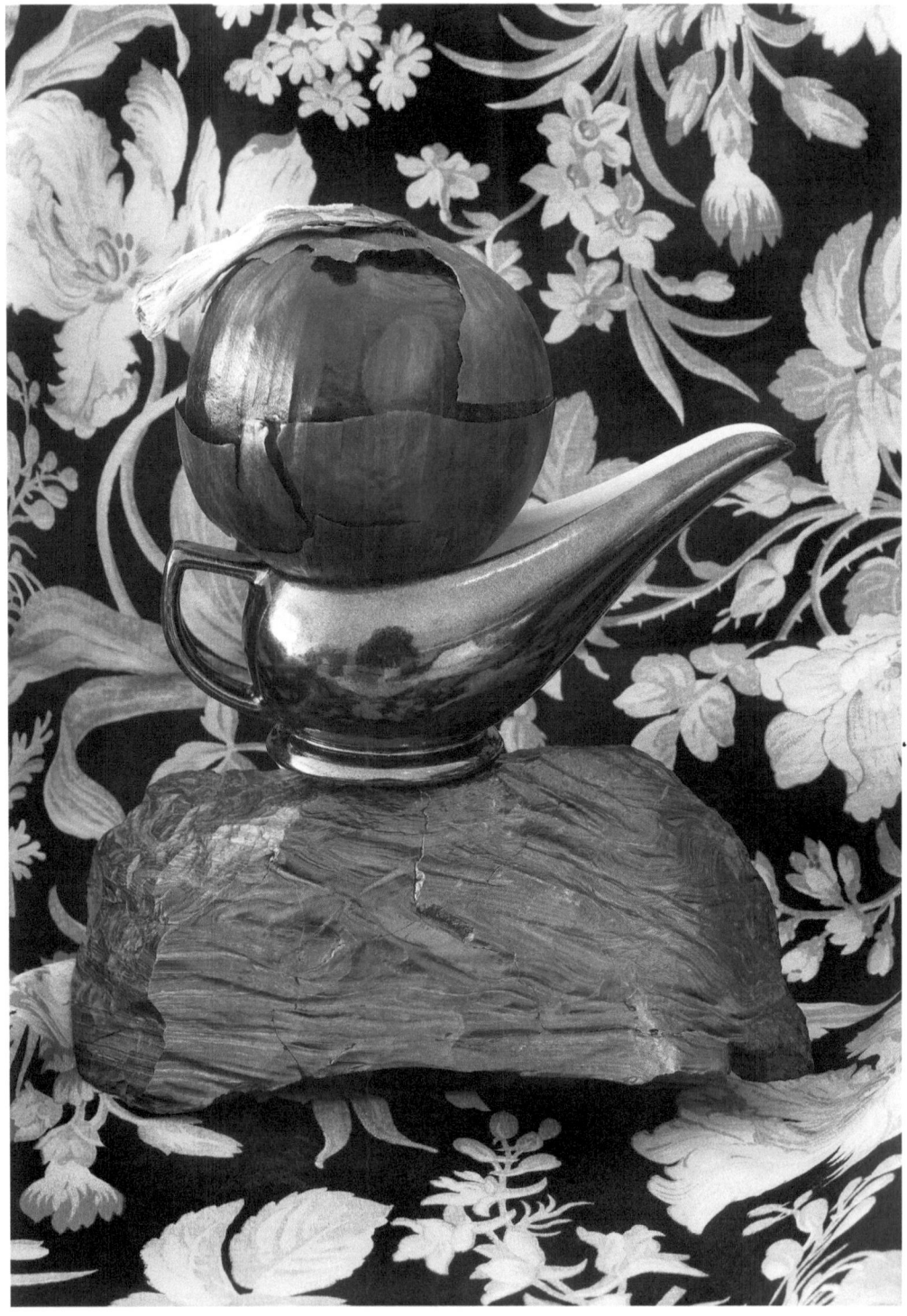

Patina on the surface of an object tells a tale much the way facial features reveal a personal history. Subtle textures, and reflective finish compare to a placid brow, the upturned corner of a mouth, and knowing eyes.

Corrie
AMK Ranch, Wyoming

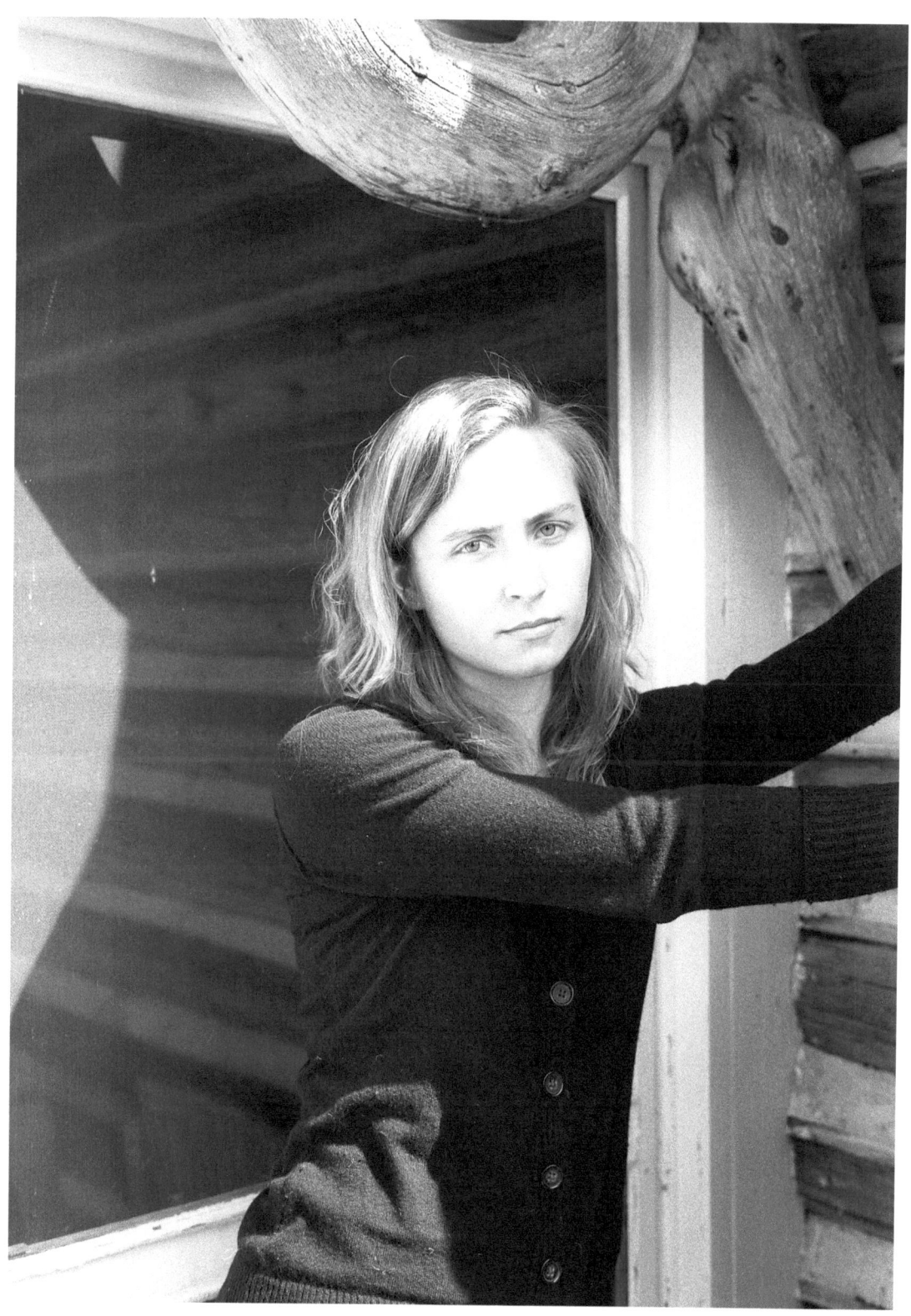

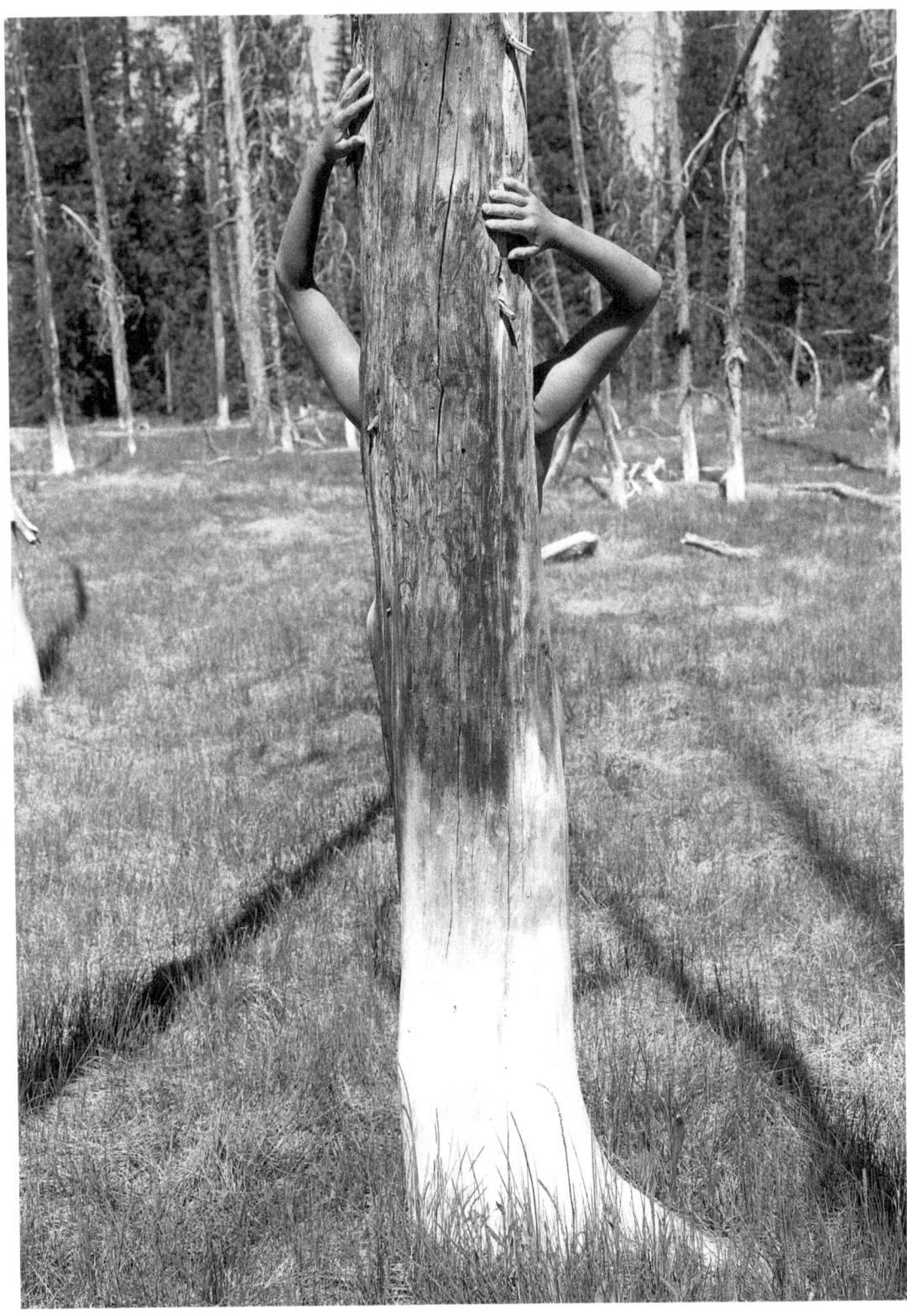

Emma's Arms

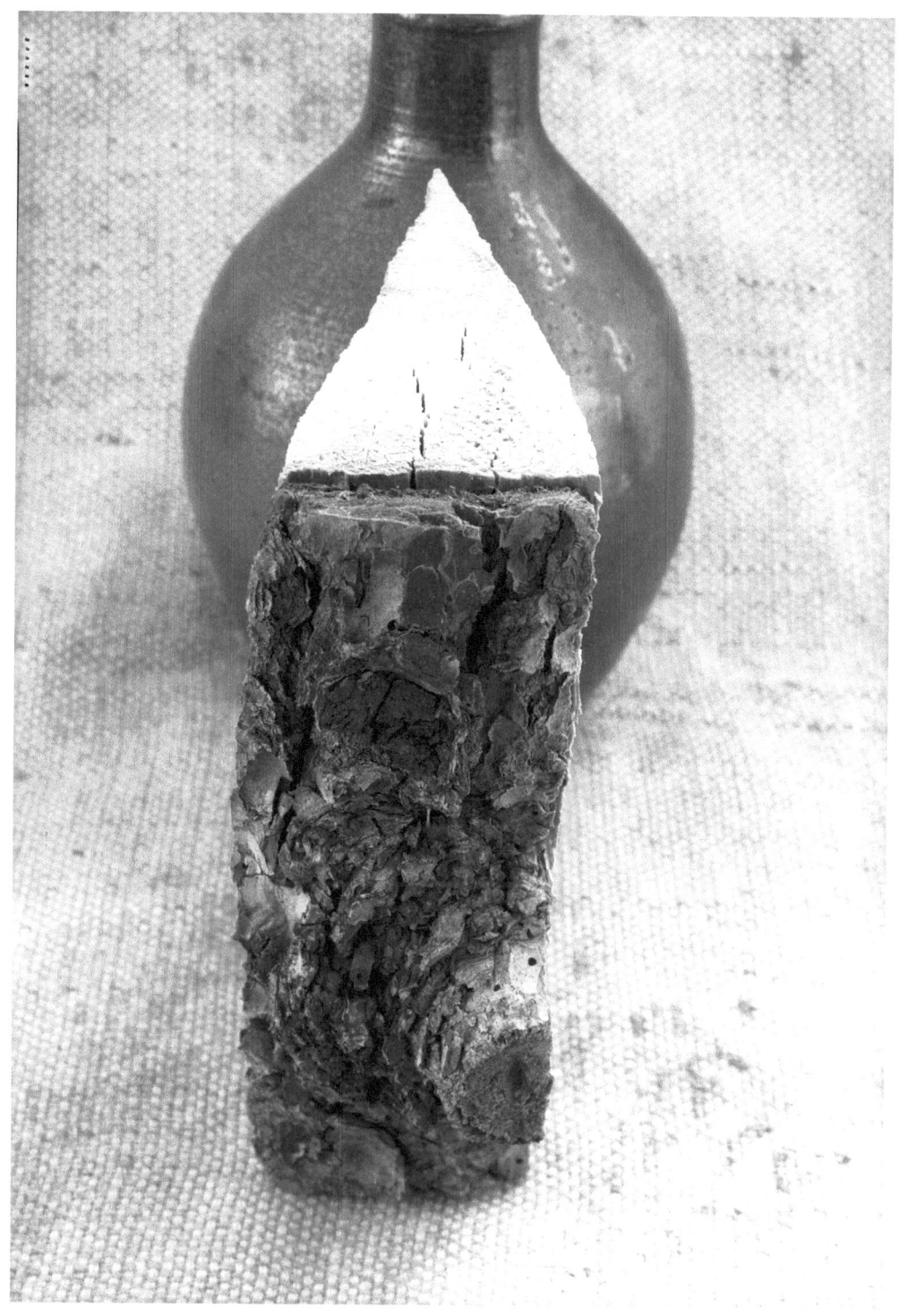

Firewood Wedge and German Jug

A sharp wedge of firewood bisects the soft silhouette of a seventeenth-century stoneware jug. A visual illusion is created as the objects merge in two dimensions, becoming nearly unrecognizable, as an abstract form.

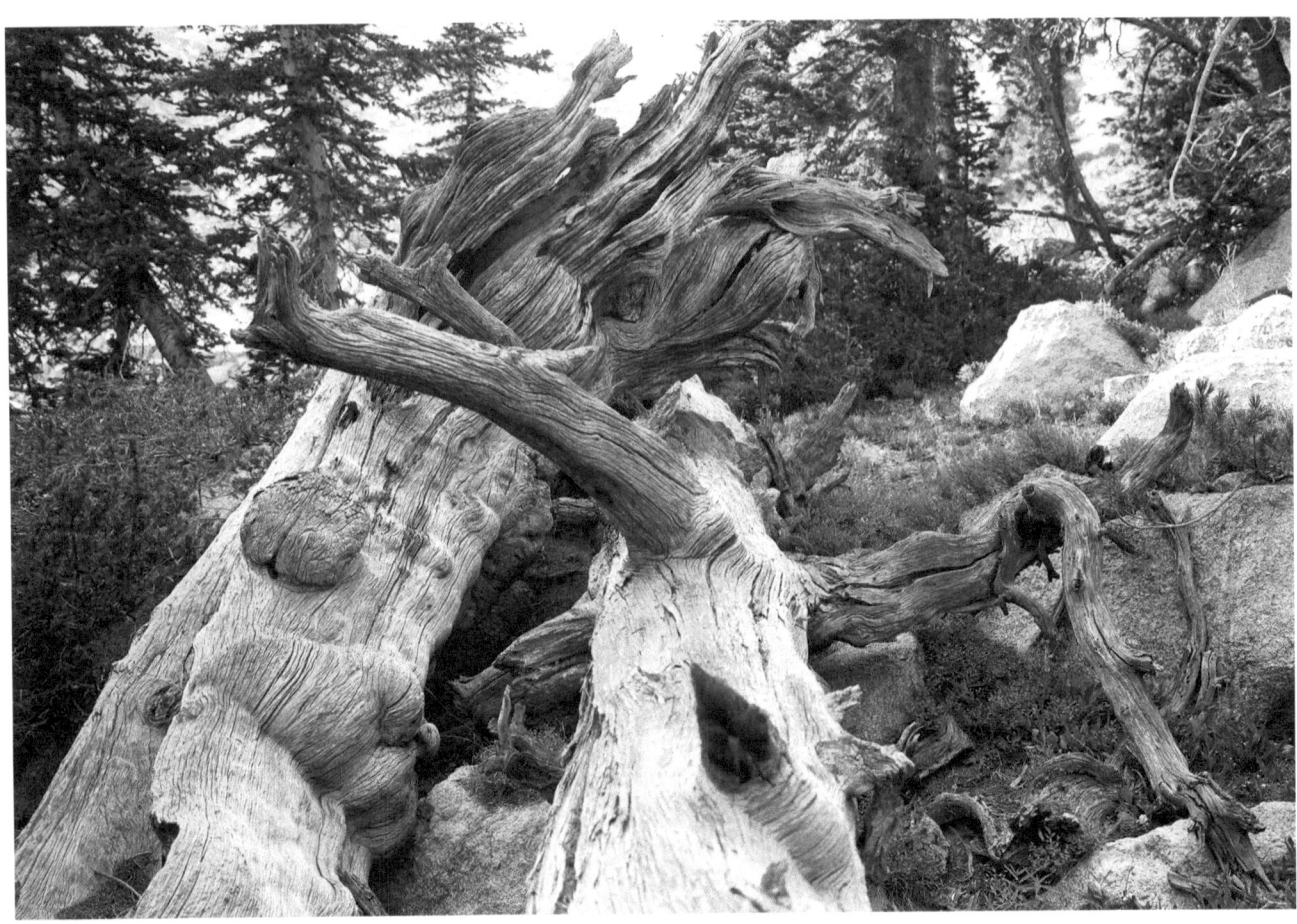

Downed Whitebark Pines
Cirque of the Towers, Wyoming

The ancient, weathered, reaching limbs of these downed trees bring to mind the experiences that fill a lifetime. Undoubtedly there were rich seasons of growth interspersed with the challenges of wind, bitter cold, drought, and disease. Whitebark pines are currently experiencing an overall decline. Reasons for this include mortality from the pine beetle, and environmental effects resulting from climate change.

Prevailing Westerlies

Emma and Driftwood Willow

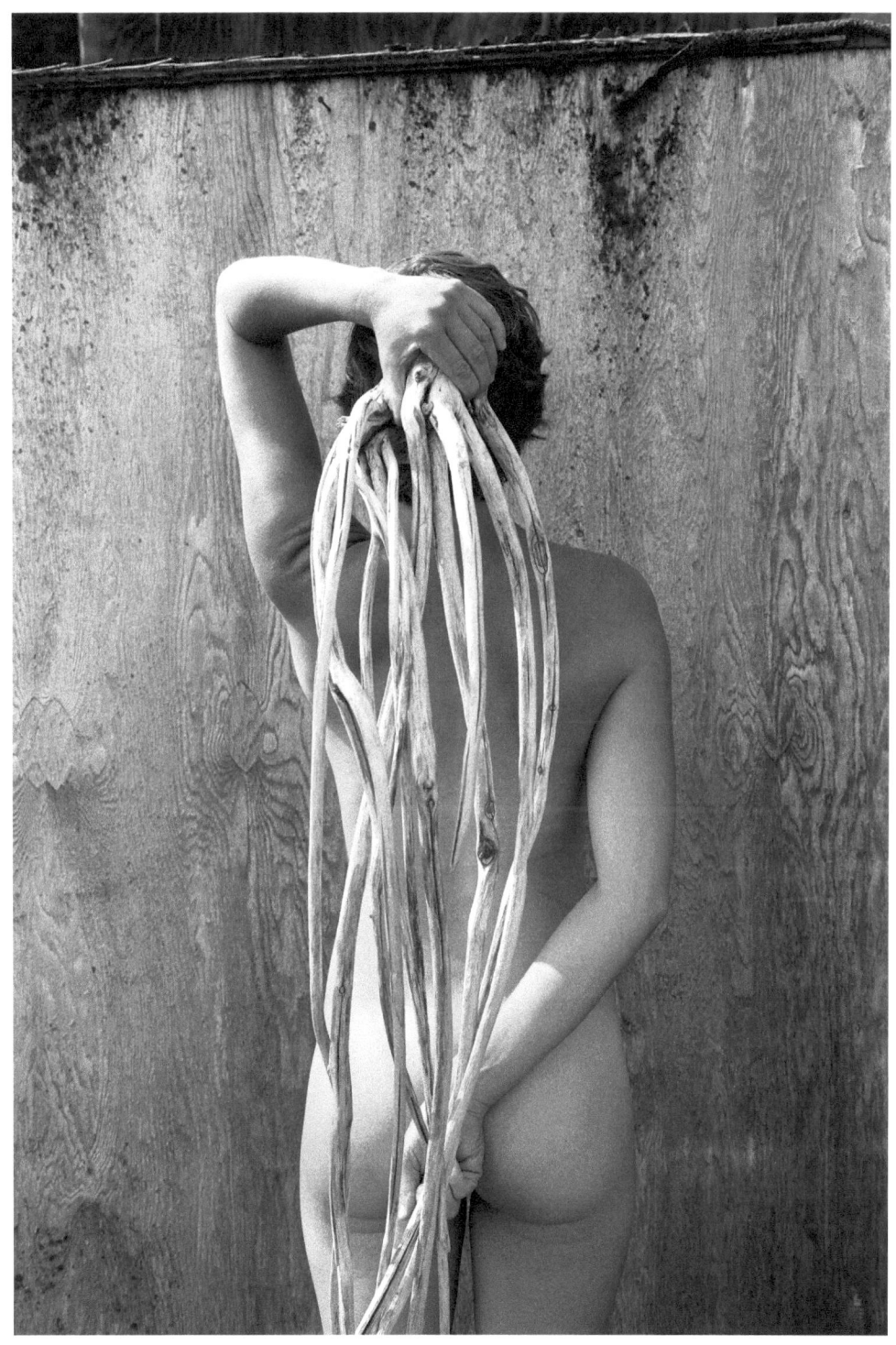

Ed Lavino

Willow Row
Elk Ranch, Wyoming

My wife and I were circumnavigating an unnamed butte near our home in Moran when I came upon this row of willows sustained by the lifeblood of an irrigation ditch. Their linear progression reminds me of an Alberto Giacometti sculpture of multiple tall figures walking in formation.

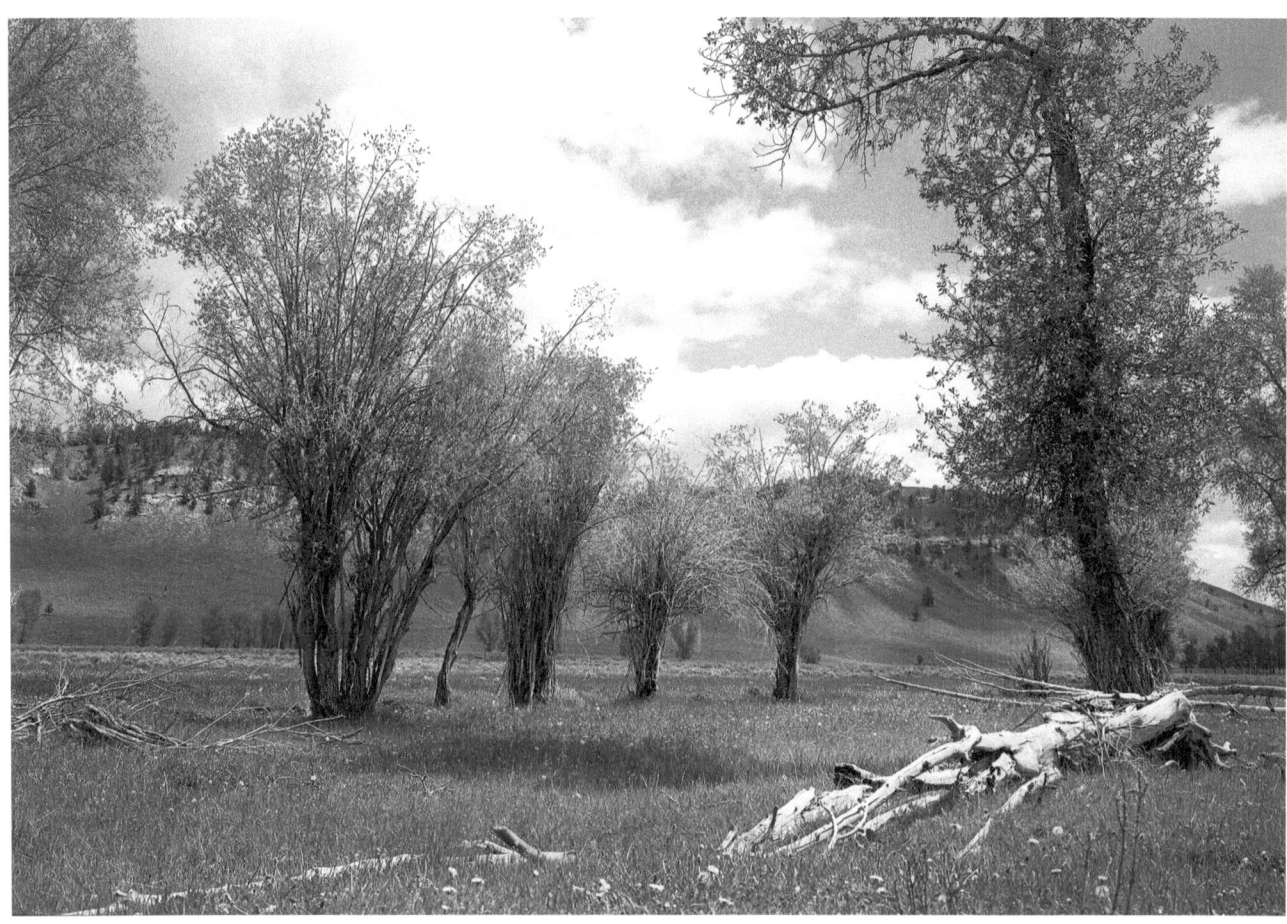

Prevailing Westerlies

Jackie and Sapling
Fremont Lake, Wyoming

This photograph was taken in the springtime, as the aspens were beginning to leaf out. Jackie effortlessly ascended the tree as the sun broke out, illuminating pale bark and delicate branches. Her figure seemed to momentarily break tether with the earth, hovering like a helium balloon temporarily snagged by a branch.

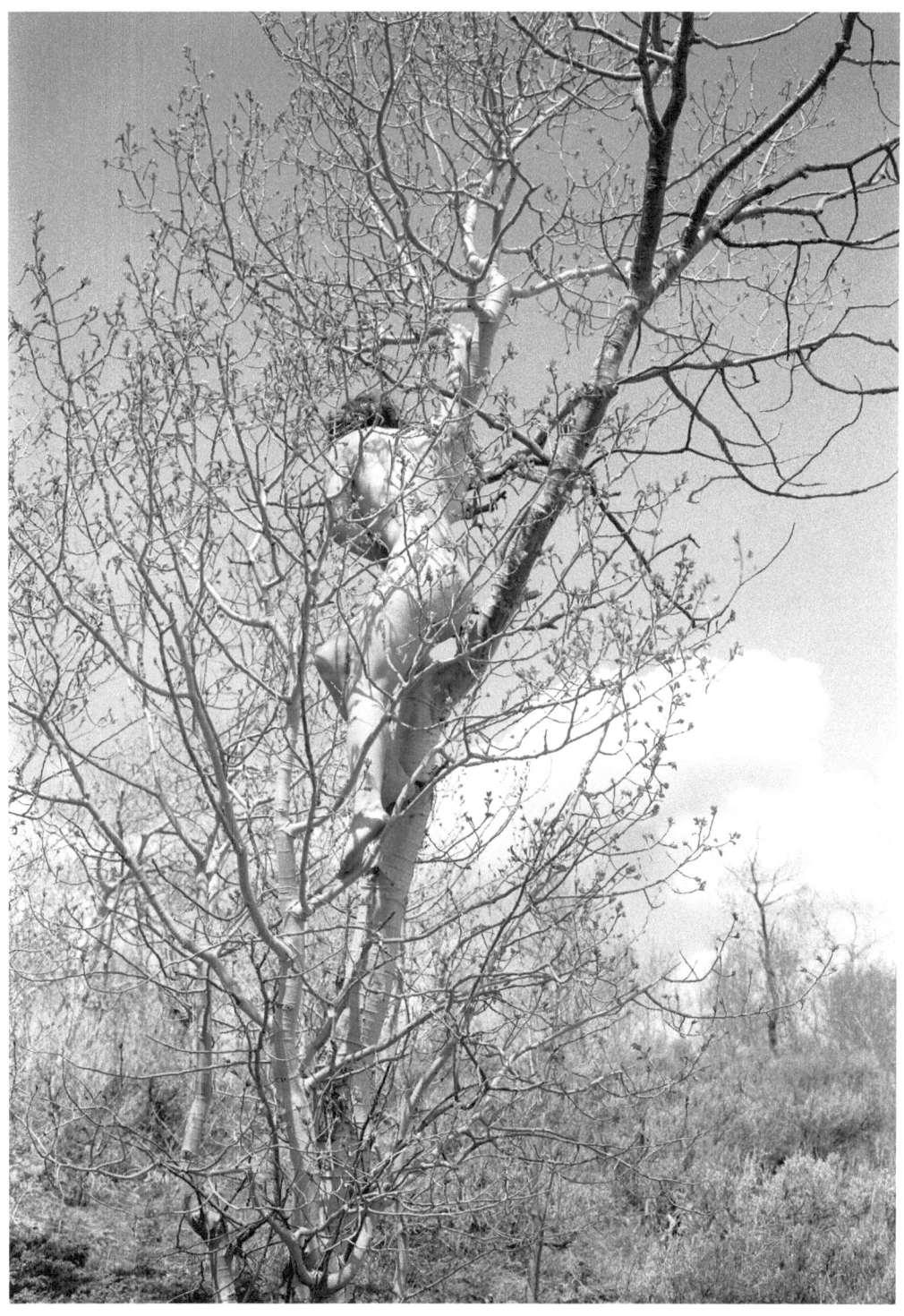

Ed Lavino

Erin
Shoreline Cavern

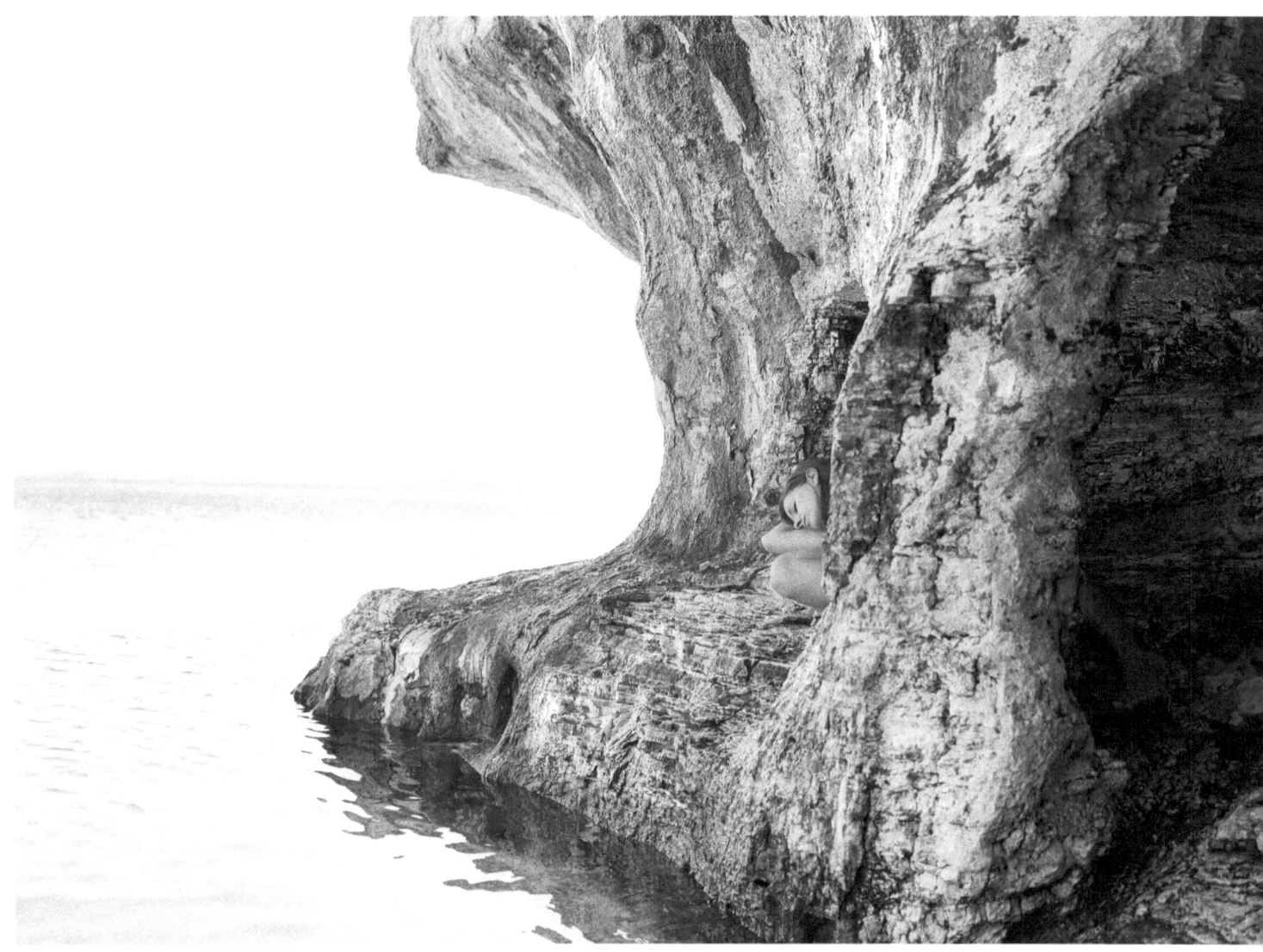

Prevailing Westerlies

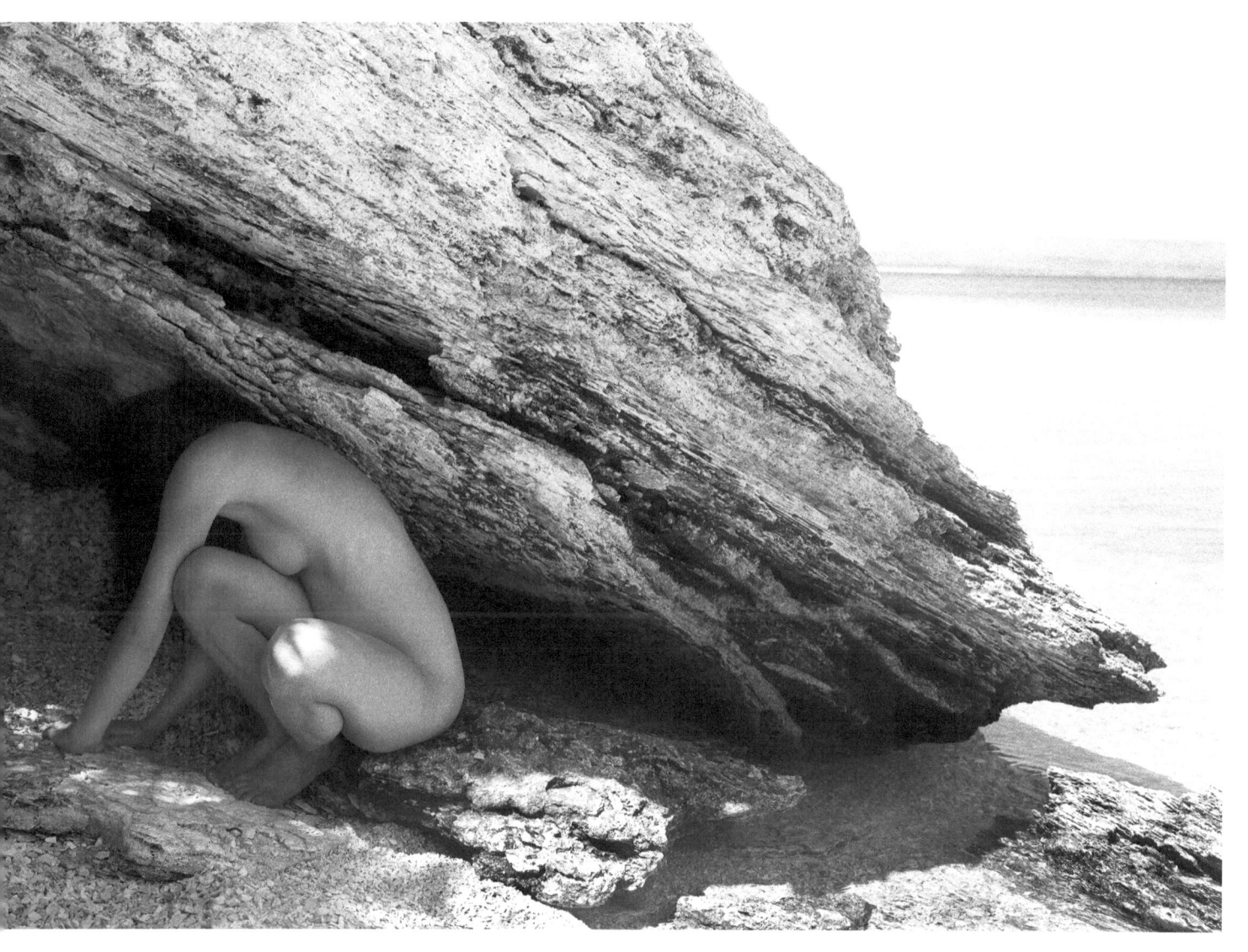

Erin
Lakeshore

Ed Lavino

West Thumb Geyser Basin
Yellowstone National Park, Wyoming

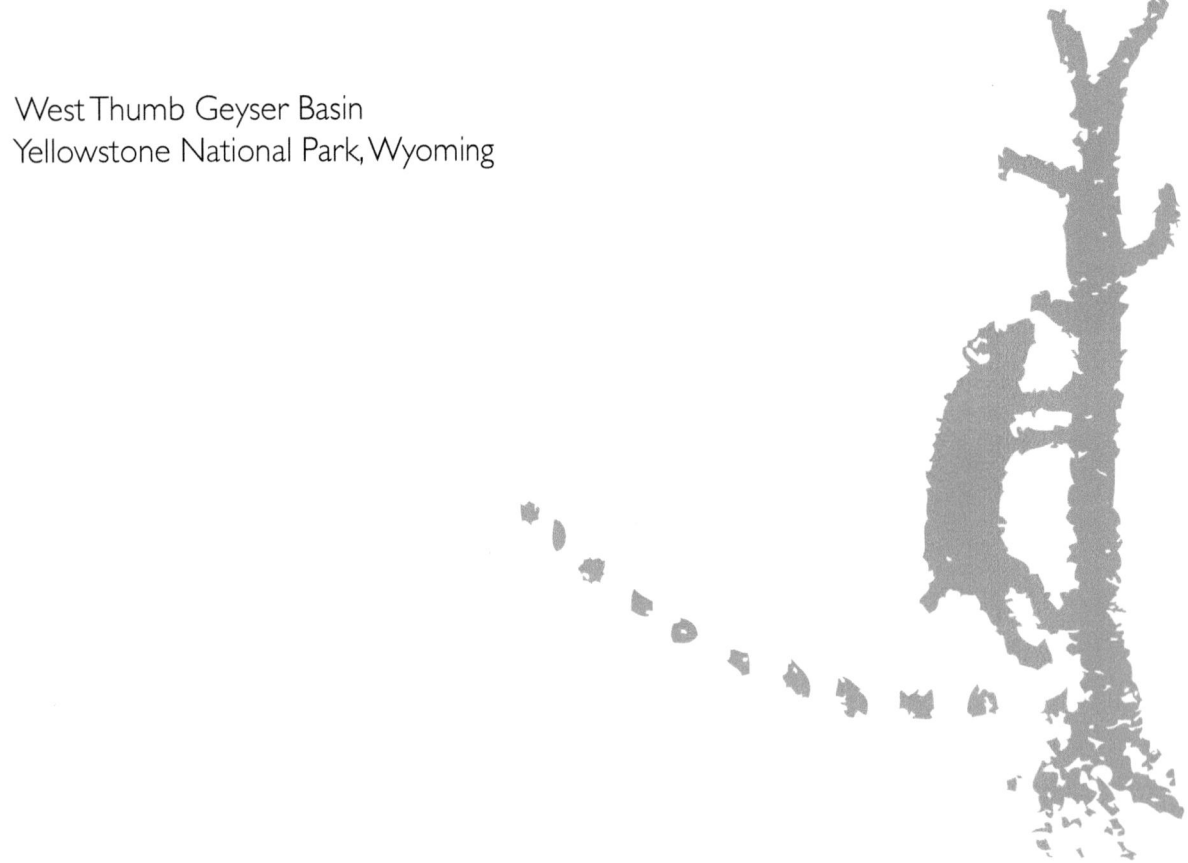

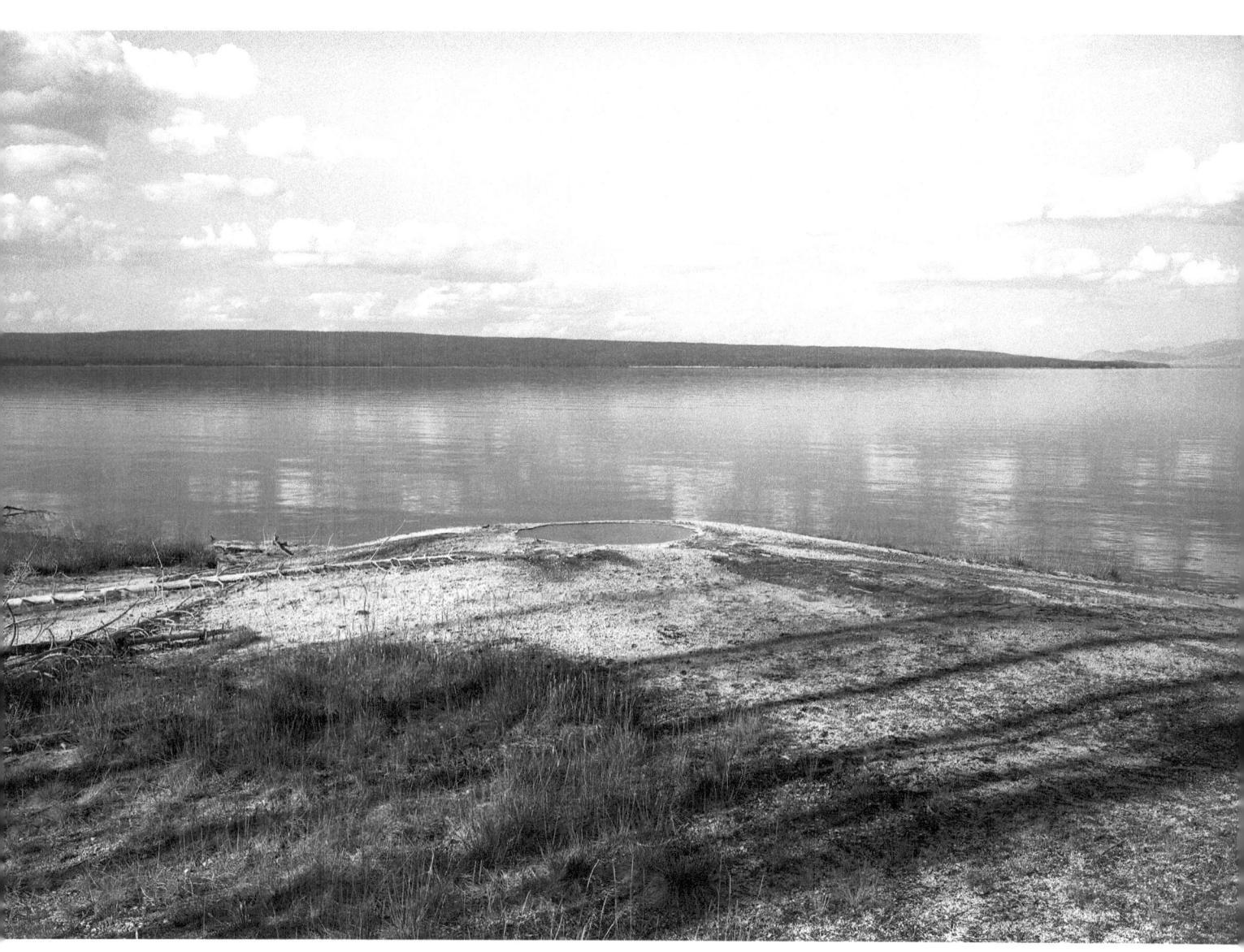

Ed Lavino

Corrie
Teton River, Idaho

"I entered a deep spring pool, braced my arms against the banks and submerged everything but my head in the cold water. As I consciously relaxed, expressing a peaceful face, Ed depressed the shutter on his huge camera—snap.... snap.
I couldn't hold back the shivers, and had to jump out and run around on the grass to warm up.
— Corrie

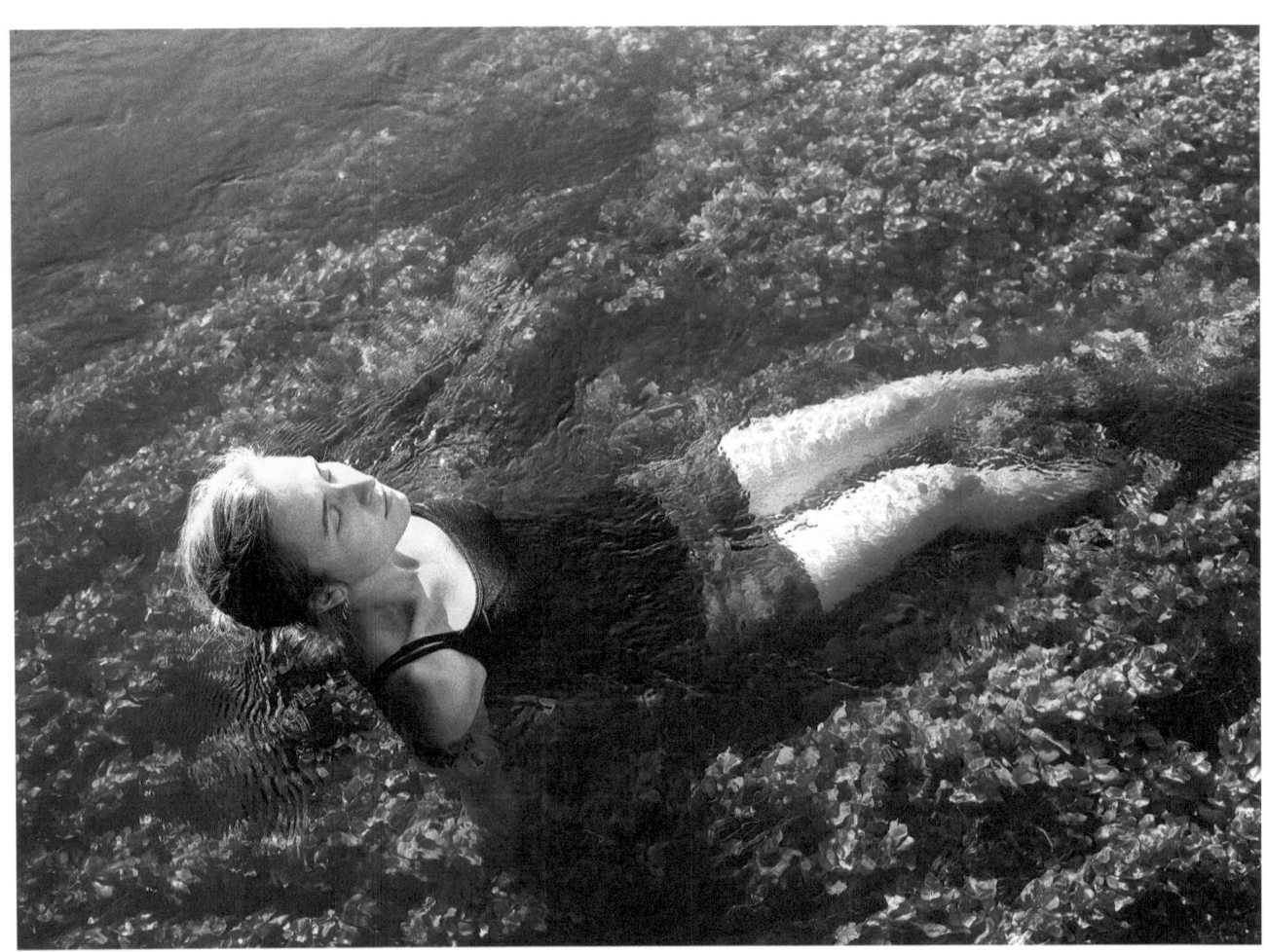

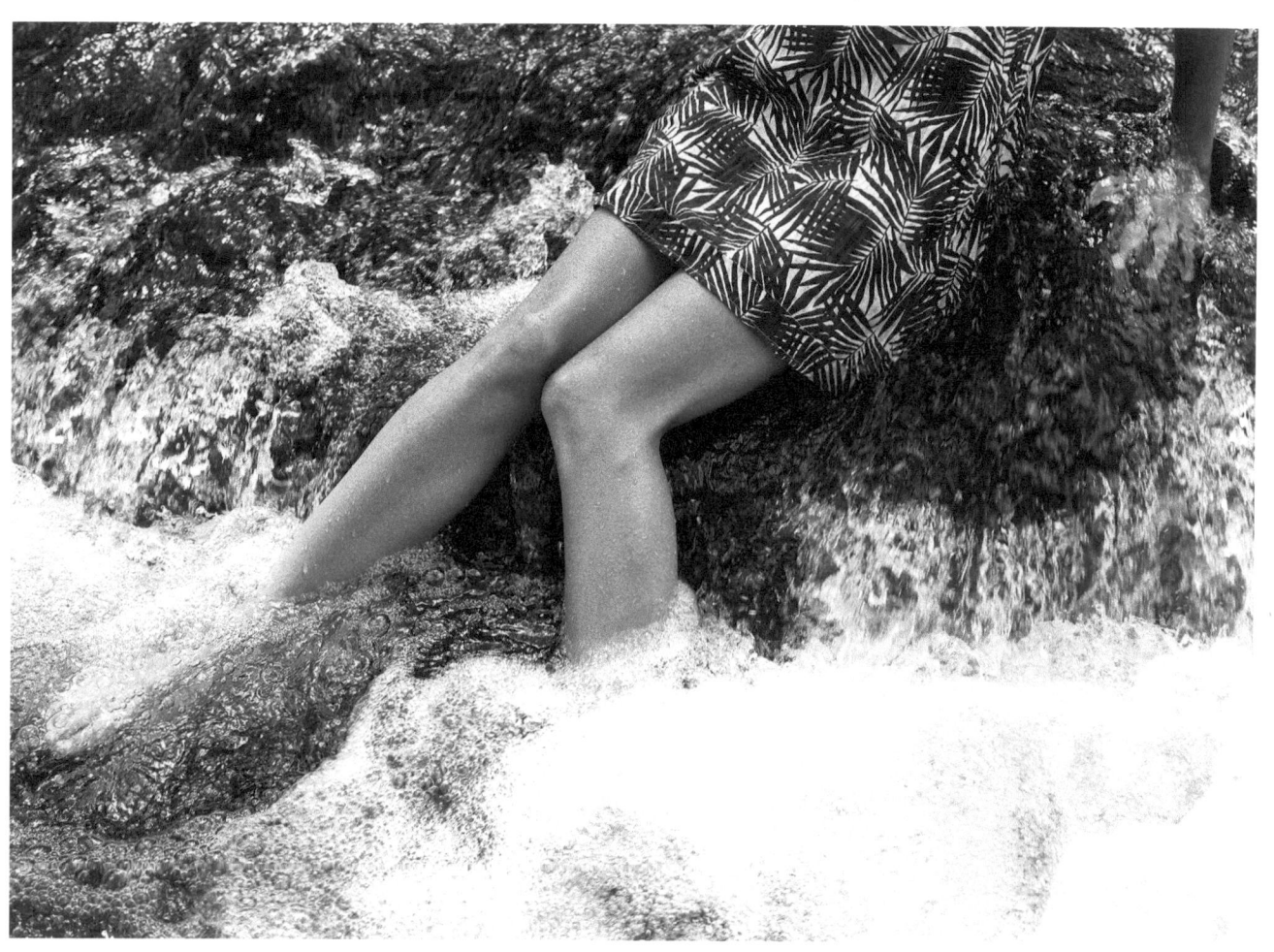

Camille and Palm Frond Dress

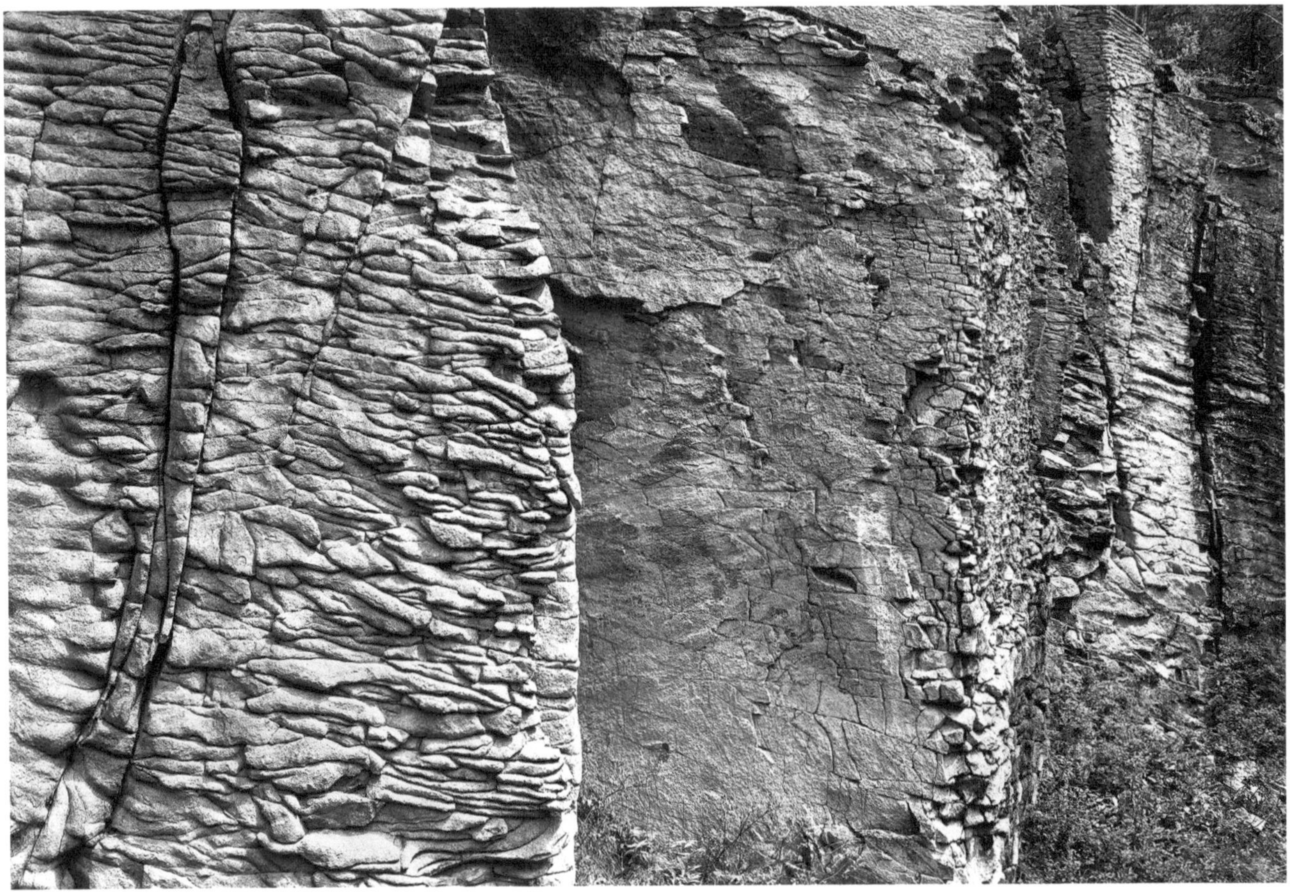

Cliff Band
Yellowstone National Park, Wyoming

Rock faces have a mesmerizing beauty reminiscent of the surfaces of abstract expressionist paintings. In place of color and brush strokes, rich textures are created in fractured planes of light and shadow.

Prevailing Westerlies

The Sinagua, a pre-Columbian people of the Desert Southwest, constructed Montezuma Castle in Arizona out of native limestone. This forty-five room pueblo seamlessly merges with the vertical rock wall of its foundation. It was abandoned circa 1425 AD, for reasons unknown.

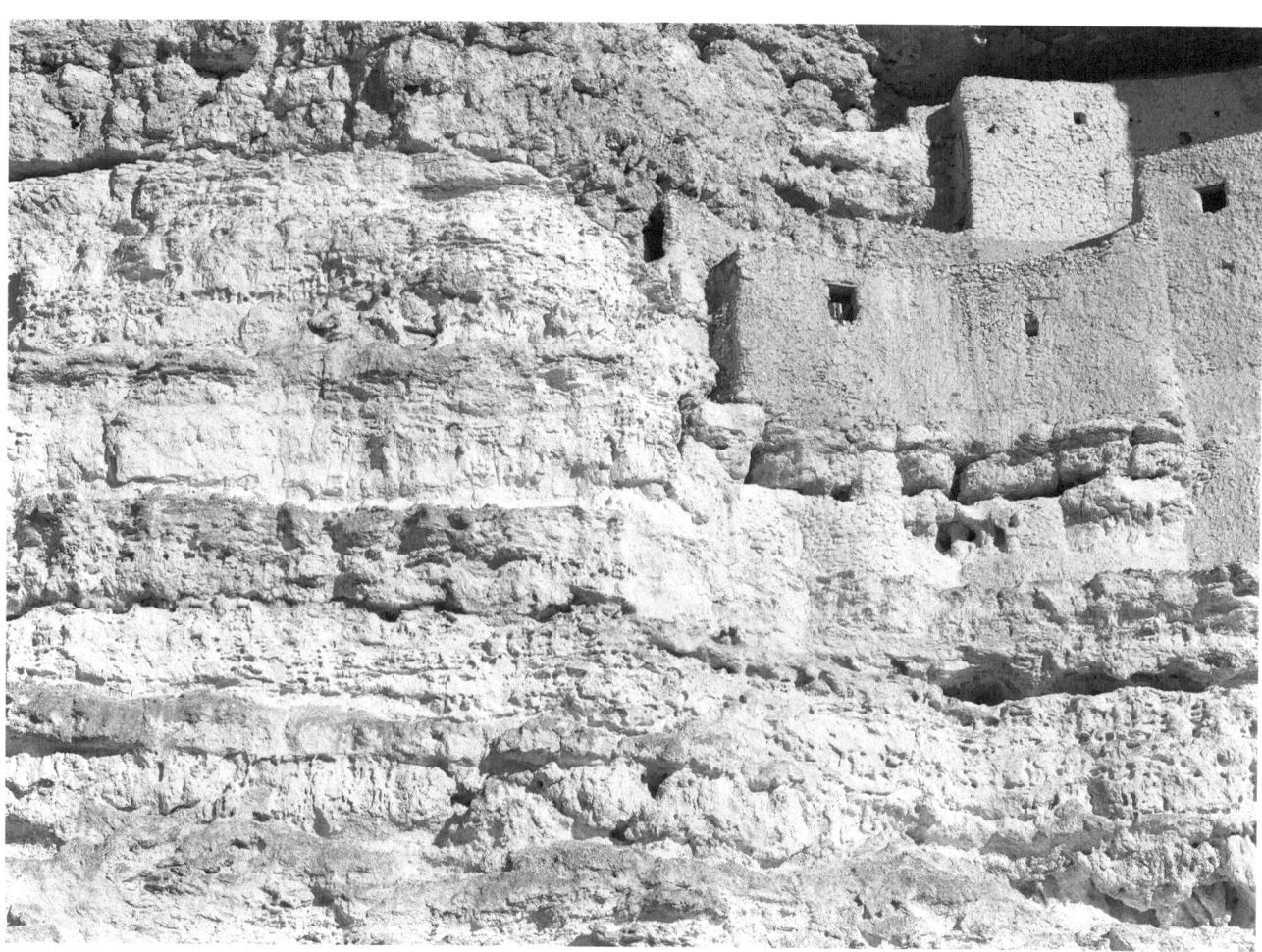

Ed Lavino

Not far from this location, my friend, George, and I were changing roll film in the shade of a whitebark pine grove. George whispered, "Look up." Over a brink crested the largest, healthiest black bear I had ever seen. His pelt glimmered in the sunlight. The bear passed within a stone's throw, never looking our way. He veered, then circled back down the steep talus slope he had recently surmounted.

The echoing clatter of loose rocks signaled the bear's retreat, as he quickly made for the forest floor a thousand feet below. Upon reaching the toe of the talus, the bear glanced back, directly into my field binoculars, thus confirming his precise knowledge of our location all along.

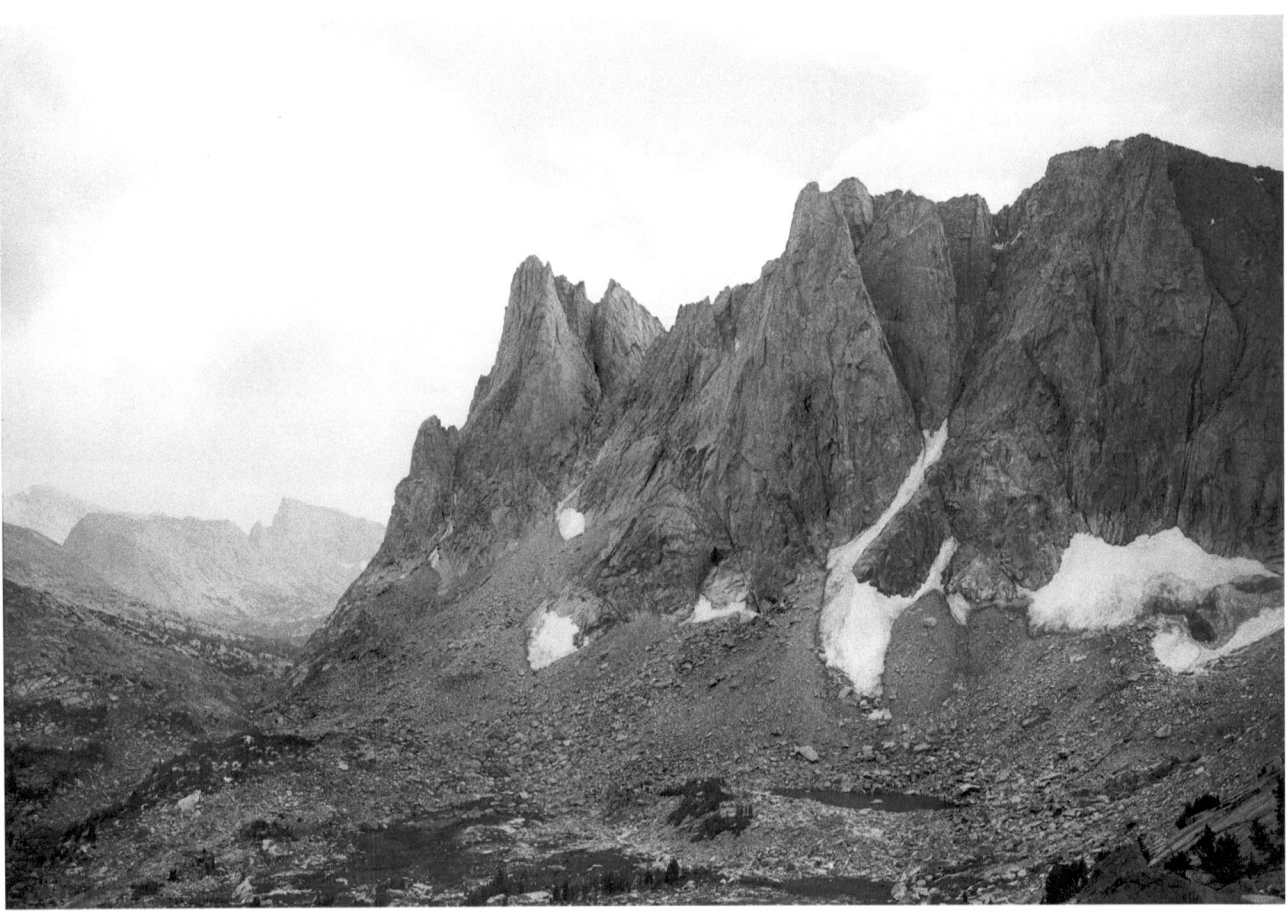

Warbonnet and Haystack Peaks
Wind River Mountains, Wyoming

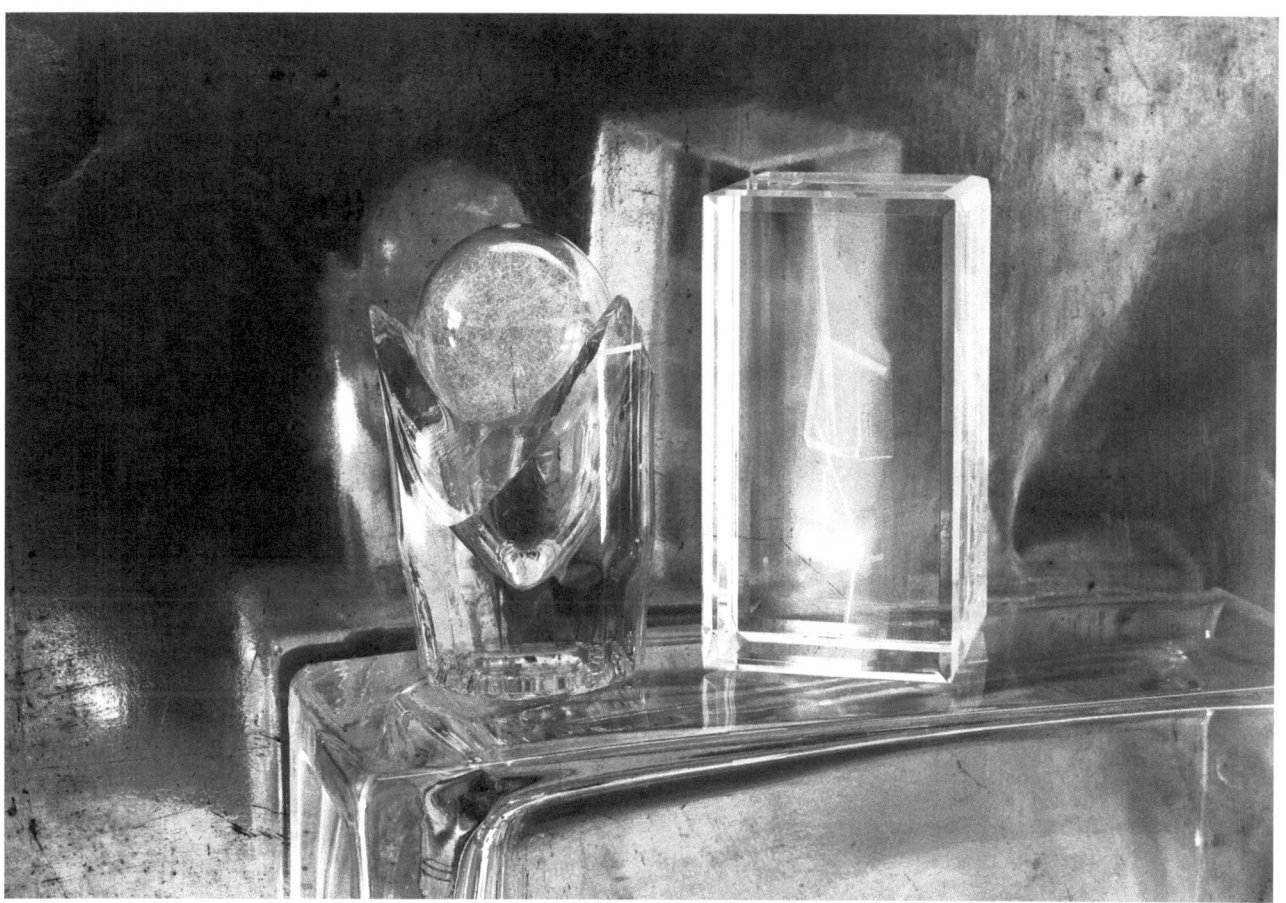

Broken Shot Glass and Light Bulb

Ed Lavino

Putter Home
Hudson River, New York

While working on a land survey of the submerged remains of a historic pier, I discovered an unusual home being remodeled. This riverfront estate was the life-long dream of the original builder. He constructed a house facade that mimics a ship's prow when seen from passing boats.

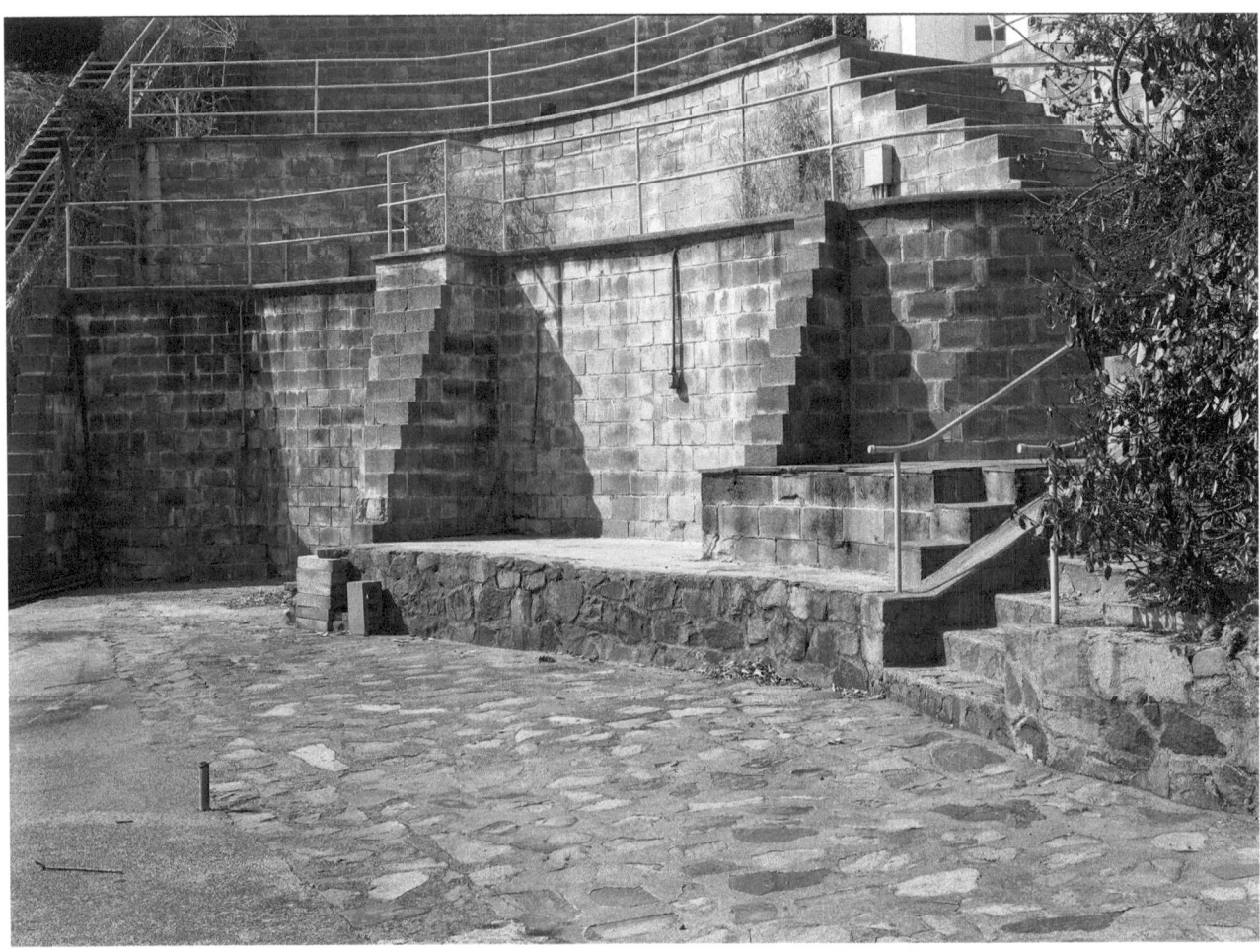

Prevailing Westerlies

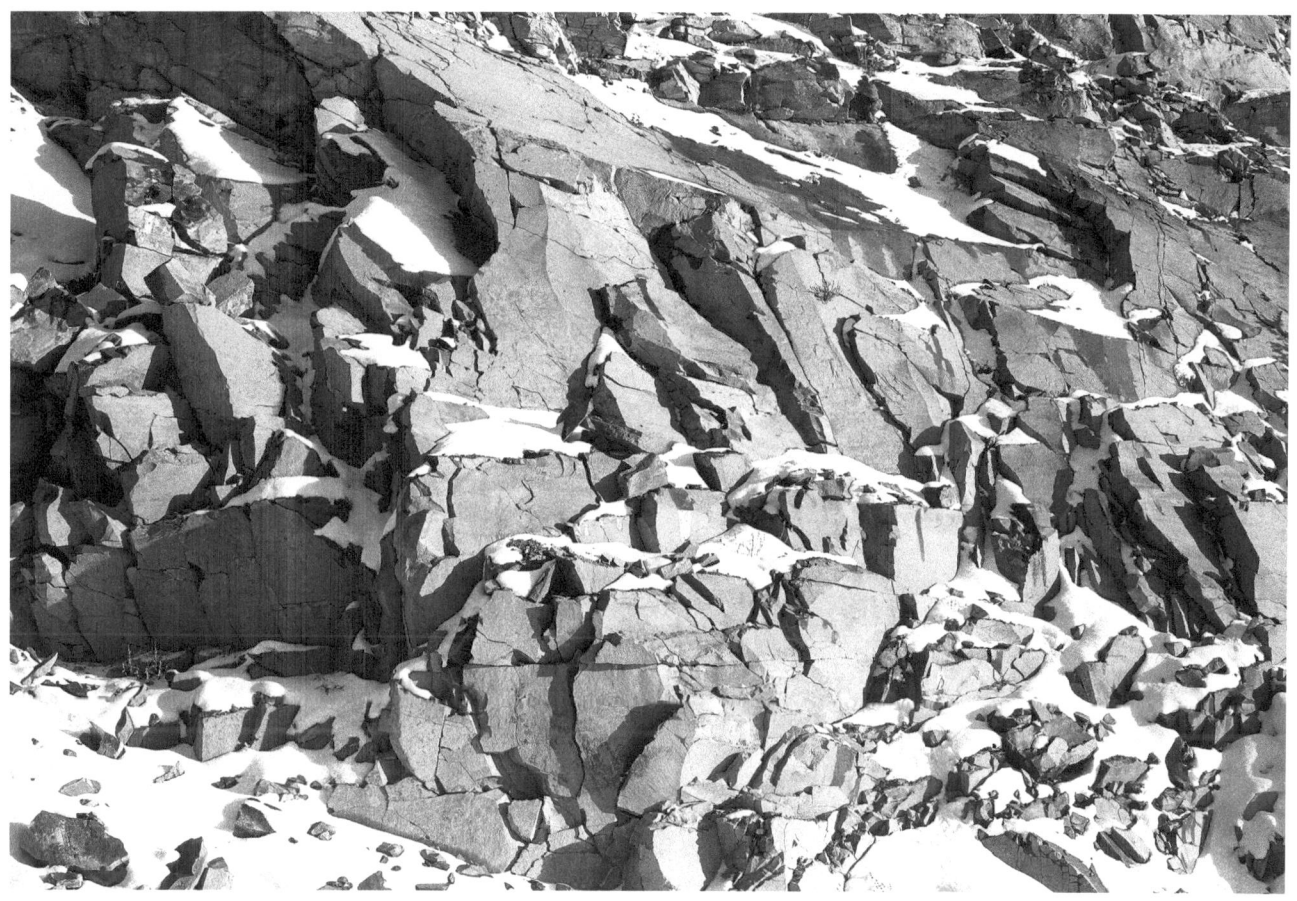

Rock Face
Teton Pass, Wyoming

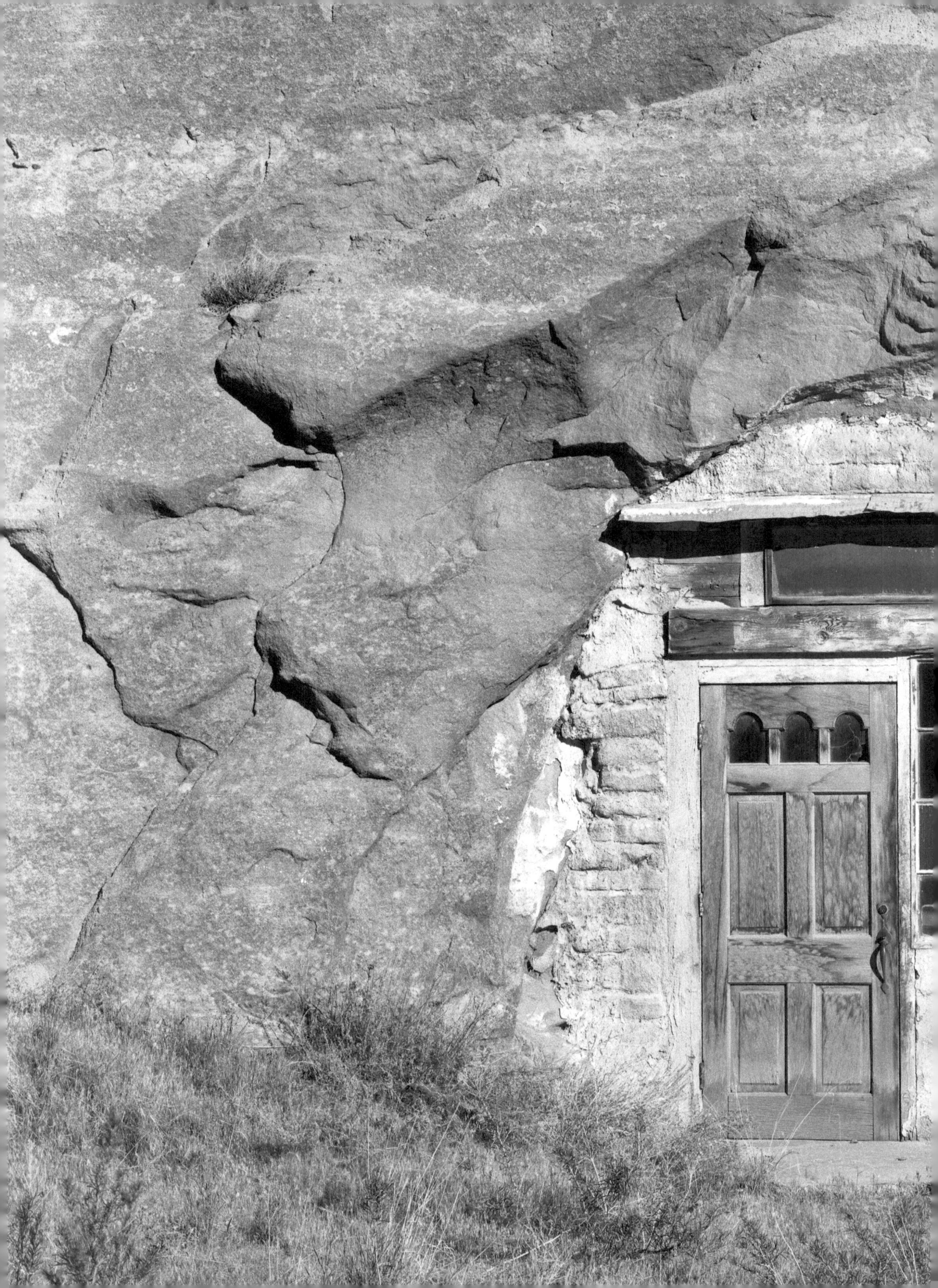

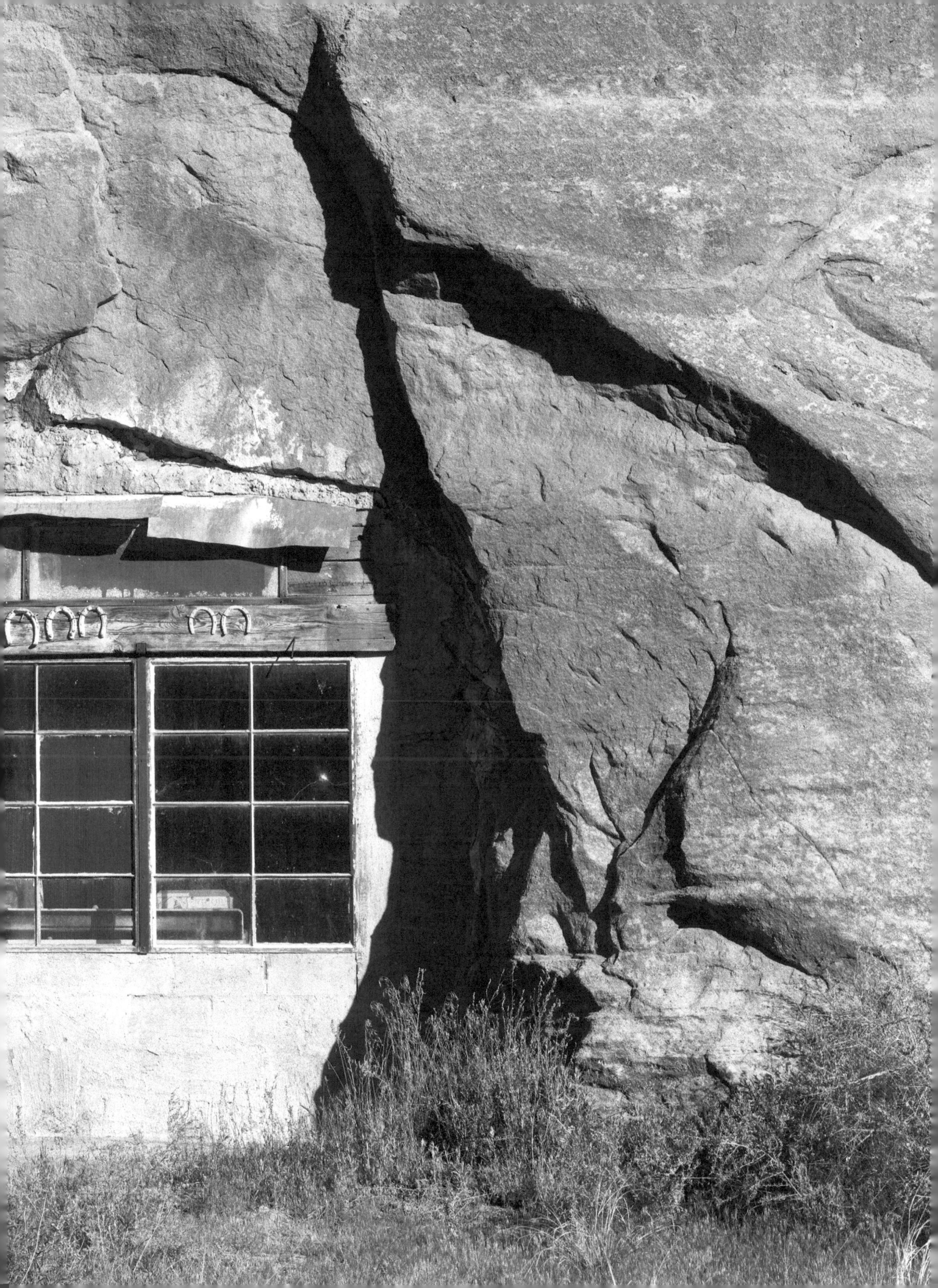

Ed Lavino

(Previous page) Cave Dwelling
Blanding, Utah

This remote dwelling was once used as a seasonal cow camp, but was unoccupied when I came across it. It is situated in an isolated canyon, formerly inhabited by an ancient Anasazi tribe. As I returned over a period of years to photograph this unusual spot, personal belongings came and went—the frame of a bicycle, a metal chair, and some old horseshoes. I never ventured inside, as I felt I would be intruding.

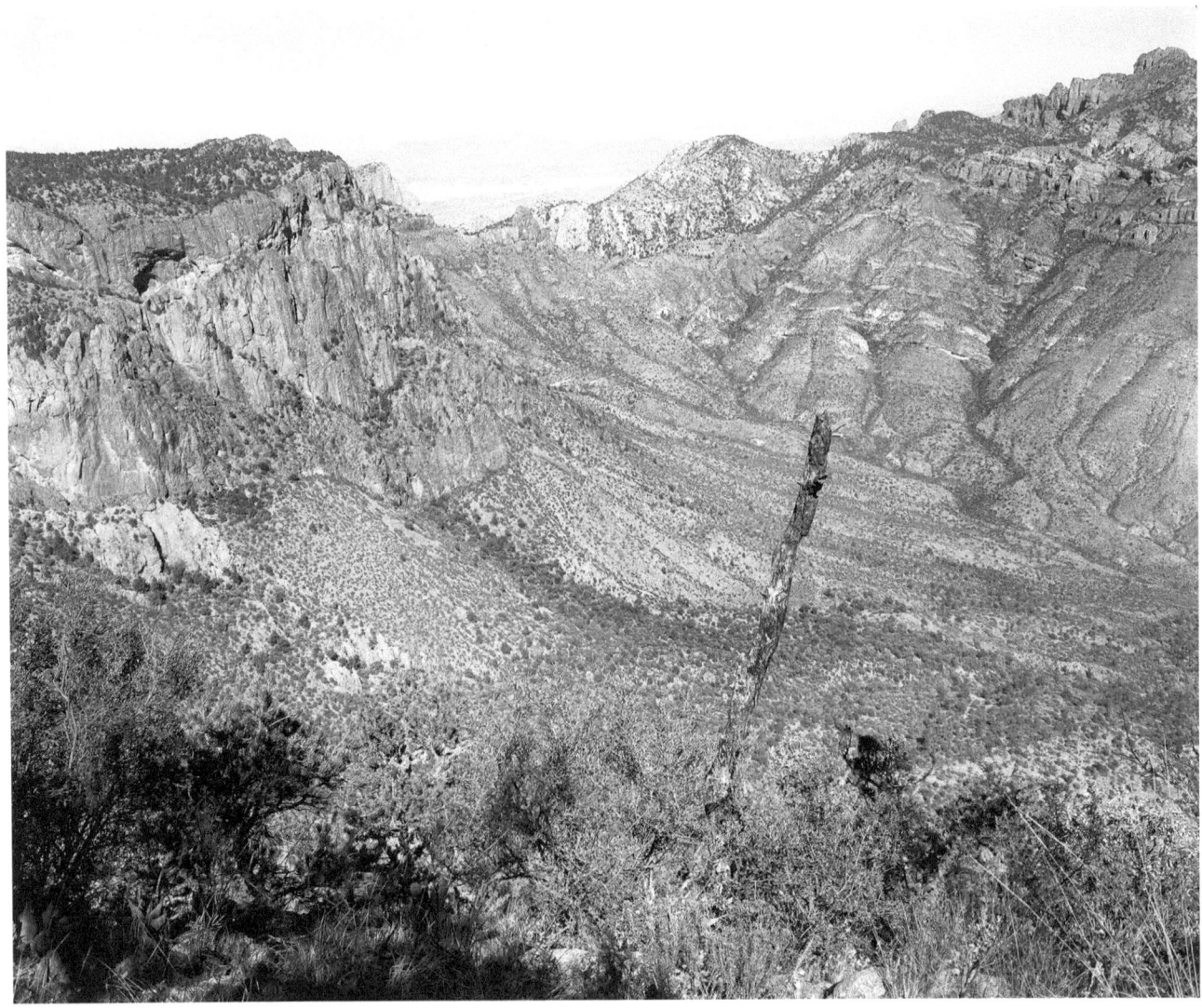

Big Bend National Park, Texas

I seek visual equilibrium; that point at which the world appears in harmony.

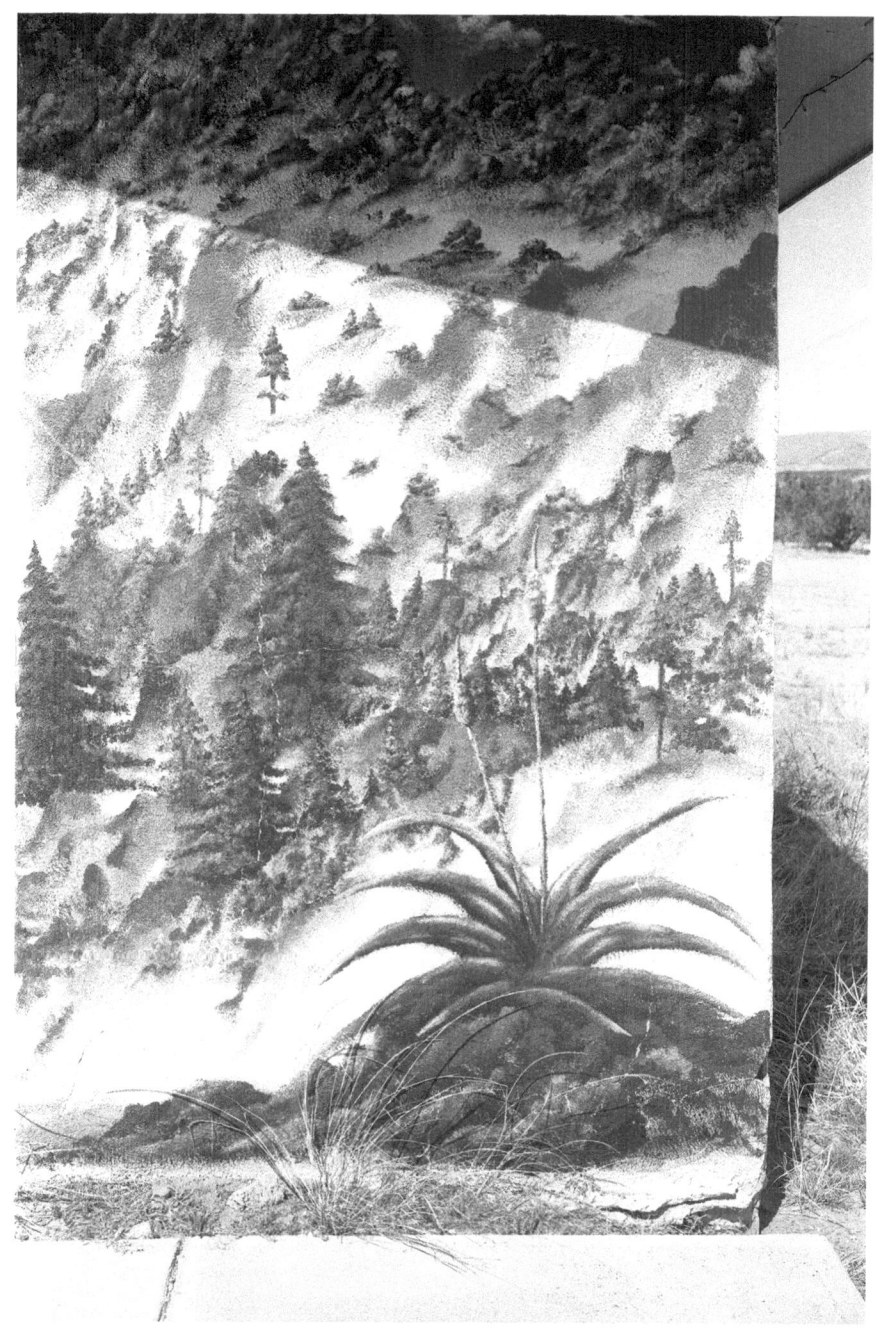

Painted Landscape
South of Abiquiu, New Mexico

Art depicting natural surroundings is common and universal. This urge to reproduce one's environment speaks to the strong affinity most people feel for it. A connection to nature is directly linked to feelings of well-being. The painted vista on the exterior of this store makes it appear as if the structure is attempting to merge back into the land.

Ed Lavino

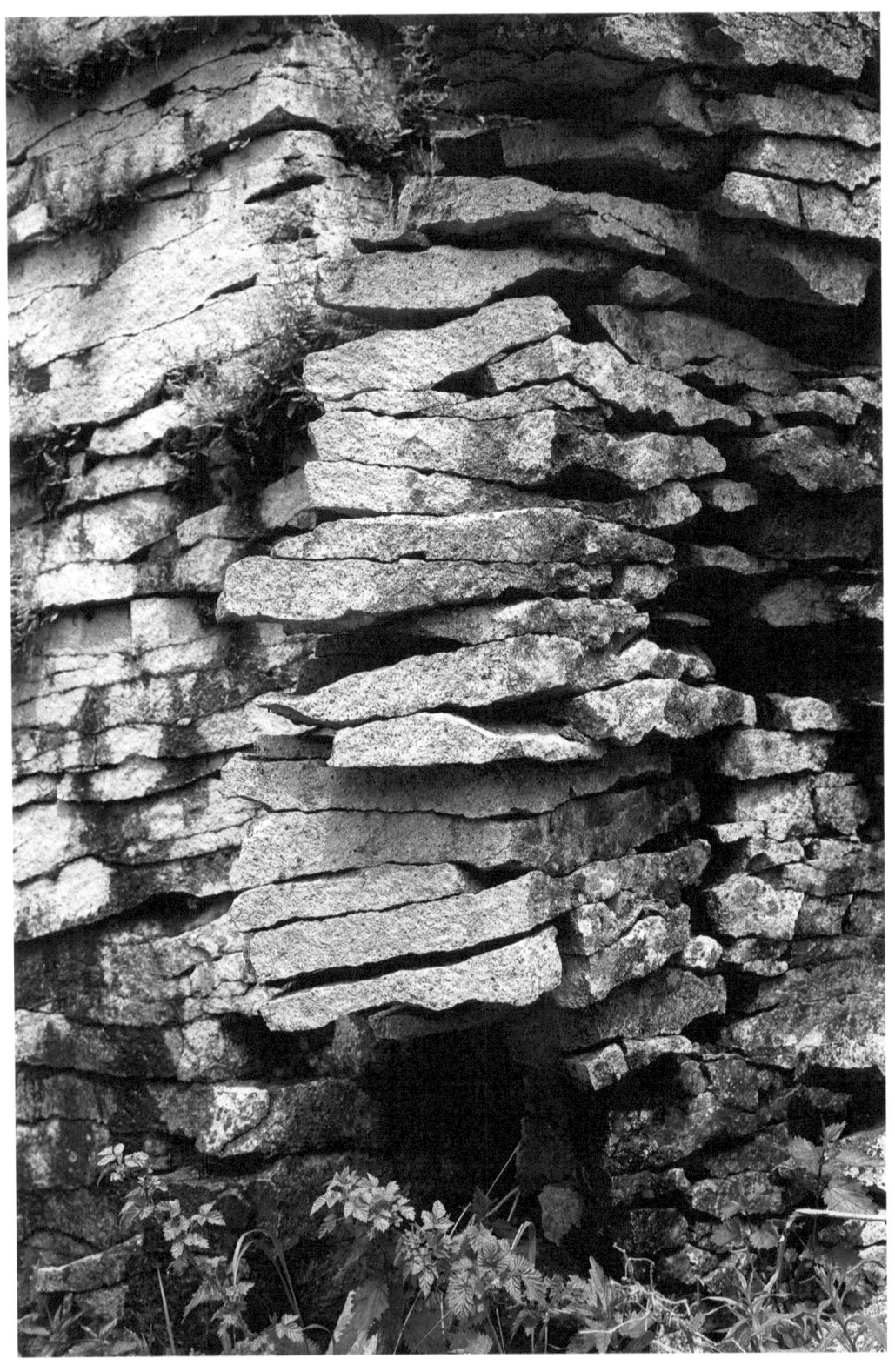

Minor Cliff Face
Yellowstone National Park, Wyoming

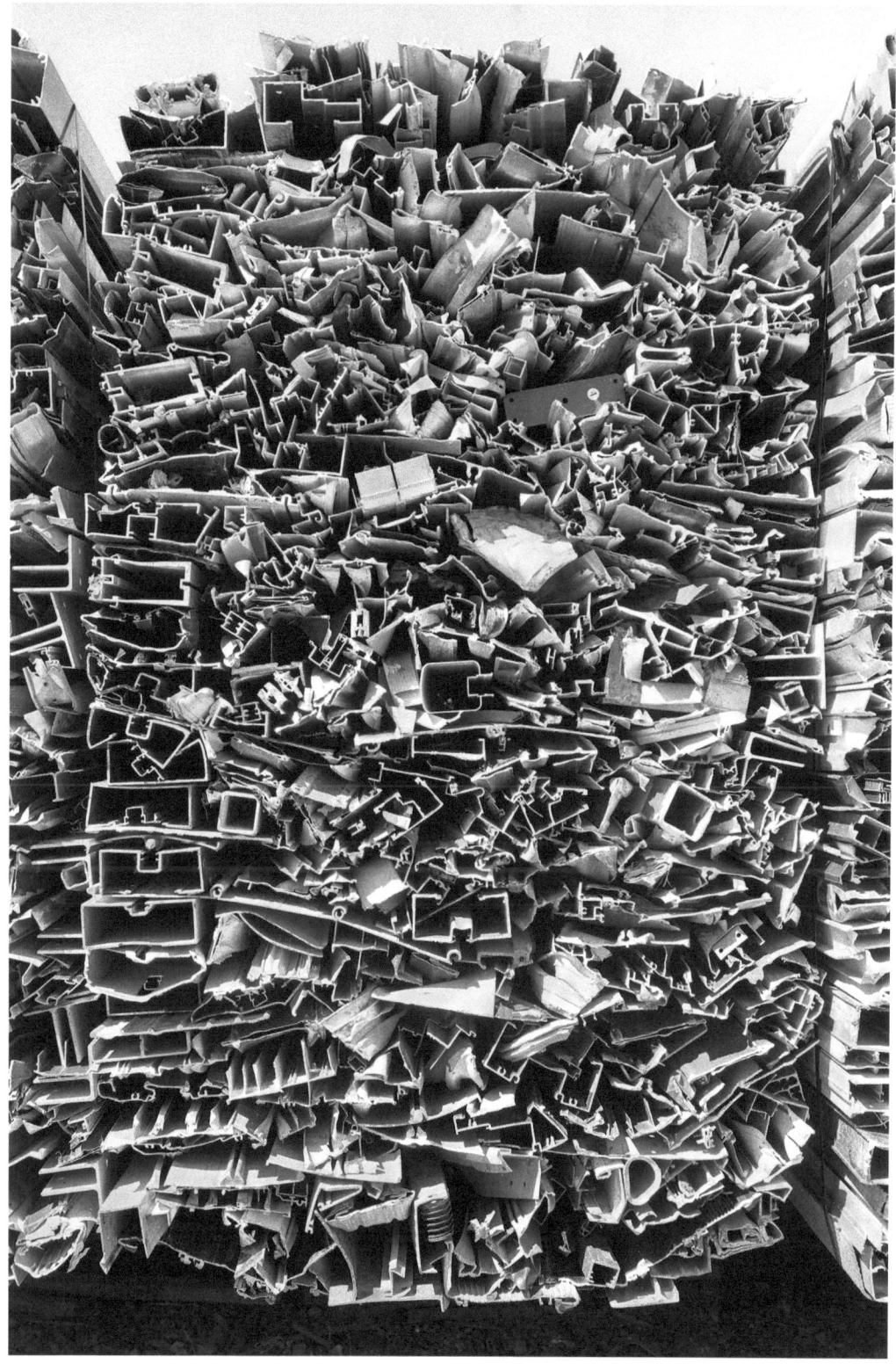

Recycled Metal
Montrose, Colorado

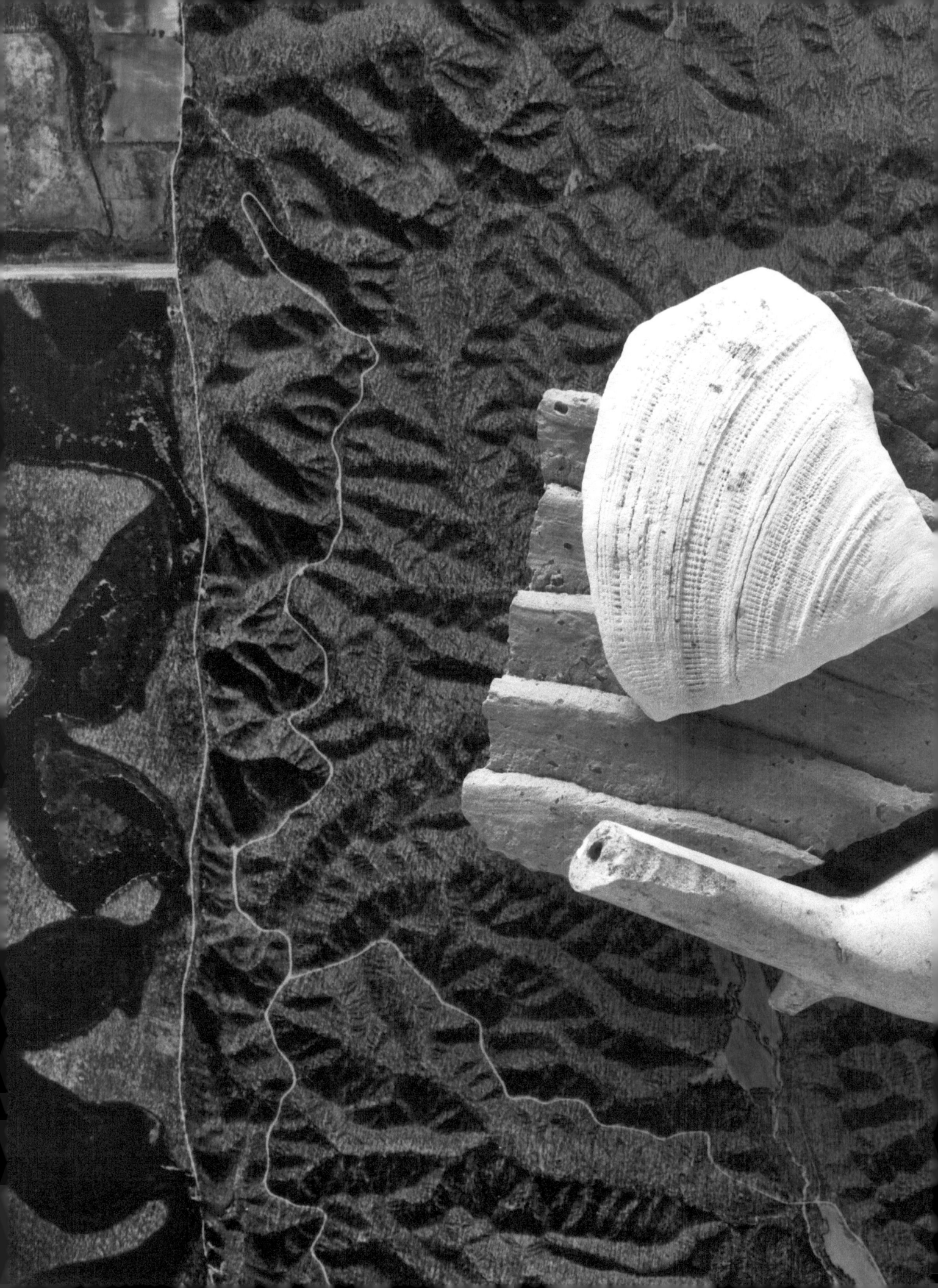

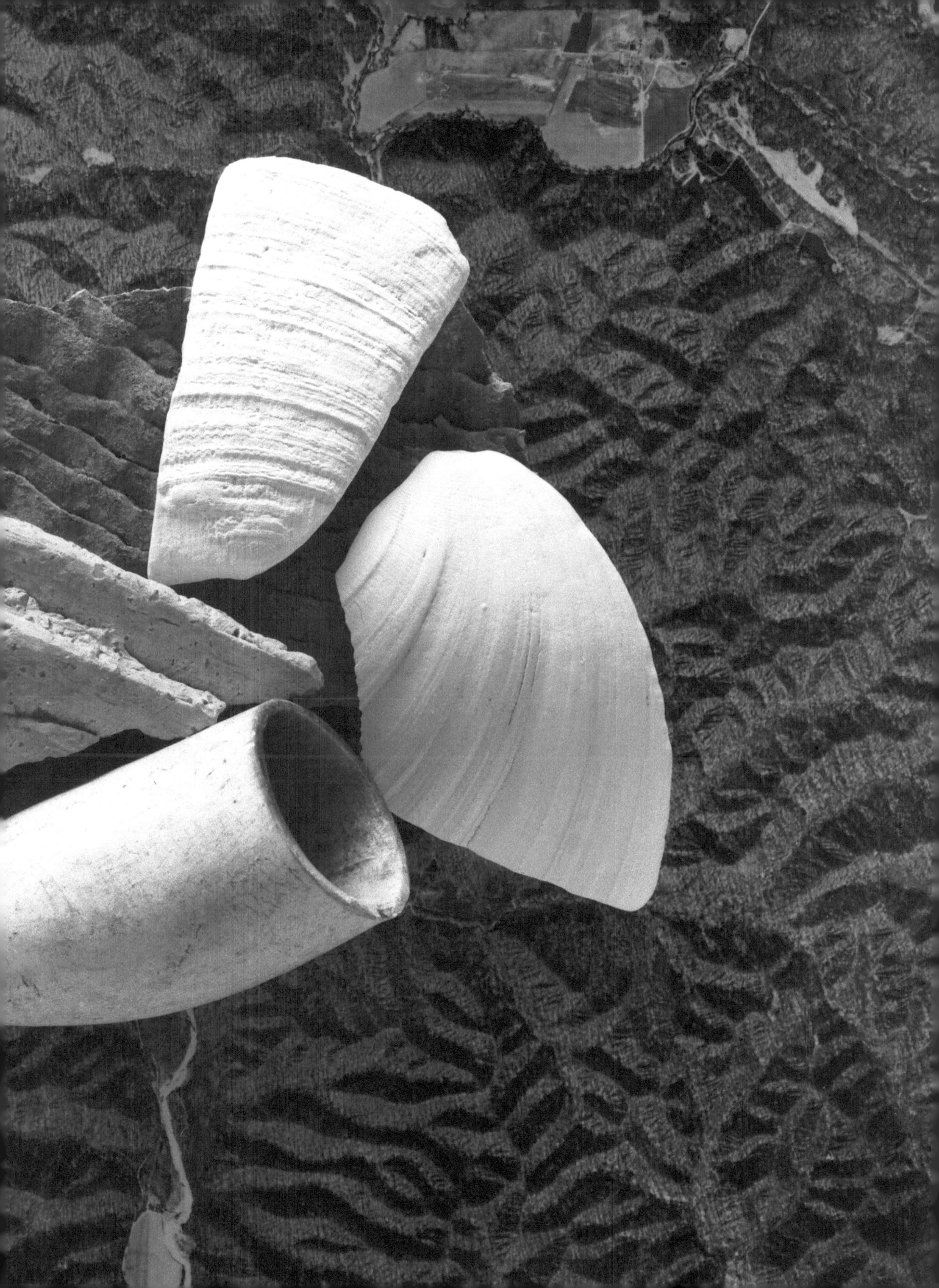

Ed Lavino

(Previous page) Pipe and Clam Shells

"Art is the objectification of feeling"
— Herman Melville

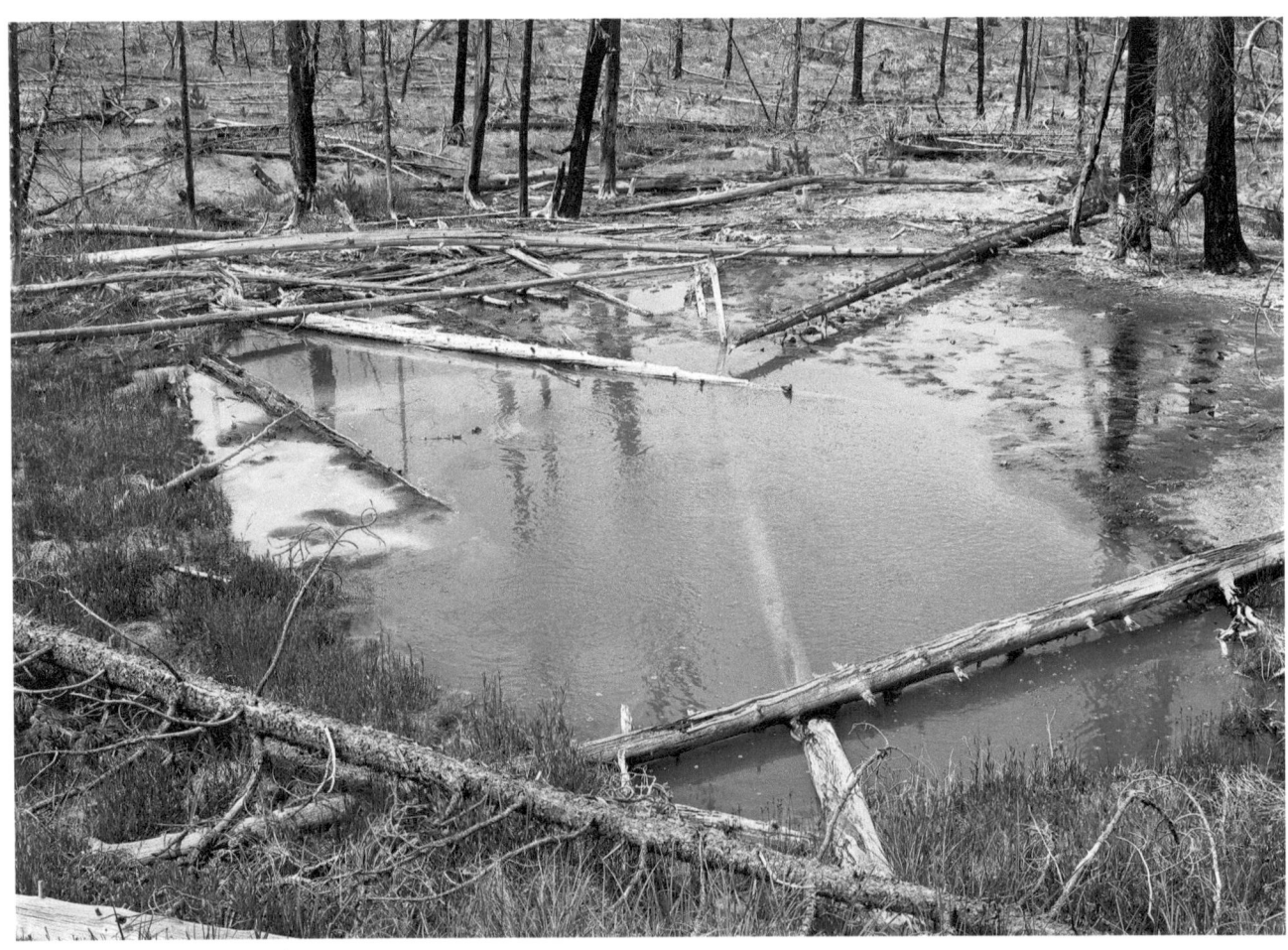

Gibbon Geyser Basin
Yellowstone National Park, Wyoming

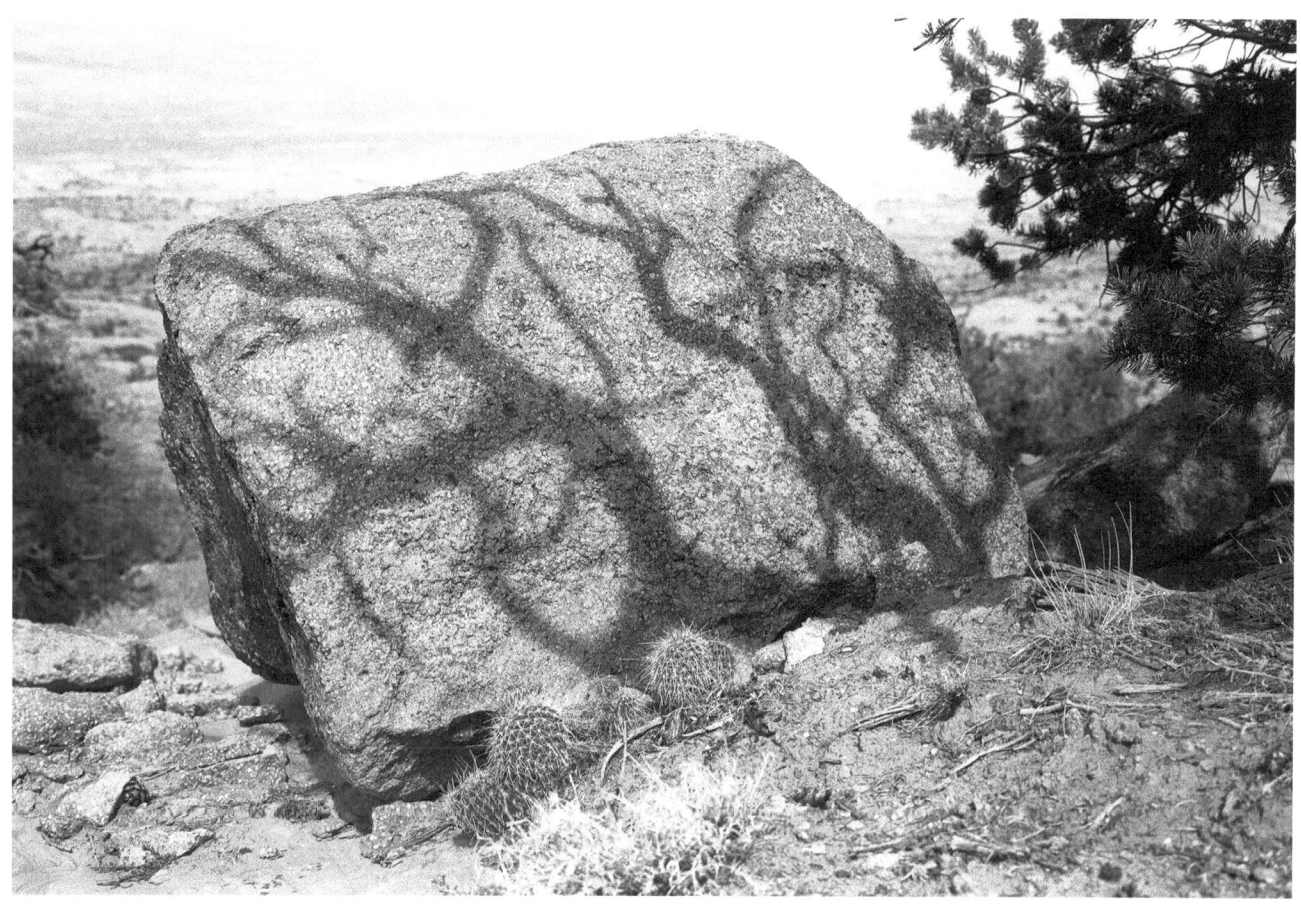

Tree Shadow on Boulder
Southern Utah

Anything can provide inspiration: a Van Gogh drawing, an article on cellular biology, or vintage snapshots. In this case, Edward Abbey's Desert Solitaire led me to this place and this image.

125

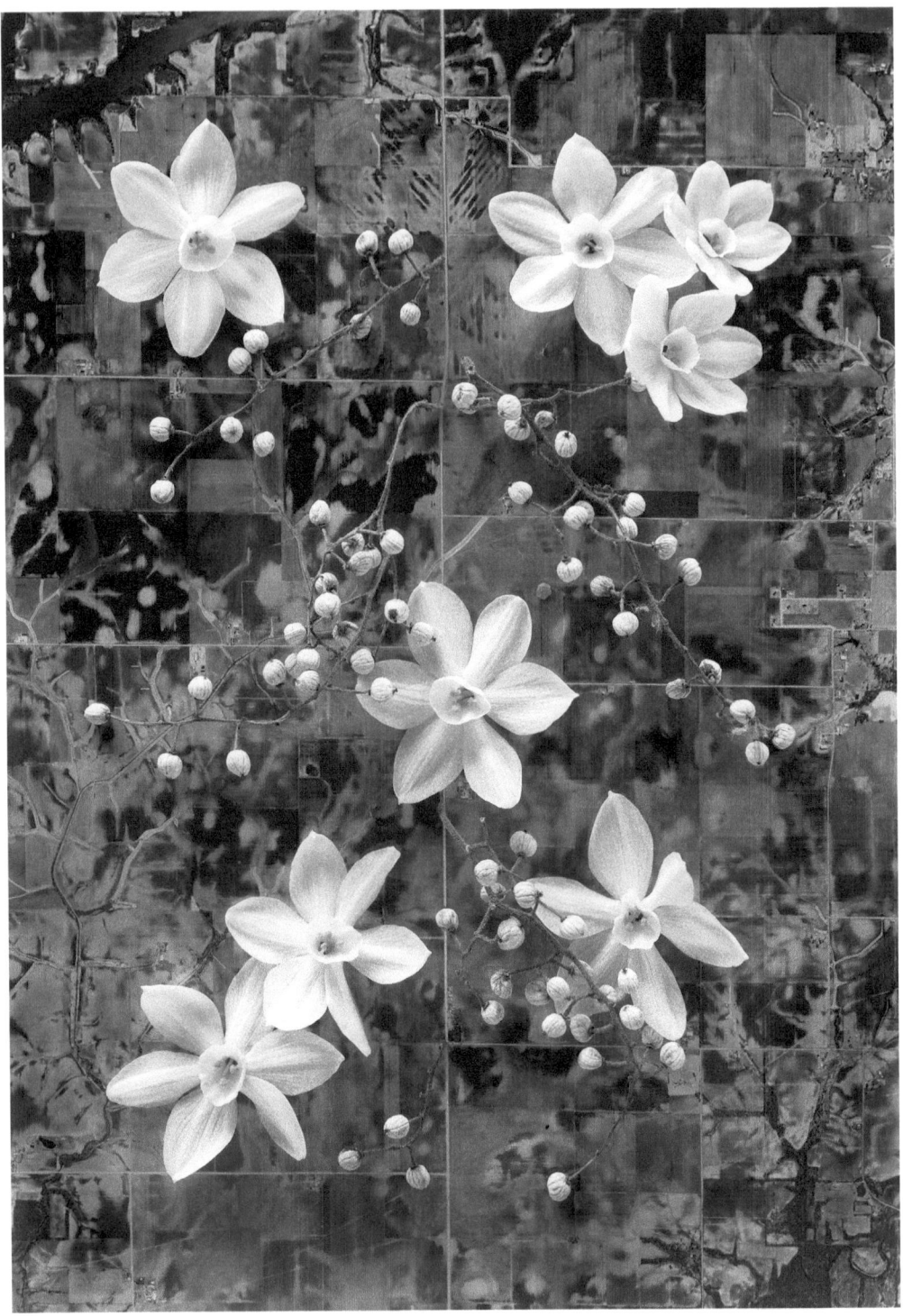

Eight Flowers and Aerial Photograph

Life retreats into itself, deep into the earth, as we pave over it. When we move on, plant life will be reconstituted through soil and seed.

"...from so simple a beginning endless forms most beautiful and most wonderful have been and are being evolved."
— Charles Darwin

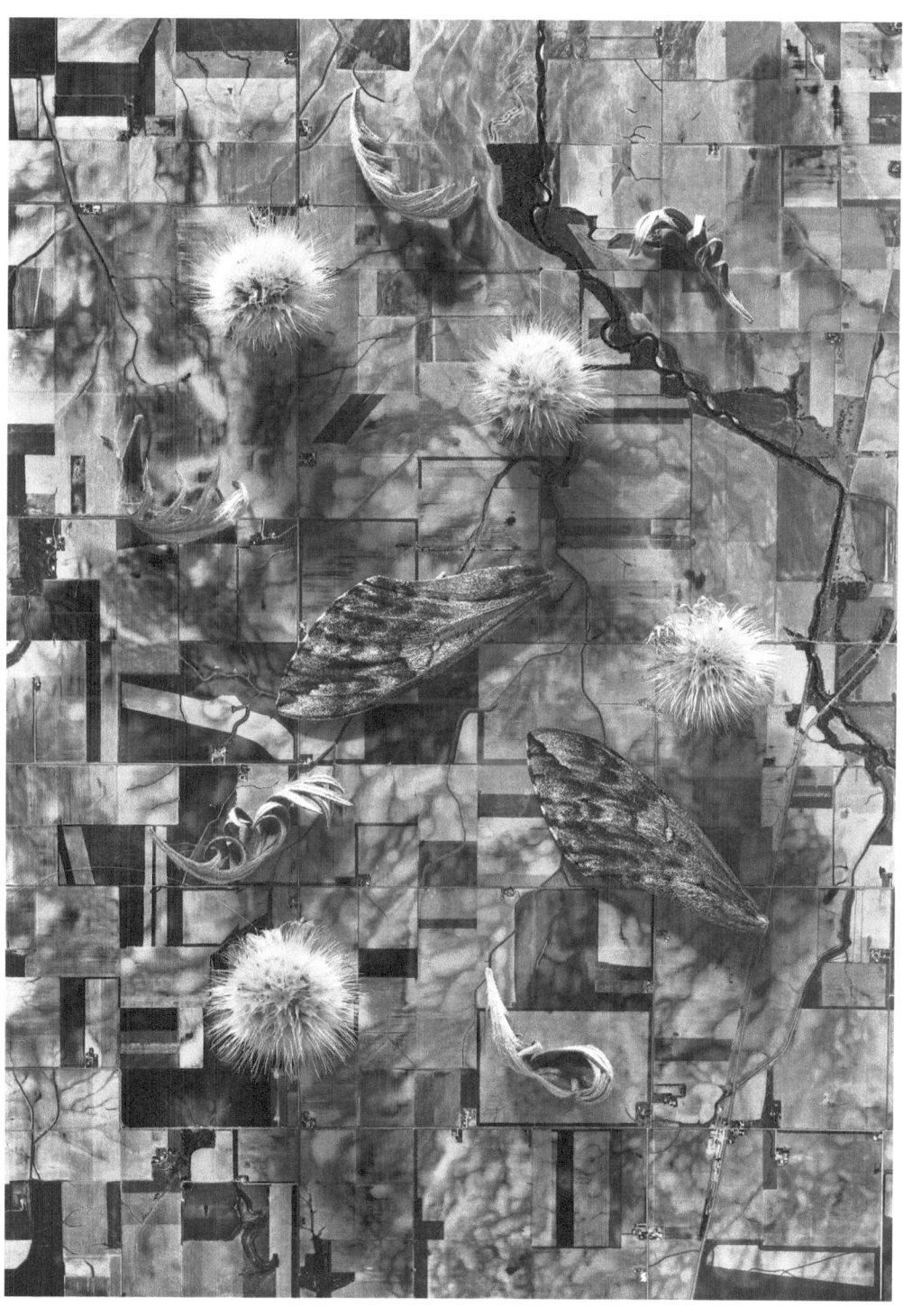

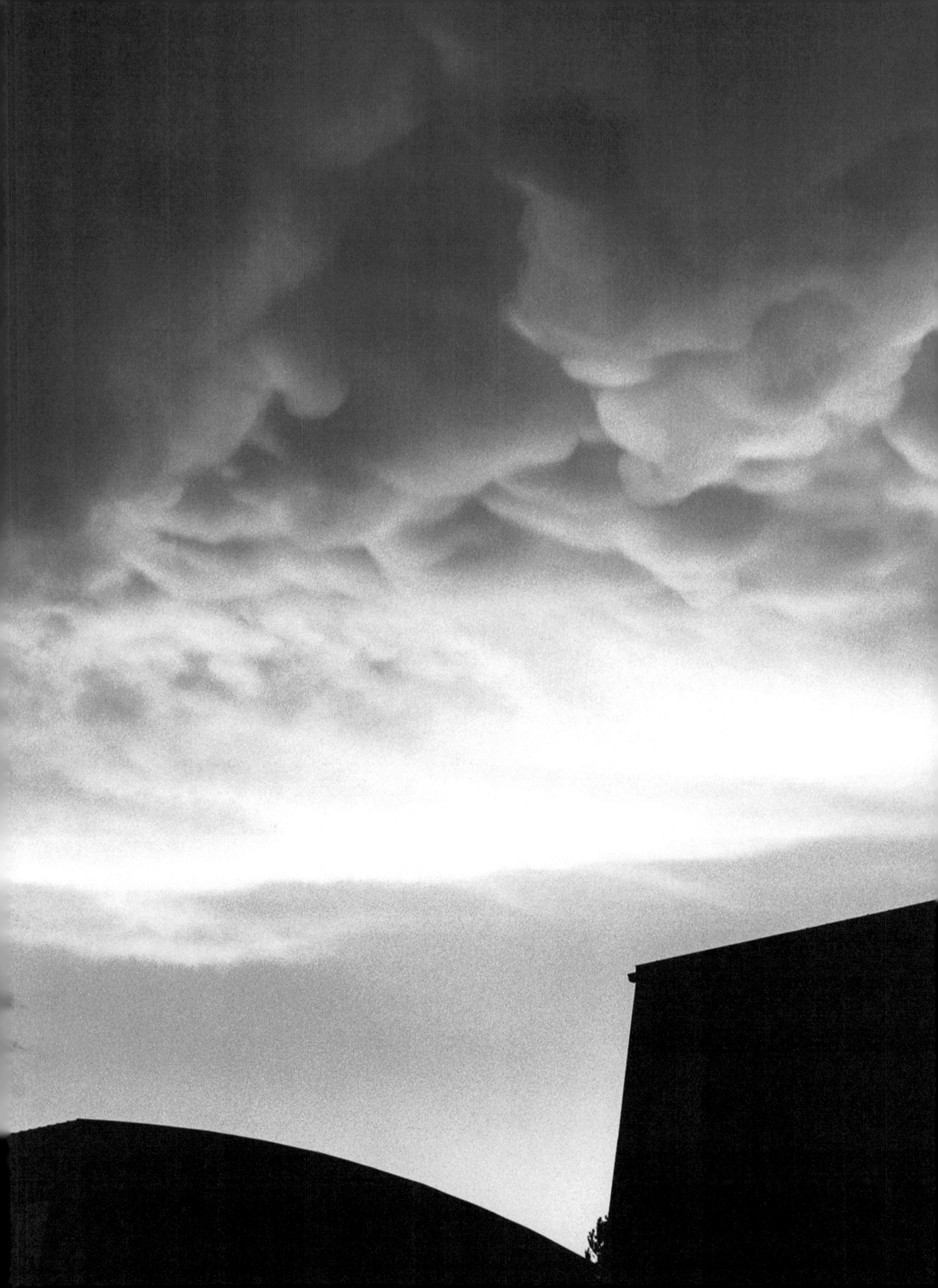

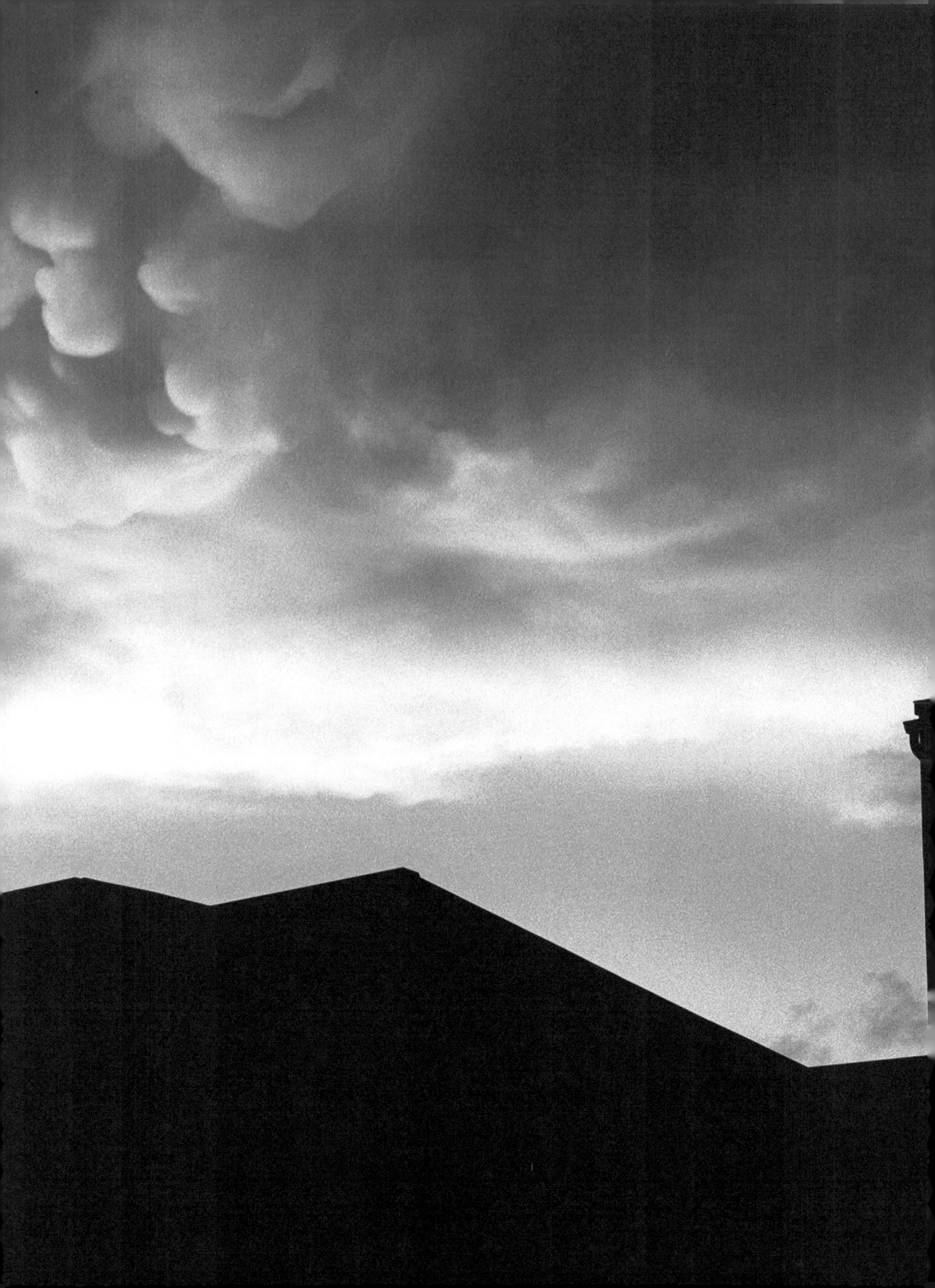

Ed Lavino

(Previous page) Storm over Housing Project
Jackson, Wyoming

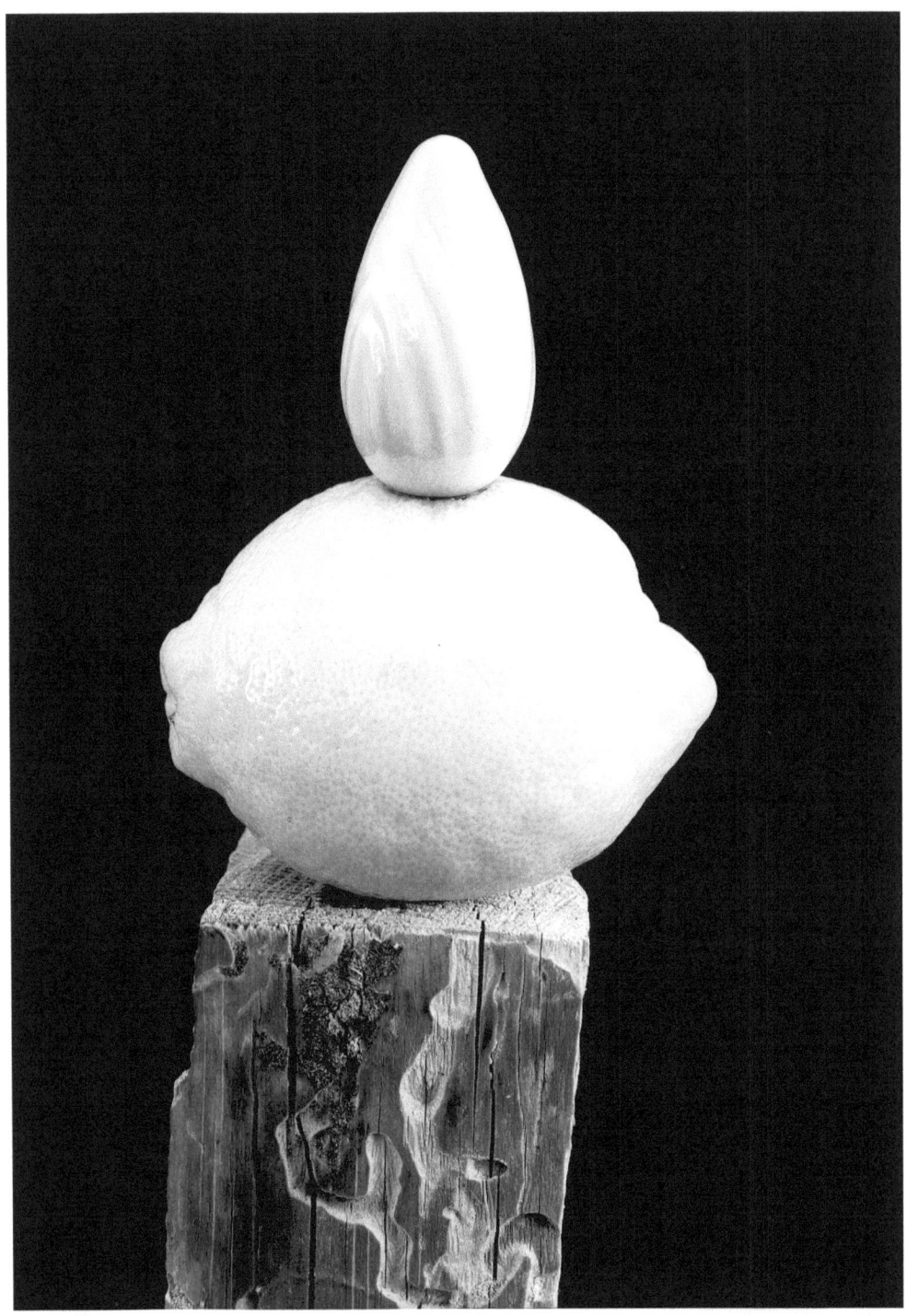

Photosynthesis

Objects can represent ideas and, at times, they are the ideas.

Prevailing Westerlies

Lily and Mussel Shells

This assemblage was made with items gathered during a day hike with my fly fishing rod on a small wooded creek.

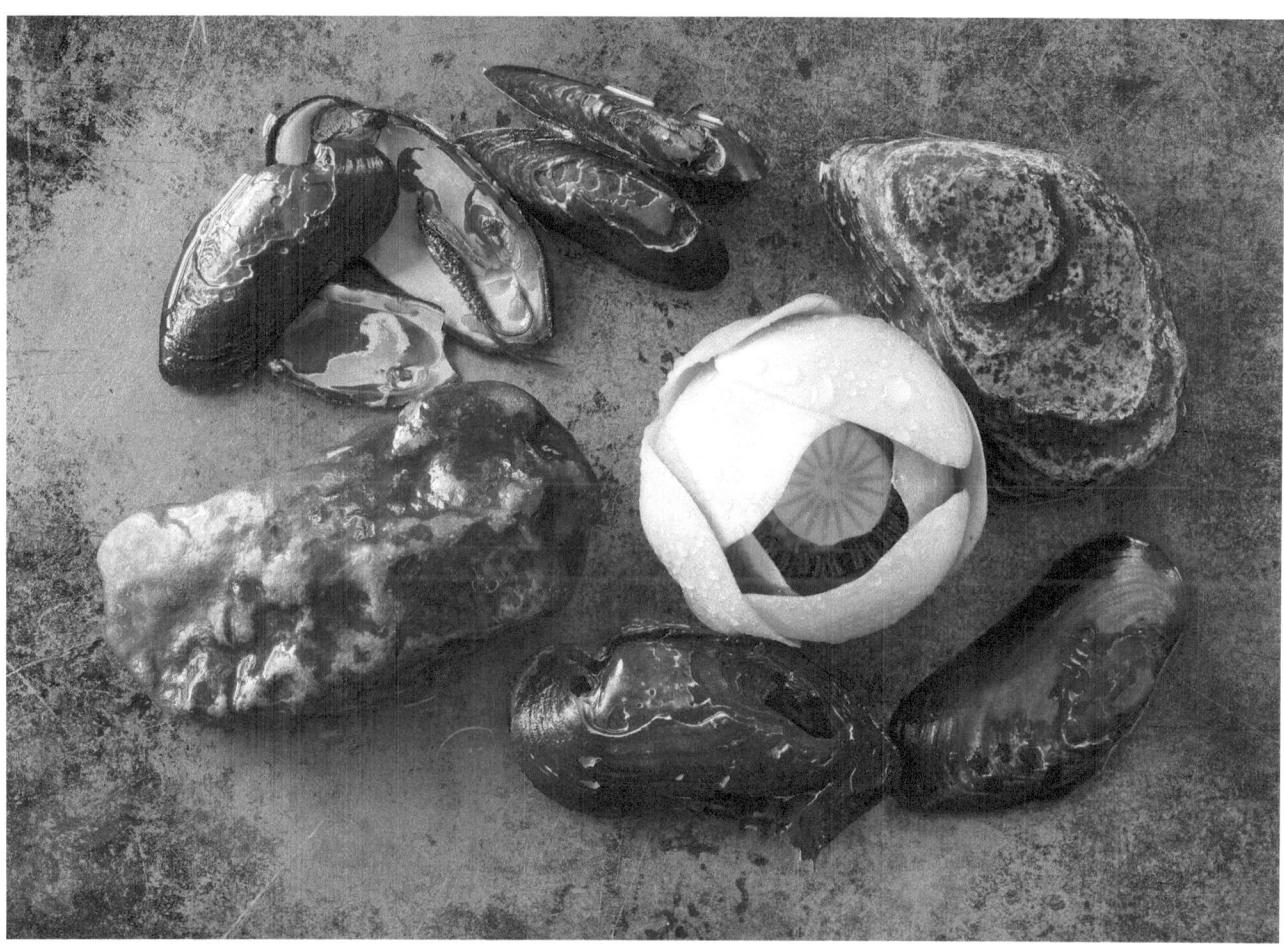

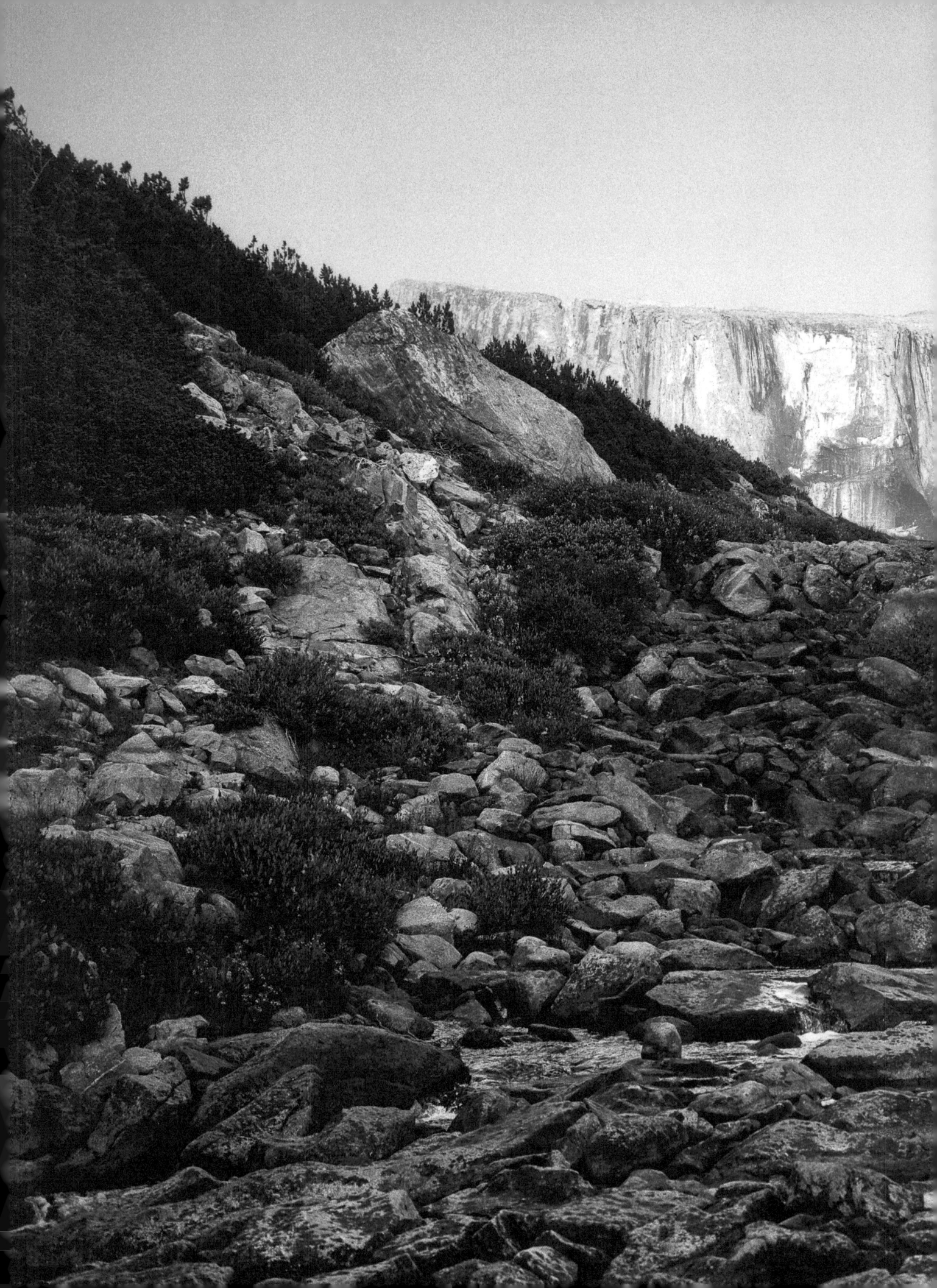

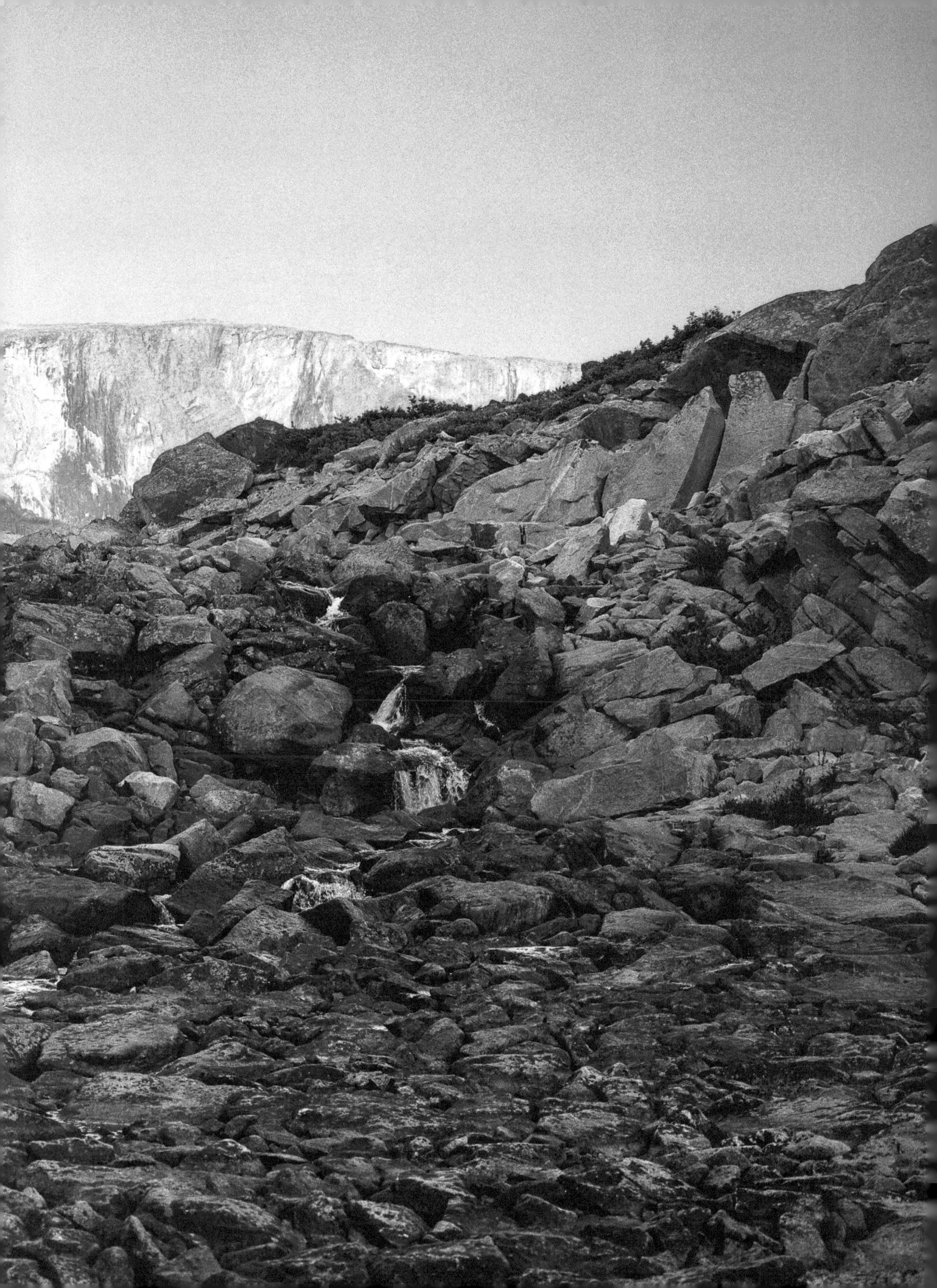

Ed Lavino

(Previous page) Roberts Mountain
Wind River Indian Reservation, Wyoming

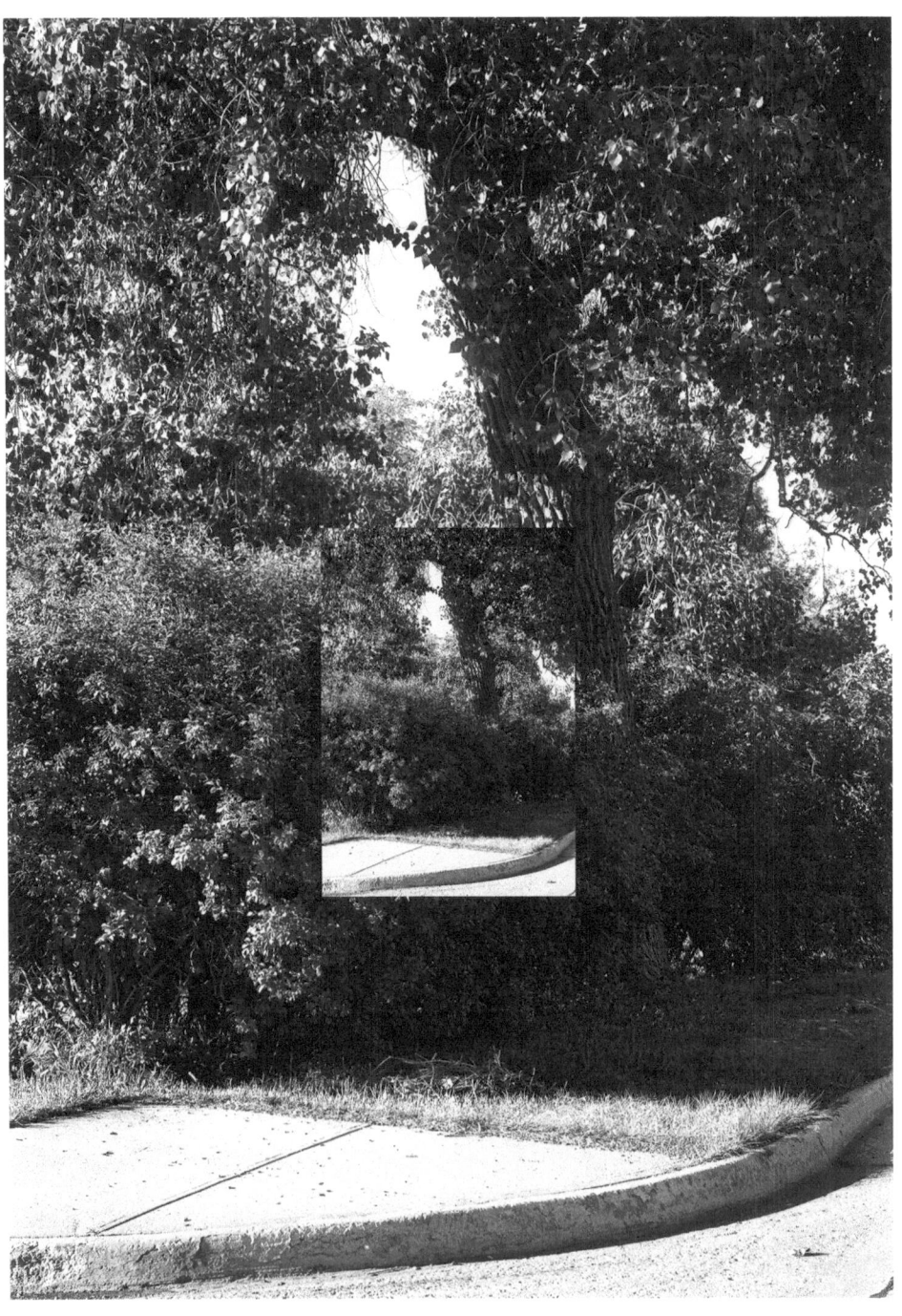

Fourth Street
Lander, Wyoming

Black Book and Galvanized Steel

"A painter should begin every canvas with a wash of black, because all things in nature are dark except where exposed by the light."
— Leonardo da Vinci

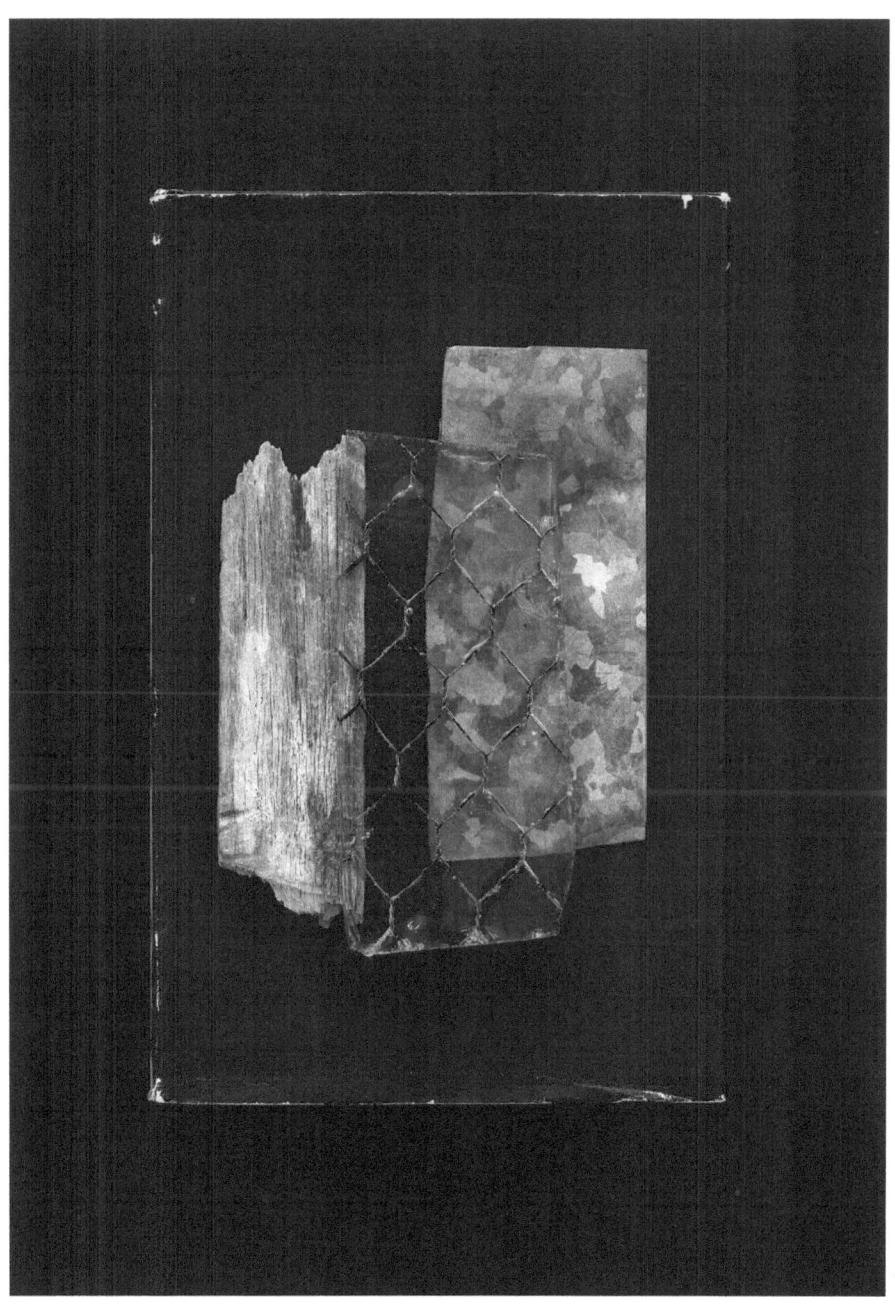

(Next page) Recreational Vehicle
Bitter Creek, Wyoming

Wyoming offers endless open space beckoning beyond the confines of four walls.

135

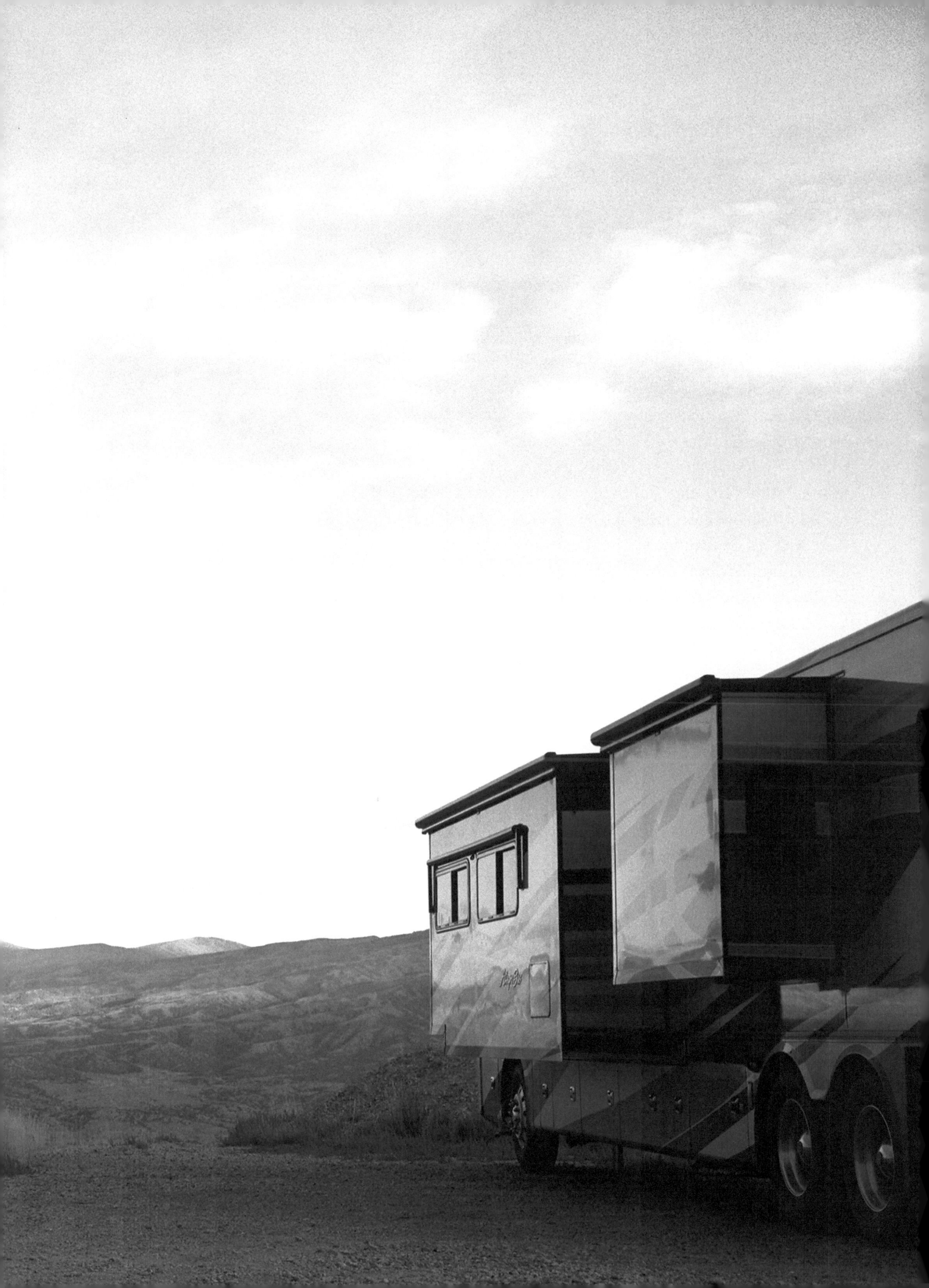

Ed Lavino Biography

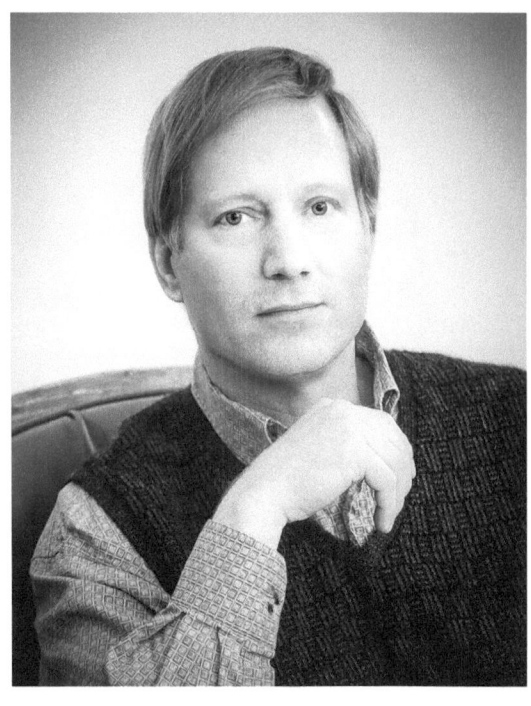

Edwin ("Ed") Lavino was born Cullen Edwin Goddard in Middletown, New York, in 1959. He was the second child and only son of Barbara Robbins and Paul Goddard (an English national). Ed's sister Paula, older by one year, was born in 1958.

Ed's earliest childhood years were chaotic. When he was one year old, his parents separated and his father left the family without financial support. Unable to care for a one-year-old and a two-year-old alone, his mother, Barbara, sent Ed to live with her Aunt Geraldine Houghtaling in the remote Catskill hamlet of Willowemoc, Sullivan County, New York. Ed lived there with his great aunt and great uncle, and their two teen-age children, for three years. Ed remembers Great Aunt Gerry fondly. Eccentric, certainly, in her wool hunter's shirts and leather logger's boots, she had been at Pearl Harbor when it was bombed and had responded by rolling up her sleeves and working during the war, like so many women of her generation. When Ed knew her, she hunted her own deer and ran her household with plucky authority and unfailing good humor.

In 1964, Ed's mother married Edward Colombo Lavino, and four-year-old Ed rejoined his mother and sister in his new stepfather's household in Oceanside, Nassau County, New York. At that point in time, Barbara began calling her son Edwin Lavino, although her new husband had not adopted her children and never would. The name change was never formalized during Ed's childhood, and in the absence of other information, Ed grew up unaware of his mother's first marriage, assuming that he was the biological son of Edward Lavino.

In 1967, the Lavino family moved back to the Catskills, settling on Red Hill near the town of Denning, New York, in Ulster County. When they moved to the country, an exotic animal veterinarian and family friend, John Swinford, gifted them with an ocelot and three African pygmy goats. Ed recalled that when his stepfather drove the goats up from Long Island, they kept getting their horns stuck in the ceiling fabric, whereupon they would toss their heads to get free. By the time they made it to Red Hill, the inside of the station wagon was ripped to shreds. The ocelot, Tash, favored Ed with his attention, lying in wait for him on top of the refrigerator, and jumping onto his head when he passed below. Tash had his fangs filed down and had been declawed, except for one claw. Still, Ed often couldn't detangle himself from the cat without calling to his mother to pull Tash off. Always a handful, Tash would nevertheless remain with the family for years, finally dying in Barbara's arms at the dignified old age of sixteen.

Rural life allowed the family to open its doors to local wildlife, too, inviting into the house tortoises, injured screech-owls, a woodchuck, an orphaned raccoon, and a flying squirrel, and so the menagerie grew. During this period, Ed became a collector of natural objects as well, and stored boxes of rocks, egg shells, and birds' nests, under his bed.

When in middle school, Ed befriended a classmate named Bill Brown, one of four brothers whose father ran the Frost Valley YMCA and environmental camp in Claryville, New York. Soon Ed became almost like one of the Brown brothers, joining them at play and at work. Throughout high school Ed earned money leading hikes and bicycle tours, working as a bicycle mechanic, and as an instructor in rock climbing and cross country skiing.

While on visits to see his grandparents in Napanoch, New York, Ed met a local handyman, an old man named George Olsterhoust, whom he befriended. George talked about how his parents had been slaves, and he had only kind words for the people who would give him a lift in their cars. Over time, Ed visited George at his cabin, a coal-heated shelter with no running water, and took a series of photographs of George in his home. By this time, Ed had progressed from his first Instamatic camera to a used Hasselblad, purchased with money earned selling out-of-print books in high school. Inspired by the paintings of Andrew Wyeth, Ed's early portraits were similarly personal, depicting friends and neighbors in a rural landscape, in a realistic style. At age eighteen, Ed won a Kodak National Achievement Award for an abstract color photograph of an abandoned house with chicken wire over a broken window.

In 1979, Ed graduated from Tri-Valley Central School in Grahamsville, New York and departed immediately, with six hundred dollars in his pocket, on a two-month solo bicycle trip across Europe. He spent the summer touring France, Belgium, Germany, Switzerland, Austria and Italy, sleeping in farmers' fields and on trains. With his sights set on a climbing excursion he could not afford, he took time out from touring to earn money, moving books for two weeks at the Leuven Library in Belgium. As he traveled, he carried his Hasselblad with him. Europeans recognized the Swedish camera as a serious instrument, and one day, while exploring a tiny street in the medieval hill town of Montisi, Italy, Ed met a little old man who noticed his camera and gestured "wait," as he disappeared through a gate. A bit later, the gate reopened to release two huge swine into the alley. Making it known that he wished to have his portrait taken with his pigs, the old man struggled to make them pose. The pigs, inclined to wander off, were uncooperative. Undeterred, the old man disappeared yet again, to hasten back with a bushel of pears, which he spilled in the street to distract the pigs. Ed captured the photograph.

Ed started college at the State University of New York at New Paltz in the fall of 1979. Short on funds, he was forced to withdraw after completing his freshman year to work for two years as a baker on the graveyard shift at a Jewish bakery, and as a logger. Finally, he was able to attend school uninterrupted for three years, to graduate with a double major in Art History and Photography, and a minor in Economics, in 1985. Based on the strength of Ed's college portfolio, he won a grant from the Catskill Center for Photography in 1986 to document the abandoned uranium mines of Terlingua, Texas. For these photographs, Ed used an 8 x 10 view camera and processed the prints with platinum and palladium, a handcrafted emulsion for rich tonal effects.

A notable aside to his college years are the summers Ed spent in Yellowstone National Park. His college roommate had worked in the Park, and clued Ed in on the opportunity to work as a cook for minimum wage, with the benefits of low-cost room and board, and (most importantly), on his days off, the chance to explore the national park with a backpack, a fly rod, and a camera.

In Yellowstone Ed met Jane Petrick, a fellow college student also from New York State, and they became friends. They were surprised to meet again on the campus at New Paltz a couple of years later, where Jane was enrolled in a teacher certification program. They went on running dates and climbing dates. During this time,

Ed Lavino

Ed also befriended Jane's identical triplet sisters, Ellen and Cathy. All of the sisters had worked in Yellowstone, which further cemented Ed's friendship with Ellen and Cathy, and Ed's bond with Jane.

In 1986, Ed married Jane in an outdoor ceremony at his parents' home in Wawarsing, New York. That same year, he started working as a land surveyor for an engineering firm in Rockland County, New York; Jane found a job teaching art in Tuxedo Park, New York.

Jane and Ed saved money and dreamed of buying land near Yellowstone. In 1988, they purchased land in Moran, Wyoming, on a bench overlooking the Buffalo Fork of the Snake River, with views of the Mount Leidy Highlands.

In 1990, they moved to Wyoming, giving them the summer to build a house and a detached garage before Jane was expected to start teaching at the Kelly and Moran schools in September. They were already living on the property in a two-person tent when a lumber truck arrived on the lot and dropped an eight foot by twenty-four foot cube of lumber—everything they would need for the whole project in one delivery. Ed signed for it and the flatbed rumbled off, leaving Ed and Jane to exchange a look, wondering what they had gotten themselves into. They proceeded to build their own house, each of them equipped with a carpenter's hammer and nail apron; and they invited friends passing through to pitch a tent and pick up a hammer. Many bent nails went into that house, but Ed graciously assured his guests that crooked nails only made the house stronger.

Outdoor work, in the form of land surveying, allowed Ed to explore further afield, occasionally with his camera. While recreating too, be it fly fishing close to home, or photographing in the Wind River Range with llamas or packhorses, Ed looked for opportunities to capture the open spaces of Wyoming with 8 x 10 and 5 x 7 Deardorff view cameras.

In 1992, Ed and Jane's daughter Hillary Torrey Lavino was born. When Hillary was small, especially during the long isolating winters in the Buffalo Valley, Ed looked for ways to continue his creative work indoors. He had worked for a geomorphologist on an AutoCAD mapping project, and had collected USGS aerial photographs to use for reference. He began arranging found objects, like old beer caps, arrowheads, and fragments of antler atop the aerial photographs. The interesting visual collages inspired the still life compositions that Ed then photographed, challenging the viewer with anomalies in scale and figure-in-field camouflage.

When Hillary joined the alpine ski team during middle school, the hour-long drive into Jackson for school, ski training, work, and groceries proved burdensome. In 2004, the family moved to Jackson. Apart from the heartache of selling the home they had built themselves, the move made life easier.

In Jackson, Ed connected with a community of artists of every stripe. As fellow artists responded positively to his work, he began exhibiting in coffee shops, galleries, and art centers. For two decades, throughout Wyoming, he has participated in group exhibitions, juried shows, and solo exhibitions, attracting devoted fans at every turn.

In light of the hours spent during childhood tramping through the woods and hand-feeding wild animals, it is not surprising that Ed continues to find sustenance in nature. His early interest in collecting was prophetic. The birds' nests, turtle shells, and fossils brought indoors and meticulously arranged bring to mind 19th century British cabinets of curiosity. Yet his current work is decidedly modern in its ability to make the viewer stop and question our destructive habits, and then reimagine a world where man and nature merge in dream-like harmony.

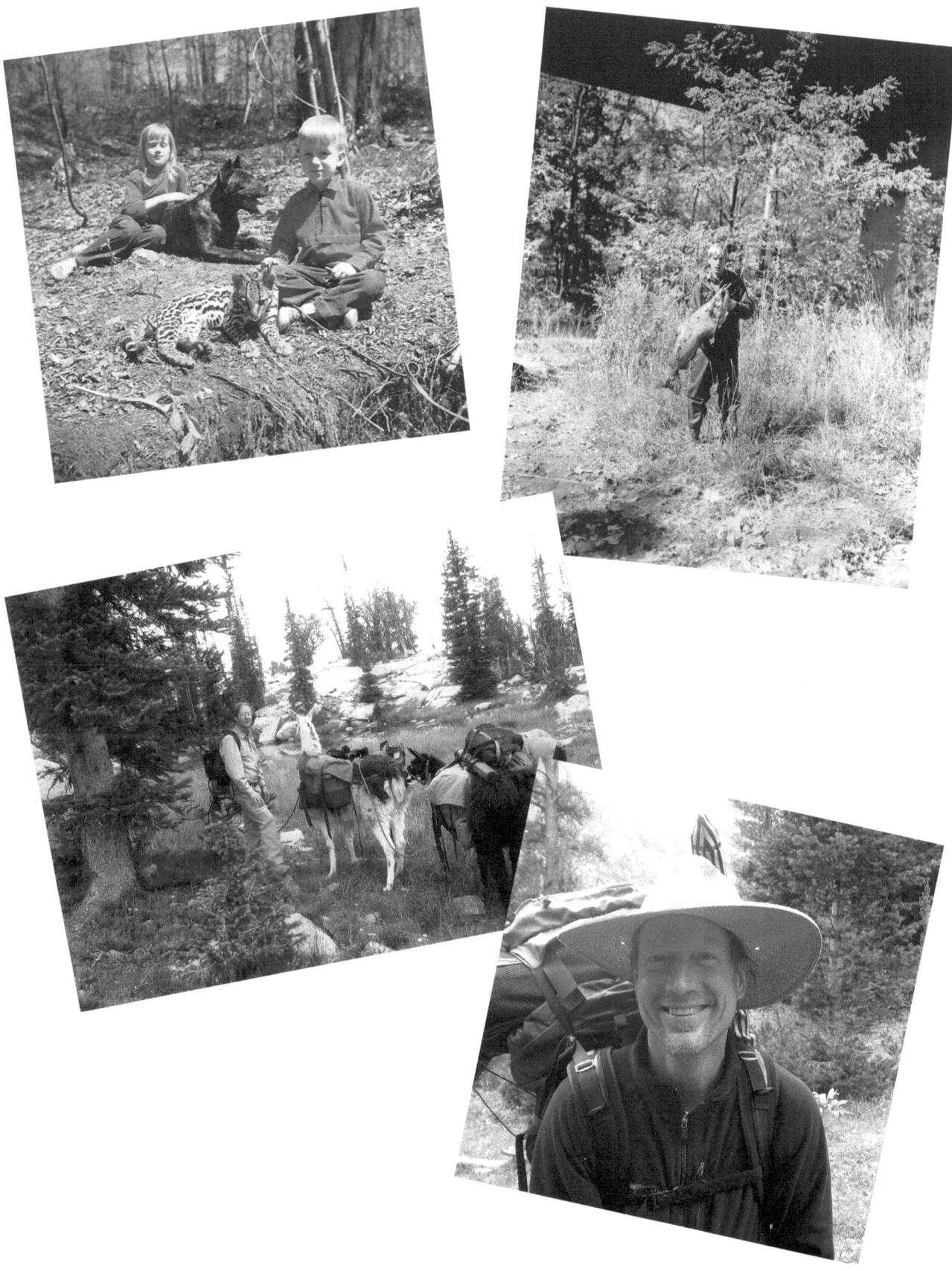

Technical Notes

Still life images were photographed with a 210mm Schneider G-Claron lens on a 5"x7" Deardorff view camera. For the landscapes I used a 305mm Schneider G-Claron lens on an 8"x10" Deardorff view camera with a yellow filter. I calculated exposures with a Pentax Spot Meter using the Zone System.

Portraits were photographed using a Fuji GW690III camera with a fixed 90mm lens and 400ASA roll film. I do not use a light meter with this camera, because a cloudless day in the Rocky Mountains is a constant f16 at 1/500th of a second, or f8 at 1/500th of a second on overcast days.

Silver gelatin prints were made on Ilford multigrade, Forte warm multigrade and Kodak Azo papers with 1:31 selenium toner or gold toner.

Silver and digital prints are available for sale at www.edlavinophotography.com

Ed Lavino, PO Box 8248, Jackson, WY 83002-8248

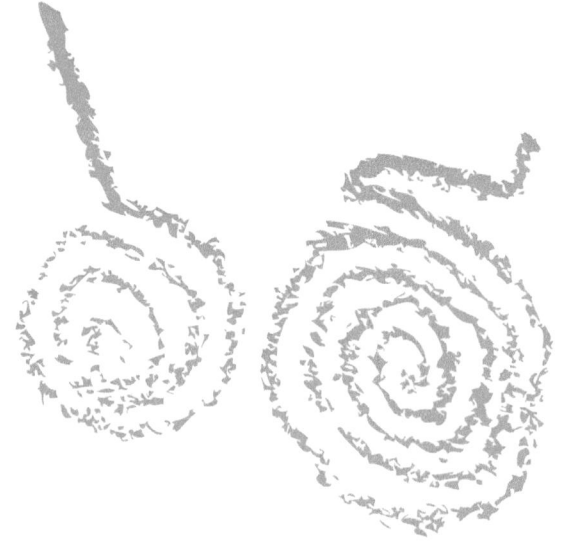

www.ingramcontent.com/pod-product-compliance
Lightning Source LLC
Chambersburg PA
CBHW050848180526
45159CB00007B/2610